BREAKING HIDDEN COVENANTS

A Guide to Identifying and Breaking Spiritual Bondages

DR. MAXWELL SHIMBA

Published in Manhattan, New York by Shimba Publishing, LLC.

Shimba Publishing LLC

Table of Contents

INTRODUCTION

Chapter 01 1
ANATOMY OF HIDDEN COVENANTS: IDENTIFICATION, MECHANISMS, AND MANIFESTATIONS 1
Chapter 02 47
THEOLOGY OF COLLECTIVE CAPTIVITY: CORPORATE BONDAGE AND GENERATIONAL STRATEGIES OF DARKNESS 47
Chapter 03 92
RELEASE FROM CURSES ATTACHED TO EVIL COVENANTS.. 92
Chapter 04 223
PRISONER OF LOCAL ALTARS 223
Chapter 05 271
DELIVERANCE FROM EVIL ALTARS: A CALL TO SPIRITUAL WARFARE 271
Chapter 06 322
THE BLOOD COVENANT TRAP 322
The Prison Without Walls 322
Chapter 07 382
PRAYER WARFARE SECTION 382

INTRODUCTION

THE ARCHITECTURE OF COVENANTS AND THE HIDDEN BONDAGES OF MODERN BELIEVERS

"And they said, We saw certainly that the LORD was with thee: and we said, Let there be now an oath betwixt us, even betwixt us and thee, and let us make a covenant with thee" (Genesis 26:28).

Let us begin this solemn discourse by confronting a theological and spiritual reality that has been obscured in much contemporary Christian teaching, yet remains critical for understanding the persistent struggles of believers. The ancient words of Ecclesiastes haunt our present condition: "For man also knoweth not his time: as the fishes that are taken in an evil net, and as the birds that are caught in the snare; so are the sons of men snared in an evil time, when it falleth suddenly upon them" (Ecclesiastes 9:12). This book represents not merely another spiritual manual, but rather a systematic theological investigation into the architecture of covenants—both divine and destructive—and their continuing operation in the lives of those who profess faith in Christ.

The contemporary Christian landscape presents us with a troubling paradox: countless believers who faithfully confess Scripture, attend worship, and pursue godliness find themselves ensnared in patterns of failure, repeated setbacks, and inexplicable bondages. There exists what can only be described as a yawning chasm between confession and fulfillment, between positional truth and experiential reality. This gap cannot be adequately explained by surface-level analyses of sin, discipline, or divine testing alone. We must venture deeper into the biblical understanding of spiritual realities, particularly the enduring nature of covenants and their consequences.

THE ONTOLOGICAL NATURE OF COVENANTS: A BIBLICAL-THEOLOGICAL FOUNDATION

Before we can properly address the issue of hidden evil covenants, we must establish a robust theological framework for understanding covenants in their proper biblical context. The concept of covenant (Hebrew: *berith*; Greek: *diatheke*) stands as one of the central organizing principles of Scripture—the very backbone of God's relationship with humanity. From the Edenic covenant to the New Covenant in Christ's blood, Scripture reveals a God who relates to His creation through covenantal structures.

Etymologically and semantically, the English term "covenant" signifies a mutual understanding between two or more parties, each binding themselves to fulfill specified obligations. It represents a legal contract, a binding agreement, a written compact, or a solemn commitment to do or refrain from doing a particular thing. Yet these English approximations barely capture the profound theological and spiritual reality embedded in the biblical concept.

In Old Testament Hebrew, *berith* carries the sense of "a pact made by passing between pieces of flesh"—a vivid, bloody, and solemn ritual that communicates the life-and-death seriousness of the commitment being made. The verbal root suggests binding, fettering, or establishing a relationship with binding force. The New Testament Greek term *diatheke*, while sometimes translated "testament" or "will," fundamentally conveys the idea of a solemn disposition or arrangement, particularly one that is unilateral in its establishment but bilateral in its implications.

The ratification ceremony described in Genesis 15:9-17 provides our paradigmatic understanding of covenant formation. Here, Yahweh instructs Abram to bring specific animals, to divide them, and to arrange the pieces opposite one another. The divine presence—manifested as "a smoking furnace, and a burning lamp"—passes between these pieces, establishing an unilateral covenant grounded in divine faithfulness. This ritual finds echo in Jeremiah 34:18-19, where covenant violators are judged for having "passed between the parts of the calf." The very imagery communicates a truth modern Christians often overlook: covenants involve the whole person—life, body, blood, and future generations.

THE MULTIFACETED PURPOSES OF BIBLICAL COVENANTS

Scripture reveals covenants serving diverse purposes in human relationships, each illustrating different dimensions of covenantal reality:

1. **Establishing Friendship**: The covenant between Jonathan and David (1 Samuel 18:3) exemplifies how covenants formalize relational bonds, creating obligations that transcend mere affection.
2. **Procuring Assistance in War**: King Asa's covenant with Ben-hadad of Syria (1 Kings 15:18-19) demonstrates the political-military dimensions of covenants as instruments of statecraft and survival.
3. **Mutual Protection**: Isaac's covenant with Abimelech (Genesis 26:28-29) and Jacob's with Laban (Genesis 31:50-52) reveal covenants as mechanisms for

establishing boundaries and security in uncertain environments.

4. **Promoting Commerce**: Solomon's covenant with Hiram of Tyre (1 Kings 5:6-11) illustrates the economic dimensions of covenants as frameworks for trade, resource exchange, and mutual prosperity.
5. **Transferring Property**: Abraham's purchase of the cave of Machpelah (Genesis 23:14-16) demonstrates how covenants formalize property transactions with enduring legal and spiritual implications.

Each of these examples reveals covenants as multidimensional realities involving spiritual, legal, social, and generational dimensions simultaneously.

THE FORMAL ELEMENTS AND PERPETUATING MECHANISMS OF COVENANTS

A thorough examination of biblical covenants reveals consistent formal elements that establish their binding nature:

1. **Clearly Specified Terms**: Covenants involve explicit conditions and obligations, as seen in Nahash's brutal terms to Jabesh-gilead (1 Samuel 11:1-2).
2. **Confirmation by Oath**: The invocation of deity as witness and guarantor, as Abraham swears to Abimelech "by God" (Genesis 21:23, 31).
3. **Witnesses**: The presence of human or divine witnesses, as in Boaz's transaction before the elders of Bethlehem (Ruth 4:9-11).
4. **Written Documentation and Sealing**: The formal recording and authentication, exemplified in Nehemiah's covenant renewal (Nehemiah 9:38-10:1).

5. **Divine Witness**: The invocation of God as ultimate witness and enforcer, as Jacob declares, "God is witness betwixt me and thee" (Genesis 31:50, 53).

The binding nature of covenants is emphasized in Galatians 3:15: "Though it be but a man's covenant, yet if it be confirmed, no man disannulleth, or addeth thereto." This Pauline statement underscores a spiritual reality modern believers often underestimate: covenants, once properly ratified, establish enduring spiritual realities that cannot be casually dismissed.

Furthermore, Scripture reveals specific mechanisms that establish the perpetuity of covenants:

- **The Blood Ritual**: The passing between divided sacrifices establishes a life-and-death commitment (Genesis 15:9-17).
- **The Salt Covenant**: The use of salt as "a covenant of salt forever" (Numbers 18:19; 2 Chronicles 13:5) symbolizes preservation and enduring obligation.
- **The Handclasp**: The joining of hands as ratification (Proverbs 11:21; Ezekiel 17:18) creates physical-spiritual connection.
- **Commemorative Feasts**: Shared meals following covenant ratification (Genesis 21:27-30; 31:54) establish fellowship and memory.
- **Token Exchanges**: The giving of presents as covenant tokens (1 Samuel 18:3-4) creates tangible connections.
- **Memorial Pillars**: The erection of stone witnesses (Genesis 31:45-46) establishes physical reminders of spiritual commitments.
- **Geographical Naming**: The designation of place names commemorating covenants (Genesis 21:31; 31:47-49) embeds covenant memory in landscape and language.

These mechanisms collectively establish covenants as multi-generational, spiritually-binding realities that transcend the immediate parties involved.

THE DUAL NATURE OF COVENANTAL REALITY: DIVINE AND DEMONIC

Here we arrive at the critical theological insight that forms the foundation of this entire study: **The spiritual principles governing divine covenants are mirrored in destructive covenants with evil spiritual powers.** Just as God established enduring covenants with humanity through specific rituals and commitments, so too can human beings—whether consciously or unconsciously—establish binding covenants with demonic powers through analogous mechanisms.

This understanding emerges from several biblical premises:

1. **The Principle of Spiritual Correspondence**: Satan operates as the "ape of God," counterfeiting divine patterns and principles for destructive purposes (2 Corinthians 11:14).
2. **The Reality of Spiritual Contracts**: Scripture acknowledges the possibility of covenants with death and hell (Isaiah 28:15, 18), indicating that spiritual agreements can be made with destructive powers.
3. **The Generational Consequences**: The Bible consistently demonstrates that covenants established by ancestors create spiritual realities affecting descendants (Exodus 20:5; 34:7).
4. **The Blood Principle**: Since "the life of the flesh is in the blood" (Leviticus 17:11), any covenant involving blood—whether divine or demonic—establishes profound spiritual connections.

The stages of covenant formation outlined in anthropological studies of blood covenants reveal this mirroring with frightening clarity:

1. **Deliberation of Terms**: The explicit or implicit negotiation of obligations and benefits.
2. **Exchange of Valuables**: The transfer of precious possessions symbolizing the exchange of lives.
3. **Blood Mingling Ritual**: The mutual incision, blood collection, shared drinking, and wound joining that establishes "blood brotherhood."
4. **Curse Pronouncement**: The invocation of terrible consequences for covenant violation.
5. **Identity Fusion**: The parties becoming "one person" with mutual representation of interests and descendants.

This precise pattern—documented across cultures and centuries—reveals a spiritual technology that operates regardless of whether the covenant partner is divine or demonic. The principles are transposable, which explains how believers can find themselves bound by covenants they never consciously made.

THE CONTEMPORARY CRISIS: HIDDEN COVENANTS AND BELIEVER'S BONDAGE

We now confront the pastoral-theological crisis that motivates this study: **Born-again Christians experiencing persistent bondage, failure, and limitation despite genuine conversion, faithful confession, and sincere discipleship.**

The testimony of countless believers reveals patterns that defy conventional explanations:

- Financial systems that consistently collapse at the threshold of breakthrough
- Marital relationships that replicate destructive ancestral patterns despite Christian commitment
- Physical ailments that resist medical treatment and prayer
- Mental-emotional struggles that persist despite counseling and spiritual discipline
- Ministry callings that encounter inexplicable obstruction and sabotage
- Generational patterns of tragedy, poverty, or dysfunction repeating in Christian families

These phenomena cannot be adequately explained by:

- Personal sin alone (though sin certainly exacerbates problems)
- Lack of faith alone (though faith is essential for deliverance)
- Divine testing alone (though God does test His children)
- Psychological factors alone (though these are relevant)

We must consider the possibility—indeed, the probability—that many believers are affected by **hidden evil covenants** established through:

1. **Conscious Ancestral Choices**: Covenants made by parents, grandparents, or earlier generations with idolatrous systems, secret societies, or occult practices.
2. **Cultural-Ritual Participation**: Involvement in traditional rituals (naming ceremonies, marriage customs, burial practices) that inadvertently establish covenants with territorial spirits.

3. **Personal Pre-Conversion Activity**: Occult involvement, sexual immorality, substance abuse, or other behaviors that established spiritual contracts.
4. **Unconscious Symbolic Participation**: The wearing of ritual jewelry, possession of consecrated objects, or consumption of dedicated foods that maintain covenant connections.
5. **Dream State Manipulation**: Spiritual interactions during sleep states where consent may be given without waking awareness.

The biblical warning "My people are destroyed for lack of knowledge" (Hosea 4:6) takes on profound significance in this context. Ignorance of covenant realities does not nullify their effects; it merely leaves believers vulnerable to their operations.

THE STRUCTURE OF OUR INVESTIGATION

This volume represents a systematic effort to:

1. **Define and Describe** the nature of covenants from biblical, historical, and anthropological perspectives.
2. **Identify and Analyze** twenty-one specific categories of hidden evil covenants affecting modern believers.
3. **Diagnose and Recognize** the symptoms and manifestations of covenant bondage in personal and family systems.
4. **Prescribe and Equip** with biblical strategies for covenant identification, renunciation, and breaking.
5. **Restore and Establish** believers in the freedom of Christ's New Covenant.

Our investigation will proceed through seven comprehensive chapters:

Chapter One examines twenty-one specific hidden evil covenants, detailing their mechanisms of establishment, their symptomatic manifestations, and their destructive consequences.

Chapter Two explores collective captivity—the phenomenon of corporate or familial bondage resulting from group covenants, ancestral agreements, or territorial dedications.

Chapter Three addresses the curse mechanisms attached to evil covenants, analyzing how curses operate, their legal-spiritual basis, and their specific effects on human life.

Chapter Four investigates the role of local altars as covenant centers, examining how geographical locations, ritual sites, and dedicated objects maintain covenant enforcement.

Chapter Five provides deliverance strategies from evil altars, detailing prayer approaches, renunciation protocols, and spiritual warfare techniques.

Chapter Six analyzes the blood covenant trap—the most profound and binding form of evil covenant—exploring its establishment through blood rituals, sexual immorality, and sacrificial practices.

Chapter Seven constitutes a comprehensive prayer warfare manual, providing specific prayer points, fasting guidelines, and spiritual exercises for covenant breaking and deliverance.

METHODOLOGICAL PRINCIPLES AND THEOLOGICAL SAFEGUARDS

As we proceed, several methodological principles will guide our investigation:

1. **Biblical Primacy**: All analysis must be grounded in and evaluated against Scripture. Experiences and phenomena are interpreted through biblical revelation, not vice versa.
2. **Christological Center**: The person and work of Jesus Christ—particularly His blood shed on the cross—remains the ultimate answer to every covenant problem. All deliverance finds its basis in His finished work.
3. **Discernment Orientation**: The goal is not to foster demonic obsession but to cultivate spiritual discernment—the ability to distinguish between psychological, physiological, and spiritual factors.
4. **Pastoral Responsibility**: Our approach emphasizes personal responsibility, ethical living, and ongoing discipleship as essential components of lasting freedom.
5. **Ecclesiastical Context**: Deliverance ministry properly occurs within the context of the local church, under spiritual authority, with accountability and follow-up.

We must also establish crucial theological safeguards:

- The believer's fundamental identity in Christ remains secure regardless of covenant issues.
- Not every problem is demonic; proper diagnosis requires wisdom and discernment.
- Deliverance is a process, not merely an event, involving renewing of the mind and transformation of lifestyle.
- The cross of Christ provides complete victory, but appropriation of that victory requires active faith and obedience.

THE URGENT NEED FOR THIS INVESTIGATION

The contemporary church faces a critical moment. We have often emphasized the blessings of the New Covenant while neglecting to adequately address how pre-existing evil covenants continue affecting believers. We have proclaimed freedom in Christ while sometimes failing to provide the specific spiritual tools needed to appropriate that freedom in areas of entrenched bondage.

This investigation proceeds from a sobering realization: The devil, as a legalistic spirit, often operates through established covenant structures. Where legitimate covenants exist—whether divine or demonic—he claims legal rights to enforce terms. The good news of the gospel includes not only forgiveness of sins but also release from every curse (Galatians 3:13) and deliverance from every bondage (Luke 4:18).

As we embark on this detailed examination, let us hold two truths in tension: First, the reality and potency of evil covenants that can affect believers. Second, the superior power and efficacy of Christ's blood to break every bondage and annul every contrary covenant. This is not a journey into fear but into the greater revelation of our completeness in Christ (Colossians 2:10).

The pages that follow will confront uncomfortable realities and challenge theological assumptions. They will require us to think deeply about spiritual mechanisms many would prefer to ignore. But they will also lead us to a more profound appreciation of the comprehensive victory Christ accomplished through His death and resurrection—a victory that extends to the breaking of every hidden covenant and the release from every concealed bondage.

Let us proceed with biblical courage, spiritual discernment, and confident faith in the superior covenant established through the blood of Jesus—a covenant that cannot be broken, that requires no supplementation, and that provides complete deliverance for all who approach God through it.

Dr. Maxwell Shimba
Shimba Theological Institute
New York, NY 10005

CHAPTER 01

ANATOMY OF HIDDEN COVENANTS: IDENTIFICATION, MECHANISMS, AND MANIFESTATIONS

"As soon as they hear of me, they shall obey me: the strangers shall submit themselves unto me. The strangers shall fade away and be afraid out of their close places" (Psalm 18:44-45).

THE PARADOX OF HIDDEN SPIRITUAL REALITIES

We commence this crucial investigation by acknowledging a profound spiritual paradox: The very entities that assert power and dominion in the spiritual realm exhibit marked vulnerability when confronted with authentic Christian authority grounded in Christ's finished work. The Psalmist's declaration establishes a theological premise that will govern our entire exploration: spiritual forces that operate in hiddenness and obscurity maintain their power precisely through concealment, but when exposed to the light of divine authority and the proclamation of Christ's victory, they must retreat, fade, and submit.

This chapter constitutes a systematic, scholarly examination of twenty-one specific categories of hidden evil covenants—those spiritual contracts, agreements, and binding arrangements established between human beings and demonic powers, often without full conscious awareness or understanding of their implications. Our approach must be simultaneously academic in its rigor and pastoral in its application, theological in its foundation and practical in its diagnostic utility.

Before proceeding, we must establish a critical methodological principle: The classification and analysis presented herein does not represent mere speculative spiritual taxonomy, but rather emerges from decades of pastoral observation, deliverance ministry experience, cross-cultural anthropological study, and—most importantly—rigorous biblical exegesis. Each category corresponds to observable patterns of spiritual bondage with identifiable mechanisms of establishment, consistent symptomatic manifestations, and documented pathways to freedom through Christ.

THE ONTOLOGICAL NATURE OF COVENANTS REVISITED

Let us briefly recapitulate our foundational understanding of covenants as established in our introduction. A covenant (*berith* in Hebrew, *diatheke* in Greek) represents far more than a casual agreement or temporary arrangement. It constitutes a binding, solemn commitment between parties that establishes enduring obligations, mutual responsibilities, and—crucially—spiritual and legal realities that transcend the immediate circumstances of its establishment.

From a biblical-theological perspective, covenants possess several definitive characteristics:

1. **Legal-Spiritual Hybridity**: Covenants operate simultaneously in legal and spiritual dimensions, creating obligations enforceable in both realms.
2. **Transgenerational Implications**: Properly established covenants bind not only the immediate parties but their descendants, creating what might be termed "spiritual DNA" that passes through family lines.
3. **Blood-Based Ratification**: The most binding covenants involve blood—either literally through sacrifice or symbolically through oath—because "the life of the flesh is in the blood" (Leviticus 17:11).
4. **Witnessed and Memorialized**: Covenants involve witnesses (human or divine) and memorials (pillars, altars, names) that perpetuate memory and obligation.
5. **Curse-Blessing Mechanism**: Covenants inherently contain enforcement mechanisms—blessings for fulfillment and curses for violation.

This understanding becomes critically important when we recognize that **the spiritual principles governing divine covenants are precisely the same principles that govern destructive covenants with demonic powers**. The enemy operates not by creating new spiritual laws but by hijacking and corrupting existing ones. This explains why covenants with evil spirits can possess such enduring power—they operate according to legitimate spiritual principles corrupted for destructive purposes.

THE HIDDENNESS PARADOX: WHY EVIL COVENANTS REMAIN UNDETECTED

A foundational question must be addressed: Why do these covenants remain "hidden"? Why do intelligent, sincere believers remain unaware of spiritual contracts affecting their lives? Several factors contribute to this concealment:

1. **Generational Distance**: Many covenants were established by ancestors three, four, or more generations removed. The original context, participants, and even memory of the covenant may have been lost, but its spiritual effects persist.
2. **Cultural Normalization**: Practices that establish covenants (traditional rituals, naming ceremonies, marital customs) are often so culturally normalized that their spiritual implications remain unrecognized.
3. **Unconscious Participation**: Many covenants are established during altered states of consciousness (dreams, trances, drug-induced states, intense emotional experiences) where full awareness and consent are compromised.
4. **Symbolic Misinterpretation**: Objects, gestures, and rituals that carry covenant significance in the spiritual realm are often misunderstood as mere cultural traditions or aesthetic choices in the natural realm.
5. **Theological Incompleteness**: Much contemporary theology inadequately addresses the reality and operation of evil covenants, leaving believers without conceptual categories to recognize their influence.
6. **The Fear Factor**: As Psalm 18 suggests, evil spirits maintain their power through operating in "close places"—hidden, dark, obscured areas of life and consciousness. Exposure threatens their operational capacity.

This hiddenness constitutes not merely an inconvenience but a strategic advantage for destructive spiritual forces. As Hosea 4:6

declares, "My people are destroyed for lack of knowledge." Ignorance of spiritual realities does not nullify their effects; it merely leaves believers vulnerable to their operations.

MECHANISMS OF COVENANT ESTABLISHMENT: THREE PRIMARY PATHWAYS

Before examining specific covenant categories, we must understand the primary mechanisms through which individuals become bound by hidden covenants. Our research identifies three overarching pathways:

1. ANCESTRAL OR GENERATIONAL TRANSFERENCE

The biblical principle of generational consequence (Exodus 20:5; 34:7) establishes that spiritual conditions—both blessings and curses—can pass through family lines. This occurs through several mechanisms:

- **Conscious Ancestral Agreements**: Deliberate covenants made by ancestors with idolatrous systems, secret societies, or territorial spirits.
- **Unconscious Ancestral Patterns**: Repeated sinful behaviors or traumatic experiences that create "open doors" for spiritual oppression to become familial patterns.
- **Birthright Transfers**: The spiritual implications of birth order, naming practices, and familial roles that may carry covenant significance.
- **Geographical Connections**: The spiritual environment of one's lineage—locations, lands, dwellings that carry covenant history.

The critical insight here is that **an inherited covenant, even if established unconsciously or by previous generations, carries the same binding force as a covenant entered consciously and personally**. Spiritual realities are not diminished by temporal distance or lack of contemporary awareness.

2. PERSONAL AND CONSCIOUS CHOICE

Contrary to popular assumption, many individuals enter destructive covenants through deliberate, conscious choice, though often without full understanding of the spiritual implications:

- **Secret Society Initiation**: The formal rituals of fraternal orders, occult organizations, or cultural secret societies that involve oath-taking, blood rituals, or symbolic deaths.
- **Relationship Covenants**: The exchange of blood, vows, or binding promises in romantic relationships outside marriage.
- **Economic Agreements**: The acceptance of "strange money" or participation in unethical economic practices that carry spiritual strings.
- **Religious Commitment**: The taking of vows, sacraments, or initiations in religious systems that, while appearing benign, establish covenants with spirits other than Christ.

These covenants are particularly binding because they involve the exercise of human will—the God-given faculty of choice being directed toward destructive spiritual alliances.

3. UNCONSCIOUS OR COERCED ESTABLISHMENT

Perhaps the most pastorally challenging category involves covenants established without full conscious consent or through coercive means:

- **Dream State Manipulation**: Spiritual interactions during sleep where consent may be given without waking awareness.
- **Ritual Participation Unawareness**: Involvement in cultural or religious rituals whose full spiritual significance remains unknown to participants.
- **Trauma-Based Openings**: Severe physical, emotional, or sexual trauma that creates spiritual vulnerabilities exploited by evil spirits to establish footholds.
- **Object-Based Connections**: Possession or use of objects previously dedicated to idolatrous purposes, creating unconscious spiritual linkages.

These covenants raise complex theological questions about consent and responsibility, yet their effects remain equally real and require similar processes for resolution.

DIAGNOSTIC INDICATORS: RECOGNIZING THE FOOTPRINTS OF HIDDEN COVENANTS

Before proceeding to specific covenant categories, we must equip ourselves with diagnostic tools. How does one recognize the possible presence of hidden covenants? Our clinical and pastoral observations reveal consistent symptomatic patterns:

RESISTANCE TO CONVENTIONAL SPIRITUAL REMEDIES

The most telling indicator involves persistent problems that resist normal spiritual interventions:

- Conditions unresponsive to prayer, counseling, or spiritual discipline
- Patterns that persist despite genuine repentance and lifestyle change
- Issues that improve temporarily only to return with equal or greater intensity
- Spiritual experiences (prayer, worship, Scripture reading) that consistently encounter unusual obstruction

PSYCHO-EMOTIONAL MANIFESTATIONS

Hidden covenants often manifest through identifiable psychological and emotional patterns:

- Unexplained anxiety, depression, or emotional volatility
- Recurrent nightmares or sleep disturbances with consistent themes
- Memory gaps or "lost time" particularly around significant life events
- Compulsive behaviors or thought patterns resistant to therapeutic intervention
- Unusual fears or phobias without identifiable traumatic origins

RELATIONAL AND VOCATIONAL PATTERNS

Covenants frequently establish themselves in relational and vocational dimensions:

- Repeated relational failures following identical patterns despite different partners
- Vocational obstruction at threshold moments of advancement or success
- Unexplained opposition from individuals who would normally be supportive
- Geographic or demographic patterns in life difficulties

PHYSICAL AND PHYSIOLOGICAL INDICATERS

While not all physical issues have spiritual causes, certain patterns suggest covenant influence:

- Chronic conditions unresponsive to medical treatment
- Symptoms that manifest in relation to specific locations, times, or relationships
- Family medical histories with consistent patterns across generations
- Unexplained physiological reactions to spiritual activities (prayer, worship, etc.)

SPIRITUAL AND EXPERIENTIAL MARKERS

Most directly, certain spiritual experiences may indicate covenant presence:

- Recurrent dreams with covenant-establishing content (eating with dead, ritual participation)
- Unusual spiritual manifestations during prayer or worship
- Specific spiritual sensitivities or aversions (to certain places, objects, or activities)
- Awareness of spiritual presences or influences not explained by psychological factors

These diagnostic indicators must be applied with wisdom and discernment, recognizing that multiple factors—psychological, physiological, spiritual—often interact in complex ways. However, when persistent patterns emerge across multiple dimensions, the possibility of hidden covenant influence warrants serious consideration.

TWENTY-ONE CATEGORIES OF HIDDEN EVIL COVENANTS: A COMPREHENSIVE TAXONOMY

We now proceed to our central task: the detailed examination of twenty-one specific categories of hidden evil covenants. This taxonomy emerges from extensive cross-cultural ministry experience, anthropological research, and biblical analysis. Each category will be examined according to a consistent framework: definitional parameters, mechanisms of establishment, symptomatic manifestations, biblical references, and pastoral implications.

CATEGORY 1: SPIRITUAL BURIAL COVENANTS

Definition and Mechanism: This covenant involves the symbolic or ritual burial of an individual—either through physical effigy (coffin construction), representative object (hair, nail clippings, photographs), or spiritual declaration—thereby consigning them to premature spiritual death or confinement. The mechanism operates on the spiritual principle of identification: what happens to the representative happens to the person.

Biblical Foundation: Isaiah 28:15-18 explicitly references covenants with death and agreements with Sheol, indicating the spiritual reality of such arrangements. The passage further declares God's intention to annul such covenants, establishing both their reality and their vulnerability to divine intervention.

Establishment Pathways:

- Parental or ancestral rituals seeking protection through symbolic burial
- Occult rituals targeting individuals for destruction or limitation
- Self-cursing through declarations of worthlessness or desire for death
- Participation in rituals involving coffin symbolism or grave association

Symptomatic Manifestations:

- Chronic health conditions with "wasting" or degenerative characteristics
- Premature aging or vitality loss without medical explanation
- Recurrent dreams of confinement, burial, or suffocation
- Persistent feelings of being "dead while alive" or emotional numbness
- Vocational or relational death at threshold moments

Pastoral Considerations: This covenant represents one of the most severe forms of spiritual oppression, as it attacks the fundamental God-given right to life and vitality. Breaking requires not only renunciation but deliberate "resurrection" prayers invoking Christ's victory over death.

CATEGORY 2: DEMONIC MARRIAGE CEREMONY COVENANTS

Definition and Mechanism: Traditional marriage ceremonies, particularly in certain cultural contexts, incorporate elements derived from or dedicated to idolatrous systems. The use of specific numbers, materials, or rituals—often appearing as mere cultural traditions—actually establishes covenants with territorial or familial spirits.

Cultural-Anthropological Analysis: The Yoruba example of 42 items (yam, fish, kolanut) illustrates this phenomenon. Numerologically, 4+2=6, connecting to the biblical number of incompleteness and rebellion (666). Historically, this number derives from Ifa divination systems, explicitly connecting the ritual to spiritual forces outside Christ.

Establishment Pathways:

- Provision of ritually prescribed marriage items
- Performance of traditional ceremonies with spiritual roots
- Consumption of dedicated foods during marriage rituals
- Ritual gestures (water pouring, cloth spreading) with spiritual significance

Symptomatic Manifestations:

- Marital discord following specific patterns (financial, communication, infidelity)
- Infertility or reproductive issues without medical cause
- Financial struggle despite adequate income and management
- Spiritual oppression specifically manifesting in the home environment

- Generational replication of marital dysfunction

Theological Implications: This category raises crucial questions about cultural preservation versus spiritual purity. Believers must exercise discernment, recognizing that not all traditions are neutral—some carry spiritual implications that may conflict with allegiance to Christ.

CATEGORY 3: COVENANTS THROUGH DEMONIC LAYING ON OF HANDS

Definition and Mechanism: The biblical practice of laying on of hands—for blessing, healing, ordination, or impartation—represents a transfer of spiritual substance. When performed by individuals in spiritual compromise or with wrong motives, this transfer can involve negative spiritual elements, establishing covenants of limitation, oppression, or transference of specific spiritual conditions.

Biblical Contrast: Scripture records fourteen distinct purposes for laying on of hands, all positive (Genesis 48:14; Exodus 17:11; Deuteronomy 34:9; Psalm 134:2; 141:2; Matthew 19:13; Mark 16:18; Acts 6:6; 13:3; 19:6; 14:3; Galatians 2:9; 1 Timothy 2:8; 4:14; 2 Timothy 1:6). The enemy counterfeits this practice, using similar mechanisms for destructive purposes.

Establishment Pathways:

- Blessing or prayer by individuals involved in occult practices
- Ordination or commissioning by spiritually compromised leaders
- Therapeutic touch by practitioners incorporating non-Christian spiritual elements
- Family blessings by ancestors involved in idolatry

Symptomatic Manifestations:

- Development of specific conditions following particular prayers or blessings
- Transference of generational patterns through parental blessing
- Spiritual oppression correlating with specific relational connections
- Ministry limitations following improper ordination or commissioning

Pastoral Protocol: This category necessitates careful discernment in spiritual leadership and the ministry of laying on of hands. Leaders must maintain personal purity, and recipients should exercise discernment about whose spiritual impartation they receive.

CATEGORY 4: SERPENTINE POISON COVENANTS

Definition and Mechanism: This covenant involves the transfer of spiritual poison—often symbolized by serpentine imagery—through physical contact, particularly in contexts like hair salons, beauty treatments, or therapeutic practices where practitioners may (knowingly or unknowingly) be channels for spiritual contamination.

Symbolic Theology: The serpent represents deception, poison, and spiritual death from Genesis onward. The transfer of serpentine poison symbolizes the implantation of destructive spiritual influences that progressively undermine life and vitality.

Establishment Pathways:

- Beauty treatments involving spiritually compromised practitioners
- Use of products previously dedicated to idolatrous purposes
- Therapeutic practices incorporating non-Christian spiritual elements
- Physical contact with individuals carrying specific spiritual assignments

Symptomatic Manifestations:

- Unexplained physical deterioration following specific treatments
- Dreams of snakes, poison, or contamination
- Development of conditions with "poisonous" characteristics (toxicity, spreading)
- Spiritual sensitivity to specific places or practitioners

Contemporary Relevance: This category has particular significance in modern contexts where personal care and therapeutic services may inadvertently involve spiritual elements. Believers must exercise discernment beyond mere physical considerations.

CATEGORY 5: DREAM STATE COVENANTS

Definition and Mechanism: Covenants established during sleep states where the dreamer participates—willingly or unwillingly—in rituals, agreements, or symbolic actions that establish spiritual contracts. The spiritual principle operates that activities in the dream realm can establish realities in the spiritual realm, which then manifest in the natural.

Biblical Precedent: Scripture contains numerous examples of significant spiritual occurrences in dreams (Jacob's ladder, Joseph's dreams, Pharaoh's dreams, Nebuchadnezzar's dreams). These establish that the dream state constitutes a legitimate arena for spiritual communication and activity.

Establishment Pathways:

- Participation in rituals or ceremonies within dreams
- Consumption of food or substances in dreams
- Sexual encounters in dreams
- Making agreements or promises in dreams
- Receiving objects or symbols in dreams

Symptomatic Manifestations:

- Waking with specific physical symptoms following dreams
- Progressive spiritual oppression correlating with dream content
- Recurrent dream themes with covenant-establishing elements
- Unexplained knowledge or abilities following dreams

Theological Considerations: This category requires balanced understanding. Not all dreams are spiritually significant, and not all significant dreams establish covenants. However, recurrent patterns with specific content warrant discernment and potentially spiritual intervention.

CATEGORY 6: RELIGIOUS SYSTEM COVENANTS

Definition and Mechanism: Participation in religious systems, practices, or sacraments that—while appearing Christian or benign—actually establish covenants with religious spirits rather than with Christ. This includes certain forms of ritualism, legalism, or tradition that substitute for genuine relationship with Christ.

Biblical Framework: Paul's warning about "another gospel" (Galatians 1:6-9) and "different spirit" (2 Corinthians 11:4) establishes that not all religious activity connects with the true God. The book of Revelation addresses churches that maintain religious form while compromising spiritual substance.

Establishment Pathways:

- Participation in sacraments administered by spiritually compromised leaders
- Adherence to religious systems emphasizing ritual over relationship
- Use of religious objects (garments, icons, etc.) with idolatrous connections
- Consumption of ritually dedicated elements in religious contexts

Symptomatic Manifestations:

- Spiritual dryness despite religious activity
- Legalistic approach to faith rather than relational
- Difficulty experiencing grace and forgiveness
- Judgment toward other expressions of Christianity
- Spiritual pride based on religious performance

Ecumenical Sensitivity: This analysis requires careful distinction between legitimate denominational differences and genuinely compromised religious systems. The issue is not variation in worship style but actual spiritual allegiance.

CATEGORY 7: SPIRITUAL MARRIAGE THROUGH OBJECTS

Definition and Mechanism: The use of rings, jewelry, or other objects to establish or symbolize spiritual marriages with demonic entities. These objects become points of contact maintaining the covenant relationship.

Biblical Principle: Objects can become "high places" or "idols"—points of spiritual contact that maintain connections (Deuteronomy 7:25; 1 Corinthians 10:14). While objects themselves have no inherent power, they can become focal points for spiritual realities.

Establishment Pathways:

- Wearing of rings or jewelry with spiritual marriage significance
- Acceptance of objects as symbols of spiritual commitment
- Retention of objects from previous occult relationships
- Use of objects in rituals establishing spiritual marriages

Symptomatic Manifestations:

- Inability to form healthy human marital relationships
- Spiritual oppression specifically relating to marriage or sexuality
- Dreams involving the object with spiritual marriage themes
- Physical reactions to removal of the object

Pastoral Approach: This category often requires both spiritual intervention (breaking covenants) and practical action (removing or destroying objects). The physical act reinforces the spiritual declaration.

CATEGORY 8: JEWELRY AND ADORNMENT COVENANTS

Definition and Mechanism: The wearing of jewelry, adornments, or symbols that carry specific spiritual significance in occult or idolatrous systems, thereby establishing covenant connections with the spirits represented.

Symbolic Analysis: Specific symbols carry centuries of occult association:

- Pentagram/pentacle: Witchcraft and occult symbolism
- Ankh: Egyptian sun god worship
- Zodiac symbols: Astrological systems
- Crescent moon and star: Initiation into specific occult traditions

Biblical Principle: The prohibition against bringing "abominable things" into one's house (Deuteronomy 7:26) extends spiritually to what one places on one's body. The body as temple of the Holy Spirit (1 Corinthians 6:19) should not be adorned with objects connecting to other spirits.

Establishment Pathways:

- Conscious use of symbols with known occult meaning
- Unconscious wearing of jewelry with spiritual significance
- Acceptance of jewelry as gifts from spiritually compromised sources
- Retention of culturally significant jewelry with spiritual roots

Symptomatic Manifestations:

- Spiritual oppression correlating with wearing specific items
- Dreams involving the jewelry with spiritual themes
- Unexplained resistance to removing certain adornments
- Spiritual manifestations during prayer or worship while wearing items

Cultural Considerations: This category requires discernment between mere cultural adornment and items with genuine spiritual significance. Not all jewelry is problematic, but specific symbols with occult history warrant caution.

CATEGORY 9: EAR PIERCING AND SPIRITUAL SLAVERY COVENANTS

Definition and Mechanism: The practice of ear piercing—particularly in specific cultural or ritual contexts—as a symbol and mechanism of establishing covenants of servitude or slavery to spiritual entities.

Biblical Foundation: Exodus 21:6 and Deuteronomy 15:17 explicitly connect ear piercing with perpetual servitude. The slave who chooses to remain with his master has his ear pierced against the doorpost, establishing a visible, permanent sign of voluntary slavery.

Cultural-Anthropological Context: Many cultures practice ritual ear piercing as initiation into servitude to specific deities or spirits. The piercing creates a permanent opening that symbolizes ongoing access and obligation.

Establishment Pathways:

- Ritual ear piercing in cultural or religious initiation

- Multiple piercings as progressive levels of spiritual commitment
- Piercing with ritually prepared instruments
- Piercing at specific ages or life stages with spiritual significance

Symptomatic Manifestations:

- Dreams of servitude or slavery following piercing
- Spiritual oppression with themes of constraint or limitation
- Difficulty hearing or responding to God's voice
- Compulsive behaviors following piercing events

Contemporary Application: This analysis does not condemn all ear piercing but recognizes that in specific ritual contexts, piercing can carry spiritual significance beyond mere adornment.

CATEGORY 10: DEMONIC BAPTISM COVENANTS

Definition and Mechanism: Participation in ritual washings, baths, or immersions that—while mimicking Christian baptism—actually establish covenants with demonic entities rather than with Christ.

Biblical Contrast: Christian baptism represents identification with Christ in His death, burial, and resurrection (Romans 6:3-4). Counterfeit baptisms establish identification with other spiritual realities.

Establishment Pathways:

- Ritual baths prescribed by non-Christian spiritual practitioners

- "Holy water" immersions in compromised religious contexts
- Therapeutic immersions incorporating spiritual elements
- Cultural cleansing rituals with spiritual roots

Symptomatic Manifestations:

- Spiritual confusion about salvation and identity
- Recurrence of conditions supposedly cleansed through rituals
- Dreams of drowning or immersion in dark waters
- Resistance to genuine Christian baptism

Sacramental Theology: This category highlights the importance of understanding the spiritual reality behind physical rituals. The efficacy of baptism derives from its connection to Christ's work, not the water itself.

CATEGORY 11: PHOTOGRAPHIC COVENANTS

Definition and Mechanism: The use of photographs—combined with spiritual rituals—to establish covenants that affect the person photographed. The photograph becomes a point of contact for spiritual activity.

Spiritual Principle: The biblical concept of "image" and "likeness" carries spiritual significance. What happens to the image can affect what it represents, particularly when combined with spiritual intentionality.

Establishment Pathways:

- Ritual manipulation of photographs (binding, piercing, burying)

- Use of photographs in altar constructions
- Combining photographs with other covenant elements
- Theft or acquisition of photographs for spiritual purposes

Symptomatic Manifestations:

- Unexplained oppression following loss of photographs
- Dreams involving photographs with spiritual themes
- Physical symptoms correlating with known photograph manipulation
- Relationship difficulties traceable to photograph rituals

Modern Relevance: In an age of digital imagery, this category may extend to digital representations. The spiritual principle remains: representations can become points of spiritual contact.

CATEGORY 12: NAME-BASED COVENANTS

Definition and Mechanism: The bearing of names—personal, family, or spiritual—that explicitly glorify or connect to idolatrous entities, thereby establishing ongoing covenant relationships through daily identification and declaration.

Biblical Theology of Naming: Scripture consistently demonstrates the spiritual significance of names. Name changes (Abram to Abraham, Jacob to Israel) signify spiritual transformation. Bearing a name connects to what or whom the name represents.

Establishment Pathways:

- Receiving names that invoke or honor non-Christian deities
- Family names with idolatrous etymological roots
- Spiritual names taken in non-Christian initiations

- Retention of names with known negative spiritual meanings

Symptomatic Manifestations:

- Life patterns reflecting the meaning of problematic names
- Spiritual oppression associated with name usage
- Difficulty establishing Christian identity while bearing contradictory names
- Dreams revealing the spiritual significance of names

Pastoral Practice: This category may require both spiritual intervention (breaking name-based covenants) and practical action (name changes or additions). The declaration of new identity in Christ is crucial.

CATEGORY 13: INCESTUOUS COVENANTS

Definition and Mechanism: Sexual relationships between close relatives that—beyond their psychological damage—establish powerful blood covenants with generational consequences due to the mixing of closely related genetic and spiritual lines.

Biblical Prohibition: Levitical law explicitly prohibits incestuous relationships (Leviticus 18:6-18), recognizing both natural and spiritual dangers. Such relationships create profound spiritual entanglements.

Spiritual Dynamics: Incest involves the mixing of similar spiritual DNA, creating reinforced patterns and intensified spiritual consequences. The blood covenant established carries multiplied generational impact.

Establishment Pathways:

- Consensual incestuous relationships
- Coerced or abusive incestuous encounters
- Spiritual incest through dream encounters
- Symbolic incest through ritual practices

Symptomatic Manifestations:

- Severe relational dysfunction following incest
- Multi-generational patterns of sexual brokenness
- Spiritual confusion about identity and relationships
- Compound psychological and spiritual trauma

Restorative Theology: This category requires profound sensitivity, recognizing the complex trauma involved. Spiritual freedom must be coupled with psychological healing and relational restoration.

CATEGORY 14: DEMONIC CONSUMPTION COVENANTS

Definition and Mechanism: The consumption of foods, drinks, or substances that have been ritually dedicated to or prepared in connection with idolatrous practices, thereby establishing covenants through ingestion.

Biblical Principle: Paul addresses food sacrificed to idols (1 Corinthians 8; 10), recognizing that consumption can establish spiritual fellowship (1 Corinthians 10:20-21). What is ingested can have spiritual implications beyond nutritional value.

Establishment Pathways:

- Participation in rituals involving dedicated foods

- Consumption of foods prepared with spiritual intentionality
- Use of substances in ritual contexts
- Accidental consumption of spiritually compromised items

Symptomatic Manifestations:

- Spiritual oppression following consumption events
- Dreams of eating or drinking in ritual contexts
- Physical reactions to specific foods with spiritual history
- Development of conditions following specific consumptions

Practical Discernment: This category requires wisdom, not paranoia. The issue is not food itself but spiritual intentionality behind its preparation and consumption.

CATEGORY 15: CHIEFTAINCY TITLE COVENANTS

Definition and Mechanism: Acceptance of traditional chieftaincy titles that involve ritual initiation, often including covenant-establishing elements that connect the recipient to ancestral spirits or territorial deities.

Cultural-Anthropological Context: In many African contexts, chieftaincy installation involves elaborate rituals with specific spiritual components: sacred groves, ancestral invocation, ritual garments, symbolic objects.

Theological Tension: Believers called to cultural leadership face tension between influence and compromise. Some titles involve minimal spiritual compromise; others require substantial covenant participation.

Establishment Pathways:

- Participation in installation rituals
- Acceptance of ritual garments or objects
- Swearing of traditional oaths
- Maintenance of traditional obligations

Symptomatic Manifestations:

- Spiritual conflict following title acceptance
- Dreams involving traditional ritual elements
- Pressure to participate in ongoing traditional obligations
- Conflict between Christian faith and traditional expectations

Missiological Approach: This category requires contextualized approaches that neither completely reject culture nor uncritically accept all traditional practices. Discerning engagement is needed.

CATEGORY 16: CIRCUMCISION-BASED COVENANTS

Definition and Mechanism: Ritual circumcision performed in contexts with spiritual significance beyond mere physical procedure, establishing covenants through blood ritual at the most intimate physical and spiritual level.

Biblical Contrast: Biblical circumcision represented covenant with Yahweh (Genesis 17). Counterfeit circumcision establishes covenant with other spiritual realities.

Cultural Variations: Different cultures practice circumcision with varying spiritual significance. The issue is not the physical act but the spiritual intentionality and context.

Establishment Pathways:

- Ritual circumcision in non-Christian spiritual contexts
- Circumcision by spiritually compromised practitioners
- Circumcision at spiritually significant times or places
- Circumcision accompanied by specific spiritual rituals

Symptomatic Manifestations:

- Sexual or relational dysfunction following circumcision
- Dreams involving the circumcision event or practitioner
- Spiritual oppression with sexual themes
- Generational patterns connected to circumcision practices

Medical-Spiritual Interface: This analysis recognizes legitimate medical reasons for circumcision while discerning potentially problematic spiritual contexts.

CATEGORY 17: TWINS-RELATED COVENANTS

Definition and Mechanism: Cultural or ritual practices specifically related to twins that establish covenants—either between the twins themselves or between the twins and spiritual entities.

Anthropological Context: Many cultures have specific spiritual beliefs and practices regarding twins, ranging from veneration to fear. These often involve ritual practices with covenant implications.

Establishment Pathways:

- Ritual separation or bonding of twins

- Special naming ceremonies for twins
- Ritual obligations for parents of twins
- Cultural practices treating twins as spiritual entities

Symptomatic Manifestations:

- Unusual spiritual connection or conflict between twins
- Dreams involving twin-specific spiritual themes
- Life patterns following twin-related cultural expectations
- Spiritual oppression with twin-specific characteristics

Developmental Considerations: This category requires sensitivity to the unique bond between twins while discerning potentially problematic spiritual elements in cultural practices.

CATEGORY 18: STRANGE MONEY COVENANTS

Definition and Mechanism: Acceptance of money or financial benefit that carries spiritual strings—either through its source (occult practices, ritual purposes) or through the intentions of the giver (to establish spiritual obligation).

Biblical Principle: The love of money is a root of evil (1 Timothy 6:10), and money can carry spiritual contamination (Deuteronomy 23:18). Financial transactions can establish spiritual relationships.

Establishment Pathways:

- Acceptance of money from occult sources or practices
- Financial transactions with spiritually compromised intentions
- Inheritance from ancestors involved in occult practices
- Business partnerships with spiritual obligations

Symptomatic Manifestations:

- Financial patterns of gain and sudden loss
- Spiritual oppression following financial transactions
- Dreams involving money with spiritual themes
- Inability to achieve financial stability despite apparent opportunities

Economic Spirituality: This category highlights the spiritual dimensions of economic activity, requiring discernment beyond mere financial considerations.

CATEGORY 19: DEMONIC PARTY COVENANTS

Definition and Mechanism: Participation in celebrations, parties, or feasts that—while appearing as mere social events—involve spiritually compromised elements: dedicated foods, ritual timing, symbolic elements that establish covenants.

Biblical Parallel: Feasts often followed covenant establishment in Scripture (Genesis 21:27-30; 31:54). Shared meals can establish spiritual fellowship.

Establishment Pathways:

- Consumption of ritually prepared foods at celebrations
- Participation in parties with spiritual timing or elements
- Celebration of birthdays with spiritual significance
- Attendance at events with underlying spiritual purposes

Symptomatic Manifestations:

- Spiritual oppression following specific celebrations
- Dreams of party participation with spiritual elements

- Life difficulties following milestone celebrations
- Unexplained aversion to certain types of celebrations

Social Discernment: This category requires wisdom in social participation, recognizing that not all celebrations are spiritually neutral.

CATEGORY 20: FIRST SEXUAL PARTNER COVENANTS

Definition and Mechanism: The first sexual encounter—particularly outside marriage—establishes a profound blood covenant that affects all subsequent relationships and spiritual condition.

Biblical Principle: Sexual union establishes "one flesh" (Genesis 2:24; Matthew 19:5-6)—a profound spiritual, physical, and emotional joining. This union creates covenant realities.

Establishment Pathways:

- Consensual premarital sexual activity
- Coerced or abusive sexual encounters
- Ritual sexual activity in occult contexts
- Dream state sexual encounters

Symptomatic Manifestations:

- Relationship patterns reflecting first sexual partner
- Spiritual oppression with sexual themes
- Difficulty establishing healthy marital intimacy
- Generational patterns following sexual choices

Restorative Theology: This category requires both spiritual cleansing and psychological healing. God's redemptive power can restore what has been damaged.

CATEGORY 21: POLYGAMY-BASED COVENANTS

Definition and Mechanism: Participation in polygamous family systems—whether as spouse, child, or descendant—establishes complex covenant networks with spiritual consequences affecting relationships, identity, and destiny.

Biblical Context: While Old Testament records polygamy, its consequences are consistently negative (strife, jealousy, generational conflict). The New Testament establishes monogamy as God's standard (1 Timothy 3:2, 12).

Spiritual Dynamics: Polygamy creates competing spiritual lines, divided loyalties, and complex generational spiritual entanglements.

Establishment Pathways:

- Direct participation in polygamous marriage
- Birth into polygamous family system
- Cultural pressure toward polygamous practices
- Spiritual marriages in polygamous contexts

Symptomatic Manifestations:

- Relational confusion and conflict
- Identity issues related to family position
- Spiritual oppression with familial themes
- Generational patterns of relational brokenness

Missiological Sensitivity: This category requires cultural sensitivity while maintaining biblical standards. Many believers come from polygamous backgrounds requiring both spiritual freedom and cultural navigation.

TOWARD DELIVERANCE: BIBLICAL FRAMEWORKS FOR COVENANT BREAKING

Having examined these twenty-one categories, we must establish the biblical framework for freedom. The work of Christ provides complete deliverance, but appropriation requires specific responses:

1. REPENTANCE: THE FOUNDATIONAL POSTURE

True repentance—metanoia, change of mind and direction—establishes the proper relational posture before God. This includes repentance for:

- Personal involvement in covenant-establishing activities
- Ancestral participation in destructive covenants
- Unconscious compliance with covenant mechanisms
- Failure to discern and resist spiritual encroachment

2. RENUNCIATION: THE SPECIFIC REJECTION

Renunciation involves the specific, verbal rejection of covenants and their effects:

- Naming specific covenants and their mechanisms
- Rejecting their claims and effects
- Revoking any consent given—consciously or unconsciously
- Disavowing ancestral participation

3. REVOCATION: THE LEGAL CANCELATION

Revocation exercises legal-spiritual authority to cancel covenant claims:

- Applying the blood of Christ as superior covenant
- Declaring the finished work of Christ as annulment
- Using the keys of the kingdom to bind and loose
- Enforcing Christ's victory over all spiritual powers

4. RESISTANCE: THE ACTIVE OPPOSITION

Resistance involves ongoing spiritual warfare against covenant enforcement:

- Binding spirits assigned to enforce covenants
- Commanding release from covenant obligations
- Resisting manifestations of covenant effects
- Maintaining freedom through ongoing spiritual discipline

5. REPLACEMENT: THE POSITIVE ESTABLISHMENT

Replacement establishes godly alternatives to broken covenants:

- Claiming the blessings of Abraham through Christ
- Establishing new covenants with God through Christ
- Creating godly generational patterns
- Walking in newfound freedom and authority

CONCLUDING OBSERVATIONS AND CONTINUING INVESTIGATION

This comprehensive examination of twenty-one hidden evil covenants establishes several critical conclusions:

1. **The Reality and Diversity of Hidden Covenants**: Our investigation demonstrates that hidden evil covenants

constitute a diverse, complex spiritual reality affecting believers in multiple dimensions.

2. **The Mechanisms Are Knowable**: While often hidden, covenant mechanisms follow identifiable patterns and principles that can be discerned through biblical study, spiritual discernment, and cross-cultural understanding.
3. **Symptoms Provide Diagnostic Clues**: Persistent patterns of spiritual, emotional, relational, and physical difficulty often indicate underlying covenant issues requiring specific intervention.
4. **Freedom Is Available and Complete**: Christ's finished work provides complete deliverance from every form of covenant bondage, but appropriation requires specific application of biblical principles.
5. **Discernment Must Balance Wisdom and Revelation**: Effective ministry in this area requires both biblical wisdom and spiritual revelation, avoiding both naive denial and excessive demonic focus.

As we proceed to subsequent chapters examining collective captivity, curse mechanisms, altar dynamics, and specific deliverance strategies, this foundation in covenant identification will prove essential. The journey from bondage to freedom begins with recognizing the chains that bind—only then can they be specifically broken through the power of Christ's superior covenant.

The prayer section that follows provides initial practical application, but represents merely the beginning of a comprehensive deliverance process that will unfold throughout this volume. Let us proceed with both sober recognition of spiritual realities and confident faith in Christ's complete victory.

PRAYER SECTION

A LITURGY OF DELIVERANCE AND COVENANT BREAKING

Beloved, what follows is not merely a collection of words to be recited, but a spiritual engagement of the highest order. These prayers are theological declarations, legal-spiritual petitions, and warfare pronouncements that engage with the realities we have just examined. Approach them not as incantations, but as faith-filled applications of Christ's victory to the specific bondages we have identified. Pray with understanding, with authority born of your position in Christ, and with the fierce conviction that the One within you is greater than all opposing forces.

PREPARATORY CONFESSION AND POSTURE

Before you begin, center your heart with these foundational truths. Speak them aloud:

"I come before the throne of grace not in my own merit, but clothed in the righteousness of Jesus Christ. My authority is derived from His Name, my standing secured by His blood, and my victory assured by His resurrection. I am a child of God, an heir with Christ, and a citizen of the Kingdom of Light. Every spiritual legal right to address these hidden things flows from my union with Him. I declare that His blood speaks better things than any covenant of darkness. I stand firm in the liberty for which Christ has set me free."

SECTION ONE: REPENTANCE AND RENUNCIATION

Prayer of Comprehensive Repentance:

Heavenly Father, Eternal God who reveals hidden things, I approach You in humility and truth.

I repent for every avenue—known and unknown—through which covenant ties with darkness have been established in my life and lineage. I repent for the sins of my ancestors that opened doors to these bondages. I repent for my own ignorance, compliance, or participation in practices, traditions, or relationships that forged unholy alliances. I turn away from every idolatrous attachment and choose this day to serve the Lord alone.

I renounce, reject, and revoke any and all covenants, pacts, oaths, promises, or agreements made with any spirit, power, or entity other than the Lord Jesus Christ. This includes covenants made consciously by me or my ancestors, and covenants entered unconsciously through ritual, tradition, trauma, or deception. I declare them null, void, and broken by the superior blood of the Lamb.

(Pause here. In silence, allow the Holy Spirit to bring to mind any specific covenant, practice, or name that requires personal mention. Speak it out and renounce it specifically.)

SECTION TWO: TARGETED REVOCATION OF THE TWENTY-ONE COVENANTS

Now, with the authority of a believer, address each category we have studied. Pray aggressively, with the conviction that you are serving legal notice in the spiritual realm.

1. Against Spiritual Burial Covenants:

In the name of Jesus Christ, I revoke and shatter every covenant with death and agreement with hell spoken over my life or lineage. I cancel every symbolic burial, coffin ritual, or curse of premature death. I command every spirit of death, hell, and the grave to release me and my generations. I declare that I am alive unto God and my life is hidden with Christ. I am resurrected with Him into newness of life.

2. Against Demonic Marriage Ceremony Covenants:

I break every covenant established through traditional marriage rituals that honored spirits other than God. I nullify the power of every ritually presented item—yams, fish, kola nuts, alcohol, or any other element. I sever the ties formed through ceremonial gestures like water-pouring or cloth-spreading. I declare my marriage (or future marriage) is sanctified and covenanted to Christ alone.

3. Against Covenants Through Demonic Laying on of Hands:

I break and reverse every negative transfer, curse, or covenant imparted through the laying on of hands by any person in spiritual compromise, idolatry, or occult involvement. I revoke any imparted spirit of failure, poverty, sickness, or bondage. I command every unclean thing transferred to me to be flushed out by the fire of the Holy Spirit. I receive anew the pure impartation of the Holy Spirit.

4. Against Serpentine Poison Covenants:

I break every covenant of poison transferred through beauty treatments, salons, or physical contact with spiritually contaminated practitioners or objects. I command every serpentine spirit and every spiritual toxin deposited in my system to be neutralized by the blood of Jesus and expelled by the fire of the Holy Ghost. I reclaim the health of my body, hair, and skin for God's glory.

5. Against Dream State Covenants:

I revoke every covenant, vow, promise, or agreement made in my dreams. I take back every consent given while asleep. I break the power of every spiritual marriage, ritual meal, or symbolic act performed in my dreams. I place the blood of Jesus over my mind and my sleep. I decree that my dreams will be under the Lordship of Christ and any demonic activity therein is rendered null and void.

6. Against Religious System Covenants:

I renounce and break free from every covenant with religious spirits formed through participation in rituals, sacraments, or systems that drew allegiance away from a pure relationship with Christ. This includes false worship, empty ritualism, and idolatrous practices disguised as religion. I declare my total allegiance is to Jesus Christ alone, and I am free from all counterfeit religious bondage.

7. Against Spiritual Marriage Through Objects:

I break every spiritual marriage covenant symbolized or maintained by any ring, jewelry, or object. I command every spirit husband or spirit wife attached to such objects to release me now. I divorce them in the name of Jesus. I destroy the legal claim of any such object over my life. I remove and renounce any such object from my possession and life.

8. Against Jewelry and Adornment Covenants:

I renounce and break every covenant connection established through wearing jewelry, adornments, or symbols dedicated to idols, occult powers, or false gods (including pentagrams, ankhs, zodiac symbols, etc.). I sever the link between my person and any such object. I command every demonic gateway opened through such items to be sealed shut by the blood of Jesus.

9. Against Ear Piercing and Spiritual Slavery Covenants:

I break every covenant of servitude or slavery to demons signified by ritual ear piercing. I reclaim my ears to hear only the voice of God. I command every spirit of slavery, servitude, and deafness to God's voice to depart. I declare I am a child of God, not a slave. I am seated with Christ in heavenly places.

10. Against Demonic Baptism Covenants:

I renounce and invalidate any ritual bath, washing, or immersion that baptized me into allegiance with any spirit other than the Holy Spirit. I declare it null and void. I affirm my true baptism into the death and resurrection of Jesus Christ, which is my only valid spiritual identification.

11. Against Photographic Covenants:

I break every covenant, curse, or spell enacted against me using my photograph or image. I revoke the power of any ritual involving my picture—whether buried, bound, burned, or placed on any altar. I reclaim my image and identity in Christ. I command every demonic link formed through such practices to be severed by the sword of the Spirit.

12. Against Name-Based Covenants:

I break every covenant attached to my life through any name—given at birth, taken in ritual, or inherited through family—that honors, invokes, or connects me to any idol, demon, or unclean spirit. I renounce the spiritual influence of that name. I declare that my true identity is found in Christ. I am who God says I am.

13. Against Incestuous Covenants:

In the name of Jesus, I break the powerful and perverse blood covenant established through any incestuous relationship (whether in the physical or spiritual/dream realm). I sever the unclean soul-ties and spiritual entanglements formed. I command every spirit of confusion, shame, and relational dysfunction stemming from this to be bound and cast out. I receive the healing and purity of Christ.

14. Against Demonic Consumption Covenants:

I break every covenant established through consuming foods, drinks, or substances dedicated to idols or prepared with demonic intentionality. I revoke the power of every ritual meal I have ever participated in. I plead the blood of Jesus over my digestive system and my entire body. I command every demonic nutrient or poison to be expelled.

15. Against Chieftaincy Title Covenants:

I renounce and break every covenant associated with any traditional title, chieftaincy, or honor that required ritual allegiance to ancestral or territorial spirits. I revoke any oaths sworn, any rituals performed, and any garments or objects received. I surrender any title or honor that conflicts with my supreme allegiance to Jesus Christ, my King.

16. Against Circumcision-Based Covenants:

I break every covenant with demonic powers established through ritual circumcision performed outside the covenant of God. I revoke any spiritual claim made through that blood ritual. I apply the blood of Jesus to that moment and that part of my body. I declare I am circumcised in heart by the Spirit, not by hands.

17. Against Twins-Related Covenants:

I break every covenant, curse, or spiritual assignment attached to my life (or the life of my twin) because of being a twin. I nullify any ritual performed at our birth or during our lives that sought to dictate our destiny. I sever any unnatural spiritual bondage or conflict between us. I decree that our lives are governed by God's unique purpose, not by cultural or demonic traditions.

18. Against Strange Money Covenants:

I break every covenant of poverty, failure, or obligation attached to money acquired from unclean, occult, or cursed sources. I renounce and revoke any spiritual strings attached to my finances. I command the spirit of poverty to loose its grip. I declare my finances are redeemed, sanctified, and under the blessing of Abraham through Christ.

19. Against Demonic Party Covenants:

I break every covenant established through participation in celebrations, parties, or feasts that had underlying idolatrous or occult significance. I revoke the power of any dedicated foods consumed, any toasts made, or any rituals observed. I reclaim every milestone birthday or celebration for the glory of God.

20. Against First Sexual Partner Covenants:

In Jesus' name, I break the powerful soul-tie and blood covenant formed with my first sexual partner outside of marriage. I sever that ungodly bond completely. I command every spirit of relational failure, comparison, or bondage linked to that union to depart. I apply the blood of Jesus to cleanse, heal, and restore my sexuality to God's original design. I receive purity and wholeness.

21. Against Polygamy-Based Covenants:

I break every complex covenant, curse, and spiritual entanglement arising from my connection to a polygamous family system (whether as child, spouse, or descendant). I sever the cords of confusion, rivalry, divided identity, and inherited strife. I command every spirit of jealousy, rejection, and familial conflict to leave my lineage now. I declare that in Christ, I am part of a chosen lineage, a royal priesthood, a holy nation belonging to God.

SECTION THREE: ACTIVE RESISTANCE AND ENFORCEMENT

Now, enforce these revocations with direct spiritual warfare.

Binding and Loosing:

In the authority of Jesus Christ, I bind every spirit, power, and principality assigned to enforce these broken covenants. I bind spirits of memory that seek to remind me of past bondage. I bind spirits of accusation that condemn me for things now under the blood. I bind spirits of repetition that try to recreate the patterns of the past. I bind every strongman overseeing these operations in my life.

I loose myself from their grip, their influence, and their legal claims. I loose the fire of God to consume every record, document, or claim they hold in the spiritual realm against me. I loose the angels of God to execute this judgment and escort these bound spirits to their appointed place.

Command of Release:

Spirit enforcing [Name a specific covenant, e.g., covenant of poverty], I command you to release me now in Jesus' name! Release my finances, release my health, release my mind, release my destiny. You have no legal right. The blood of Jesus has canceled your claim. RELEASE ME! (Repeat this command with holy aggression for each area of your life under pressure).

Pleading the Blood and Fire:

I plead the blood of Jesus Christ over every area of my life—spirit, soul, body, relationships, finances, and destiny. Let this blood annul every contrary covenant, silence every accusing voice, and cleanse every stain.

I call for the fire of the Holy Ghost to burn out every root, residue, and remnant of these broken covenants from my life. Burn out every hidden deposit, every subconscious link, every cellular memory of bondage. Let Your fire purify me completely.

SECTION FOUR: REPLACEMENT AND BLESSING

Do not leave a vacuum. Fill the cleansed space with God's truth and blessing.

Declaration of New Covenant Identity:

I now receive and walk in the blessings of the New Covenant in Christ's blood. I am forgiven, redeemed, justified, sanctified, and being glorified. I am Abraham's seed and an heir according to the promise. The blessing of Abraham—spiritual, physical, and material—is mine in Christ Jesus.

I declare that every curse is broken and replaced with blessing, every covenant of death replaced with the covenant of life, every bondage replaced with glorious liberty. I am free indeed.

Prayer of Sealing and Protection:

Heavenly Father, I thank You for the comprehensive work of deliverance. I ask that You seal this work by Your Spirit. Surround me with a hedge of protection, post angels to guard my steps, and fill me with Your peace. Grant me discernment to avoid future entanglement and the courage to walk in this new freedom.

I consecrate my entire life—past, present, and future—to You. Let every detail serve as a testimony of Your delivering power. In the mighty, matchless, and magnificent name of Jesus Christ, my Lord and Redeemer, I pray.

Amen.

POST-PRAYER INSTRUCTIONS:

1. **Give Thanks:** Spend time in heartfelt thanksgiving. Praise is the posture of victory.
2. **Be Alert:** The enemy may test or challenge your declaration in the coming days. Stand firm in your faith. Resist thoughts of doubt or fear immediately.
3. **Take Practical Steps:** If the Holy Spirit prompts you to destroy an object, change a practice, or make restitution, obey promptly. Faith without works is dead.
4. **Walk in the Word:** Immerse yourself in Scriptures about your identity and freedom in Christ (e.g., Galatians, Ephesians, Colossians). Renew your mind.
5. **Share Wisely:** Your testimony has power, but share it with discernment. Some victories are first secured in private before they are proclaimed in public.

You have engaged in a profound spiritual transaction. Now, live out your freedom. Go in the peace and power of Christ.

CHAPTER 02

THEOLOGY OF COLLECTIVE CAPTIVITY: CORPORATE BONDAGE AND GENERATIONAL STRATEGIES OF DARKNESS

"And that they may recover themselves out of the snare of the devil, who are taken captive by him at his will" (2 Timothy 2:26).

Let us begin by sitting with the profound and unsettling implication of this Pauline declaration. The apostle does not speak here of voluntary alliance or conscious rebellion, but of *captivity*—a state of being seized, held, and manipulated against one's better judgment or desire. The Greek term *zōgreō* used here paints a vivid picture: to take alive, to capture, as a hunter captures prey. And most terrifyingly, this captivity occurs "at his will"—according to the devil's desire, purpose, and timing. This is not mere temptation or harassment; this is systemic, strategic imprisonment of human lives and destinies.

We are entering now into one of the most complex and pastorally challenging dimensions of spiritual warfare: the reality of collective captivity. If Chapter One revealed how *individuals* become bound through hidden covenants, this chapter unveils how *groups*—families, lineages, communities, even nations—can become enmeshed in corporate bondage that transcends individual choices or personal sanctification. This is spiritual warfare on a genealogical, geographical, and sociological scale.

BIBLICAL FOUNDATIONS: THE REALITY OF CORPORATE SPIRITUAL CONDITIONS

Scripture establishes without ambiguity that spiritual conditions can be corporate, transgenerational, and territorial. Let us anchor our discussion in three foundational texts that form what we might call the "captivity triad":

Psalm 68:18: "Thou hast ascended on high, thou hast led captivity captive: thou hast received gifts for men; yea, for the rebellious also, that the LORD God might dwell among them."

This messianic psalm celebrates a fundamental spiritual truth: captivity exists as a spiritual reality, but there exists a Conqueror who can "lead captivity captive"—who can imprison the imprisoner, who can take the jailer captive. The Hebrew construction here is emphatic: *shabah shabiy*—you have led captive your captives. This is not merely individual liberation; this is systemic overthrow of captivity structures themselves.

2 Timothy 2:26: Our opening text reveals the mechanism: people are "taken captive by him at his will." The devil operates with intentionality, with strategy, with what might be called spiritual intelligence. He identifies vulnerabilities, exploits generational openings, and establishes strongholds that can endure for centuries.

Hebrews 2:15: "And deliver them who through fear of death were all their lifetime subject to bondage."

Here we see the psychological-spiritual mechanism: fear—particularly the fear of death—becomes the doorway to lifelong bondage. But notice the corporate implication: "them" who are subject. This is not isolated cases but patterns of captivity affecting groups of people.

From these foundations, we must develop a robust theology of collective spiritual conditions—one that avoids the twin errors of Western hyper-individualism (which denies corporate spiritual reality) and Eastern fatalistic determinism (which sees individuals as mere products of collective fate). The biblical balance recognizes both individual responsibility *and* corporate spiritual inheritance.

TYPOLOGY OF CAPTIVITY: FOUR DIMENSIONS OF BONDAGE

In pastoral practice across four decades and multiple continents, I have observed four distinct patterns of captivity that require different diagnostic and therapeutic approaches:

1. SELECTIVE CAPTIVITY: THE TARGETED PREY

Selective captivity represents the spiritual targeting of specific individuals within a group while others remain relatively unaffected. This is the "marked man" or "marked woman" phenomenon—where spiritual forces single out one member for particular harassment, oppression, or destruction.

The case study mentioned—the man repeatedly mistaken for a criminal—illustrates this perfectly. This was not random misfortune; this was spiritual assignment. The enemy had issued a "wanted poster" in the spiritual realm with this man's spiritual identity, and earthly systems were merely manifesting what had been decreed in the unseen.

Theological Mechanism: Selective captivity often operates through what I term "spiritual signature theft." Just as identity thieves in the natural realm assume someone's identity to commit fraud, demonic forces can attach spiritual markers to an individual that cause them to be identified with someone else's sin, curse, or spiritual condition. The individual becomes a spiritual proxy, bearing consequences not rightfully theirs.

Diagnostic Indicators:

- Recurrent, specific types of trouble that follow the individual regardless of location or circumstance
- Being consistently mistaken for someone else or having one's identity questioned
- Dreams of being pursued, hunted, or having one's identity stolen
- A sense of being "marked" or visibly targeted in spiritual perception

Pastoral Implication: Selective captivity requires not merely general deliverance but specific decommissioning of spiritual markers and revocation of false identities assigned by the enemy.

2. PARTIAL CAPTIVITY: THE COMPARTMENTALIZED LIFE

Partial captivity represents perhaps the most insidious form of bondage, because it coexists with genuine spiritual function. The case of the preacher who ministered effectively while visiting prostitutes exemplifies this tragedy. Here we see a person operating in genuine spiritual authority in one dimension while being utterly enslaved in another.

Theological Mechanism: Partial captivity operates through what Scripture calls "strongholds" (2 Corinthians 10:4)—fortified areas of thinking, behavior, or desire that have been surrendered to enemy control. These become compartmentalized zones where the individual's will has been effectively partitioned, creating what psychologists might call dissociation but what spiritually represents divided territory within a single life.

Diagnostic Indicators:

- Significant spiritual gifting coexisting with specific, persistent areas of sin or bondage
- A sense of being "two different people" in different contexts
- Periodic collapse of spiritual effectiveness following episodes of compromise
- Specific triggers that reliably lead to spiritual collapse in particular areas

Pastoral Implication: Partial captivity requires targeted warfare against specific strongholds, not merely general spiritual renewal. The individual must learn to extend the lordship of Christ into every compartment, allowing no "room for the devil" (Ephesians 4:27).

3. INDIVIDUAL CAPTIVITY: THE PERSONAL STRONGHOLD

Individual captivity represents bondage resulting from personal choices, traumas, or attacks specifically directed at the individual. This is the most commonly recognized form of spiritual bondage—what happens when a person through sin, victimization, or attack becomes personally ensnared.

Theological Mechanism: This operates through personal legal rights given to darkness through willful sin, through traumatic openings created by victimization, or through direct assault when spiritual defenses are lowered. The individual's own spiritual "property" has been invaded and occupied.

Diagnostic Indicators:

- Bondage clearly traceable to specific personal events or choices
- Spiritual oppression that began at identifiable moments in personal history
- Personal patterns of sin, addiction, or dysfunction with clear personal origins
- Responsiveness to personal repentance and renunciation

Pastoral Implication: Individual captivity responds most directly to personal spiritual disciplines: repentance, renunciation, resistance, and renewal. The individual holds the keys to their own deliverance through cooperation with Christ's work.

4. COLLECTIVE CAPTIVITY: THE CORPORATE UMBRELLA

Now we arrive at our primary subject: collective captivity. This represents bondage that affects groups—families, lineages, communities—as corporate entities. The members may experience the bondage differently or to different degrees, but all operate under what I call a "demonic umbrella"—a spiritual covering of oppression, limitation, or destruction that extends over the group.

Theological Mechanism: Collective captivity operates through what Scripture reveals as generational consequences (Exodus 20:5; 34:7), territorial spirits (Daniel 10:13, 20), and corporate covenants (Joshua 9:15). When a group—through representative leadership, collective agreement, or ancestral action—enters into covenant with darkness, that covenant establishes a spiritual reality that affects all under its jurisdiction, much like a national treaty binds all citizens.

Diagnostic Indicators:

- Recurrent patterns across multiple members of a group (family, community)
- Similar struggles appearing at similar life stages across generations
- Geographical or demographic patterns in difficulties (all women of a family, all firstborns, etc.)
- Group histories of specific types of tragedy, failure, or limitation
- Spiritual oppression that feels larger than personal issues

Pastoral Implication: Collective captivity requires corporate spiritual warfare—identifying group covenants, breaking generational patterns, and addressing territorial strongholds. Individuals can remove themselves from under the umbrella, but complete freedom often requires corporate repentance and warfare.

THE ANATOMY OF COLLECTIVE CAPTIVITY: HOW CORPORATE BONDAGE OPERATES

Having established the four types, let us now focus intensively on collective captivity—its mechanisms, manifestations, and spiritual architecture.

THE DEMONIC UMBRELLA: SPIRITUAL COVERINGS AND THEIR EFFECTS

The metaphor of the "demonic umbrella" is more than illustrative; it reflects spiritual reality. Just as a physical umbrella creates a zone of dryness in rain, a demonic spiritual covering creates a zone where certain spiritual conditions prevail. Under this umbrella, blessings are intercepted, curses are amplified, and specific patterns are enforced.

Consider the testimony of the family where 11 of 13 members died within one year. This was not coincidence; this was a death umbrella. Someone had invoked a curse, established a covenant with death, or opened a door that allowed a spirit of death to operate over that family line. The individuals were like people standing in a rainstorm with holes in their umbrellas—some got wetter than others, but all were affected by the same weather system.

The Spiritual Physics of Corporate Curses: A curse, in biblical terms, is not merely negative words; it is a spiritual transaction that releases destructive spiritual energy. When that curse is directed at a group or established through group covenant, it creates what we might call a "curse field"—an area of spiritual influence where the curse operates. Members of the group who enter that field are affected.

GENERATIONAL TRANSMISSION: RIVERS OF INIQUITY

The Scripture speaks of "visiting the iniquity of the fathers upon the children unto the third and fourth generation" (Exodus 20:5). This is not divine injustice; it is spiritual cause-and-effect. Sin creates openings; unrepentant sin maintains those openings; subsequent generations inherit both the spiritual vulnerabilities and often the behavioral patterns that reactivate them.

I call this phenomenon "rivers of iniquity"—continuous flows of spiritual contamination that course through family lines. Just as a polluted river affects everyone downstream, unaddressed ancestral sin affects all descendants until someone builds a dam of repentance and breaks the flow.

Case Study: The Cocoa Farmers: The example of generations dying in poverty despite successful cocoa farming illustrates this perfectly. The great-grandfather's poverty wasn't merely economic; it was spiritual. Perhaps he made a covenant with a land spirit for good harvests. Perhaps he engaged in ritual sacrifice that promised prosperity but actually established poverty. That spiritual transaction created a river of poverty that flowed to his son, his grandson, and beyond. Each generation drank from the same polluted stream.

TERRITORIAL CURSES: GEOGRAPHY AS SPIRITUAL BATTLEGROUND

Jesus' pronouncement of woe upon Chorazin, Bethsaida, and Capernaum (Matthew 11:20-23) reveals a critical dimension: territories can carry spiritual conditions. When He declares, "And thou, Capernaum, which art exalted unto heaven, shalt be brought down to hell," He's not merely addressing individuals but the city itself—its collective spiritual identity and destiny.

The Principle of Spiritual Consecration: Land, buildings, and locations can become consecrated—set apart for specific spiritual purposes. This can be positive (Bethel becoming "the house of God") or negative (tophets dedicated to Molech sacrifice). When a location is dedicated to idolatry, it becomes a spiritual stronghold that affects inhabitants.

The businessman whose office was built where two pregnant women were buried illustrates this tragically. That ground had been consecrated to death, strife, and untimely ending. No business could prosper there because the land itself was spiritually hostile to prosperity.

COLLECTIVE AGREEMENTS AND COVENANTS

Beyond ancestral and territorial factors, collective captivity can be established through group covenants. When a family, community, or society collectively enters into agreement with spiritual forces—whether through traditional religion, secret society initiation, or cultural ritual—that covenant binds all participants and often their descendants.

The African extended family system, while rich in community support, can tragically become a vehicle for transmitting collective captivity. As the observation notes, a black person considers not just immediate family but "relations from his own mother's side, and then his own father's side... his wife's relations." This beautiful web of connection becomes, under spiritual attack, a web of entanglement where one person's covenant becomes everyone's bondage.

DIAGNOSING COLLECTIVE CAPTIVITY: RECOGNIZING THE PATTERNS

How do we recognize when we're dealing with collective rather than merely individual captivity? Spiritual diagnosis requires looking for patterns:

FAMILIAL PATTERN ANALYSIS

Begin with what I call "Familial Spiritual Mapping." Take a notebook and create what genealogists call a genogram—a family tree that includes not just names and dates but spiritual conditions. Look for:

1. **Recurrent Life Patterns:**
    - At what age do family members tend to die?
    - What types of diseases recur?
    - Are there patterns in marriage (late marriage, divorce, polygamy)?
    - What vocational patterns emerge (always employees, never employers; always struggling financially despite apparent opportunity)?
2. **Generational Timing:**
    - Do certain problems appear in every generation at similar life stages?
    - Are there "jinxed" ages (early 30s, mid-40s, etc.) when trouble consistently strikes?
    - Do difficulties skip generations only to reappear?
3. **Gender-Specific Patterns:**
    - Are struggles concentrated in male or female lines?
    - Do all women in the family experience similar marital challenges?
    - Do all men struggle with similar addictions or failures?

4. **Birth Order Patterns:**
    - Do firstborns face particular challenges?
    - Do middle children or lastborns have characteristic struggles?
    - Are there patterns with twins or children born after loss?

SYMPTOM CLUSTERS OF COLLECTIVE CAPTIVITY

Beyond familial patterns, watch for these symptom clusters:

1. **The "Almost" Syndrome:** Consistent failure at the edge of success—what was called "poor finishing" in the soccer analogy. The ball is kicked over the bar at the last moment.
2. **The "Cut Down" Pattern:** Promising individuals consistently cut down at their prime—like Obi the striker targeted by four opponents. When someone shows unusual promise and is systematically destroyed.
3. **The "Memory Failure" Phenomenon:** Not mere forgetfulness but systematic spiritual dullness—inability to retain spiritual truth, consistent failure to follow through on spiritual commitments, spiritual experiences that don't "stick."
4. **The "Sleep Disturbance" Cluster:** Not occasional insomnia but generational sleep disorders—night terrors, sleepwalking, excessive sleeping, inability to wake to spiritual promptings.
5. **The "Emotional Inheritance":** Unexplained depression, anxiety, or anger that seems to run in families beyond psychological explanation.

6. **The "Geographic Sensitivity":** Spiritual oppression that intensifies in specific locations—childhood home, ancestral village, certain cities.

THE SEVEN SPIRITUAL HANDCUFFS: WHAT MAINTAINS COLLECTIVE CAPTIVITY

Understanding how collective captivity is maintained is crucial for breaking it. I have identified seven "spiritual handcuffs" that keep people under demonic umbrellas:

1. UNCONFESSED SIN: THE LEGAL GROUND

Unconfessed sin represents unrenounced legal territory given to the enemy. While all sin is covered by Christ's blood for salvation, unconfessed sin—particularly habitual, hidden sin—maintains legal grounds for enemy operation in specific areas. This is not about losing salvation but about maintaining strongholds.

The Principle: Sin we hide, God cannot heal. Sin we defend, we keep. Sin we confess, God forgives and cleanses (1 John 1:9). Corporate sin requires corporate confession.

2. UNBELIEF AND DOUBLE-MINDEDNESS: THE FAITH GAP

Hebrews 11:6 establishes that without faith it is impossible to please God. Unbelief isn't merely intellectual doubt; it's a spiritual posture that nullifies prayer and gives place to the enemy. Double-mindedness (James 1:6-8)—trying to believe while doubting—creates spiritual instability that the enemy exploits.

The Principle: Corporate unbelief can maintain corporate bondage. When a family, community, or church culture is characterized by unbelief, it creates a spiritual environment where miracles cannot flourish and bondage persists.

3. UNFORGIVENESS: THE POISONED WELL

Unforgiveness is perhaps the most potent maintainer of bondage. Jesus directly links forgiveness received with forgiveness given (Matthew 6:14-15). Unforgiveness creates what I call "spiritual acid" that corrodes our own souls and gives legal rights to tormentors (Matthew 18:34-35).

The Korean Pastor's Story: The pastor who adopted his sons' murderer understood something profound: forgiveness isn't saying what happened was okay; it's releasing the right to revenge so God can heal. Corporate unforgiveness—family feuds, ethnic hatreds, church divisions—creates corporate legal grounds for demonic harassment.

4. SPIRITUAL STARVATION: THE WEAKENED IMMUNE SYSTEM

Just as physical starvation weakens the body's defenses, spiritual starvation weakens spiritual defenses. Corporate spiritual malnutrition—when families, churches, or communities neglect prayer, worship, Scripture, and fellowship—creates vulnerability to collective captivity.

The Principle: Spiritual disciplines are not legalistic requirements; they're spiritual nutrition. A starving person cannot fight effectively. A spiritually malnourished community cannot resist corporate strongholds.

5. ADDICTION: THE VOLUNTARY SLAVERY

Addiction represents willful surrender of control—what Paul describes as being "under the power" of something (1 Corinthians 6:12). Corporate addictions—whether to substances, behaviors, or systems—create collective vulnerability.

The Principle: What controls you, owns you. What a community is collectively addicted to, it is collectively enslaved to. Breaking collective addiction requires both spiritual deliverance and practical reformation.

6. INCOMPLETE DELIVERANCE: THE PARTIALLY DEMOLISHED STRONGHOLD

Incomplete deliverance is like demolishing most of a stronghold but leaving the command center intact. The enemy retreats temporarily, regroups, and returns often stronger (Matthew 12:43-45). Corporate incomplete deliverance—addressing symptoms but not roots, individuals but not systems—ensures bondage returns.

The Principle: Deliverance must be thorough to be lasting. Corporate strongholds require corporate, comprehensive warfare that addresses all dimensions: spiritual, psychological, relational, and sometimes physical.

7. PRIDE: THE UNBOWED WILL

Pride maintains bondage by preventing the humility required for deliverance. Corporate pride—ethnic pride, denominational pride, family pride—creates spiritual blindness that prevents recognition of bondage and resistance to the humbling required for freedom.

The Disappointed Bride's Story: The woman nearly destroyed by rejection illustrates how pride can trigger collapse. Her family pride ("We don't get rejected!") made the rejection catastrophic rather than merely painful. Corporate pride makes communities vulnerable to specific types of attack.

THE STRATEGY OF THE ENEMY: UNDERSTANDING CORPORATE SPIRITUAL WARFARE

To effectively combat collective captivity, we must understand how the enemy operates at corporate levels:

1. THE CASCADE STRATEGY: POISONING THE SOURCE

The enemy understands spiritual hydrology: poison the source, and you poison everything downstream. His strategy with collective captivity often involves identifying and contaminating sources:

- **Ancestral Sources:** The founding father or mother whose decisions established spiritual patterns
- **Geographical Sources:** The land, well, tree, or building where covenants were made
- **Relational Sources:** The marriage, friendship, or partnership that created spiritual alliance
- **Conceptual Sources:** The belief system, worldview, or cultural value that opened spiritual doors

Once the source is poisoned, the poison flows to all connected. Break the connection to the poisoned source, and you begin to detoxify the system.

2. THE UMBRELLA STRATEGY: CREATING SPIRITUAL MICROCLIMATES

As noted, the demonic umbrella creates a spiritual microclimate where certain conditions prevail. The enemy's strategy involves:

- Establishing the umbrella through covenant, curse, or dedication
- Maintaining the umbrella through generational repetition of sin patterns
- Defending the umbrella through spiritual resistance to truth and light
- Extending the umbrella by drawing new members under its coverage through marriage, initiation, or alliance

3. THE COLLABORATOR STRATEGY: USING THE ENSLAVED TO ENSLAVE

Perhaps the most diabolical strategy: using those already captive to capture others. The story of the girl whose siblings were "eaten" one by one illustrates this horror. She became the means of their destruction. In collective captivity, the enemy often identifies "gatekeepers"—members who, through fear, manipulation, or shared bondage, become enforcers of the captivity on others.

4. THE CURSE-UPON-CURSE STRATEGY: BOOBY-TRAPPING DELIVERANCE

The midwife's experience reveals this vicious tactic: placing a curse upon a curse so that anyone attempting deliverance becomes targeted. This is spiritual booby-trapping—making the captive dangerous to free. This explains why some families resist help, why pastors get strangely angry when trying to help certain people, why deliverance attempts seem to trigger backlash.

THE PATH TO FREEDOM: INDIVIDUAL AND CORPORATE STRATEGIES

Given the reality of collective captivity, how do we find freedom? We must operate on two tracks simultaneously: individual responsibility and corporate warfare.

INDIVIDUAL EMANCIPATION: STEPPING OUT FROM UNDER THE UMBRELLA

The ancient proverb holds profound spiritual truth: "Try and save your country; but if it is not possible, try and save your city; if it is not possible, try and save your street; if it is not possible, try and save your house; if it is not possible, try and save your household; if it is not possible, try and save yourself."

You may not be able to free your entire family lineage today, but you can certainly free yourself. And your freedom creates a beachhead of liberty for others.

The Three-Step Individual Process:

1. **Recognition and Repentance:** Honestly assess your family patterns. Identify likely sources of collective captivity. Repent not only for personal sin but, as Daniel did, for the sins of your ancestors (Daniel 9:4-19). Stand in the gap.
2. **Renunciation and Severance:** Specifically renounce every collective covenant, curse, or dedication affecting your lineage. Verbally sever your connection to every

polluted spiritual stream. Declare yourself under the covering of Christ's blood alone.

3. **Resistance and Replacement:** Actively resist manifestations of collective captivity in your life. Replace generational patterns with godly ones. Establish new spiritual traditions for your lineage.

CORPORATE WARFARE: TEARING DOWN THE UMBRELLA

When possible, corporate deliverance is more effective. This requires:

1. **Corporate Recognition:** Getting family or group members to acknowledge the patterns together.
2. **Corporate Repentance:** Collective confession of ancestral sins and current compromises.
3. **Corporate Renunciation:** Unified rejection of generational covenants and curses.
4. **Corporate Reconstruction:** Establishing new godly patterns as a group.

The story of the five unmarried sisters who prayed together for seven days illustrates this beautifully. Their corporate warfare broke what individual prayer might not have.

SPECIAL CHALLENGES: TERRITORIAL AND DEMOGRAPHIC CAPTIVITIES

Some collective captivities are particularly challenging:

TERRITORIAL CAPTIVITIES

When your location is cursed or dedicated to darkness, you may need to:

- Engage in land cleansing prayer
- Break dedications over properties
- In extreme cases, relocate from spiritually hostile territory

DEMOGRAPHIC CAPTIVITIES

When everyone from your village, ethnic group, or social class experiences similar bondage:

- Identify the historical or cultural sources
- Engage in identificational repentance for group sins
- War against the territorial spirits over that demographic

THE ROLE OF THE BLOOD OF JESUS IN BREAKING COLLECTIVE CAPTIVITY

All our strategies find their efficacy in one reality: the blood of Jesus Christ. His blood establishes a superior covenant (Hebrews 8:6), breaks every curse (Galatians 3:13), and provides cleansing from all sin (1 John 1:7). When applied through faith, the blood of Jesus:

1. **Cancels Every Contrary Covenant:** It is the blood of a better covenant that nullifies all previous covenants.
2. **Cleanses Every Polluted Stream:** It purifies what other blood has contaminated.
3. **Covers Every Legal Claim:** It satisfies every legal demand against us.
4. **Conquers Every Enemy Stronghold:** It is the weapon of our warfare that tears down strongholds.

The prayer section that follows is designed to systematically apply the power of Christ's blood to every dimension of collective captivity we have discussed. As you pray, understand you are not merely speaking words; you are applying the most powerful spiritual substance in the universe to the most entrenched spiritual strongholds.

You are stepping from under the umbrella of generational captivity into the glorious liberty of the children of God. You are not just freeing yourself; you are establishing a beachhead of freedom for generations to come.

THINGS THAT KEEP ONE UNDER COLLECTIVE CAPTIVITY OR CORPORATE EVIL COVENANT

THE SEVEN ANCHORS OF CORPORATE BONDAGE: A DEEPER EXPLORATION

Having established the architecture of collective captivity, we must now examine with surgical precision the mechanisms that maintain individuals under these corporate spiritual umbrellas. These are not mere character flaws or spiritual weaknesses; they are specific spiritual conditions that, when present, serve as anchor points tethering the soul to generational strongholds and collective curses.

1. UNCONFESSED SIN: THE LEGAL GROUND FOR CONTINUED OCCUPATION

Unconfessed sin represents the most fundamental anchor maintaining collective captivity. We must understand this theologically: while all sin is atoned for by Christ's blood concerning our eternal salvation (justification), unconfessed sin maintains what might be called "legal occupancy rights" for demonic forces in specific areas of our lives.

The Spiritual Legal Principle: In the spiritual realm, unconfessed sin functions like unaddressed property rights.

Imagine a squatter occupying a room in your house to which you hold title but have never formally evicted him. Your ownership is not in question, but his occupancy continues because you have not exercised your legal authority to remove him. Similarly, while Christ's blood has purchased us completely, unconfessed sin—particularly habitual, hidden, or denied sin—allows demonic "squatters" to maintain strongholds.

The Corporate Dimension: When sin becomes generational—patterns of addiction, deception, sexual immorality, or occult involvement that flow through family lines—each generation's failure to fully confess and renounce these patterns reinforces the legal claim. The Korean pastor's profound act of forgiveness toward his sons' murderer demonstrates the opposite principle: radical confession and forgiveness (even of others' sins against us) dismantles legal grounds for ongoing spiritual occupation.

Pastoral Diagnostic Questions:

- What sins do I consistently minimize or excuse?
- What ancestral sins have I never specifically repented for on behalf of my lineage?
- What "secret sins" do I maintain while appearing righteous publicly?
- What corporate sins of my family, church, or nation have I never identified with in repentance?

2. UNBELIEF, DOUBT, AND DOUBLE-MINDEDNESS: THE FAITH DEFICIT

The writer to Hebrews states unequivocally: "Without faith it is impossible to please him" (Hebrews 11:6). Unbelief is not merely intellectual skepticism; it is a spiritual posture that actively nullifies God's power and gives place to the enemy. James expands this understanding with his discussion of the double-minded person who is "unstable in all his ways" (James 1:8).

The Spiritual Physics of Faith and Doubt: Faith and doubt are not neutral intellectual positions; they are spiritual forces. Faith connects us to God's power; doubt connects us to limitation. When an individual—or a collective—operates in unbelief, they create what might be called a "faith vacuum" that demonic forces rush to fill. The corporate unbelief of Israel at Kadesh-Barnea (Numbers 13-14) not only delayed their inheritance but created a spiritual environment where an entire generation perished in wilderness bondage.

Double-Mindedness as Spiritual Schizophrenia: The Greek term *dipsychos* (double-souled) describes someone whose inner being is divided. This is not ordinary uncertainty but spiritual fragmentation where part of the person believes God's promises while another part anticipates failure. This internal division creates spiritual instability that the enemy exploits like a crack in a dam.

Generational Patterns of Unbelief: Many families have what I call "generational doubt strongholds"—patterns of expecting failure, anticipating betrayal, or assuming limitation that flow through family stories and become self-fulfilling prophecies. When great-grandfather failed in business and declared "our family just has bad luck," he may have established a corporate stronghold of unbelief that affects descendants until someone breaks it with radical faith.

3. UNFORGIVENESS: THE POISONED WELL OF THE SOUL

Of all the anchors, unforgiveness may be the most potent in maintaining corporate captivity. Jesus' teaching is startlingly clear: "If you forgive others their trespasses, your heavenly Father will also forgive you, but if you do not forgive others their trespasses, neither will your Father forgive your trespasses" (Matthew 18:35). The parable of the unforgiving servant (Matthew 18:21-35) reveals unforgiveness as not merely an emotional state but a spiritual transaction that activates tormentors.

The Chemistry of Unforgiveness: Unforgiveness functions like spiritual acid—it corrodes the container (your soul) while failing to damage its object (the offender). Research in psychoneuroimmunology confirms what Scripture revealed millennia ago: unforgiveness produces measurable physiological stress, immune suppression, and increased disease risk. But beyond the physical, unforgiveness creates spiritual vulnerabilities.

The Legal Transaction of Unforgiveness: When we refuse to forgive, we inadvertently engage in a spiritual transaction:

- We claim the right to judge (usurping God's role)
- We maintain a spiritual "debt record" against the offender
- We create an open account that demonic forces can access
- We potentially activate the "tormentors" Jesus mentioned

Corporate Unforgiveness: Families, churches, and communities often have what I call "unforgiveness inheritances"—generational grudges, ethnic hatreds, or religious animosities that flow through collective memory. The Rwandan genocide, the Northern Ireland conflicts, American racial tensions—these represent corporate unforgiveness strongholds that maintain collective captivity until someone breaks the cycle through identificational repentance and forgiveness.

The Korean Pastor's Radical Example: When that pastor adopted his sons' murderer, he was doing more than emotional forgiveness; he was engaging in spiritual warfare against a generational stronghold of vengeance. His act created a spiritual breaker in what could have become another cycle of violence and counter-violence.

4. SPIRITUAL STARVATION: THE ATROPHIED IMMUNE SYSTEM

Just as physical malnutrition weakens the body's defenses against disease, spiritual starvation weakens our defenses against spiritual oppression. The metaphor is precise: prayer is spiritual breathing, Scripture is spiritual food, worship is spiritual hydration, fellowship is spiritual exercise. Neglect these, and we become spiritually anemic, vulnerable to infections that a healthy spiritual immune system would resist.

The Progressive Nature of Spiritual Malnutrition: Spiritual starvation rarely happens suddenly. It typically follows a pattern:

1. **Neglect of Private Devotion:** The "quiet time" becomes irregular, then rare
2. **Neglect of Corporate Worship:** Church attendance becomes optional, then exceptional
3. **Neglect of Scripture:** Bible reading becomes perfunctory, then non-existent
4. **Neglect of Fellowship:** Christian community becomes superficial, then avoided
5. **Neglect of Service:** Ministry becomes burdensome, then abandoned

At each stage, spiritual defenses weaken incrementally until what was once easily resisted becomes overwhelming.

Corporate Spiritual Malnutrition: Families, churches, and communities can develop collective spiritual malnutrition. The "cultural Christianity" of many Western nations represents corporate spiritual starvation—religious form without spiritual power, tradition without transformation. Such environments become breeding grounds for collective captivity because there's insufficient spiritual vitality to resist encroaching darkness.

The Sunday Golfer Syndrome: The person who plays golf while others worship isn't merely missing church; they're opting out of spiritual nutrition at a time when their spiritual immune system may already be compromised. Corporate captivity often maintains its grip because the collective spiritual immune system is too weak to mount effective resistance.

5. ADDICTION: THE VOLUNTARY SLAVERY

Addiction represents perhaps the most insidious anchor because it involves the voluntary surrender of will—what Paul describes as being "under the power" of something (1 Corinthians 6:12). The Greek term *exousiazō* means to be under the authority or control of another. Addiction creates what might be called "spiritual allegiance transfer"—where what should be submitted to God becomes submitted to a substance, behavior, or relationship.

The Neuro-Spiritual Dynamics of Addiction: Modern neuroscience confirms addiction's powerful grip through dopamine reward pathways and neural plasticity. But Scripture reveals the spiritual dimension: addiction creates "strongholds"

(2 Corinthians 10:4)—fortified patterns of thinking and behavior that resist rational intervention and require spiritual warfare for complete freedom.

Generational Addiction Patterns: Many families have what addiction specialists call "generational transmission" of addiction—not merely genetic predisposition but learned coping mechanisms, family systems that enable addiction, and spiritual strongholds that maintain addictive patterns across generations. The "family drunk" or "family gambler" represents not just individual weakness but often corporate spiritual bondage.

Addiction as Spiritual Allegiance: At its core, addiction represents misplaced worship. The addict looks to the substance or behavior for what only God can provide: comfort, escape, pleasure, meaning. This misdirected worship creates spiritual openings that demonic forces exploit, often creating what deliverance ministers call "spirits of addiction" that reinforce the physical/psychological dependence.

6. INCOMPLETE DELIVERANCE: THE PARTIALLY DEMOLISHED STRONGHOLD

Incomplete deliverance represents one of the most frustrating anchors because it often follows genuine spiritual progress. Jesus' warning about the empty house swept clean (Matthew 12:43-45) reveals the danger: partial deliverance can leave a spiritual vacuum that becomes reinfested with greater oppression.

The Demolition Metaphor: Imagine demolishing a terrorist stronghold but leaving the command center and weapons cache intact. The enemy retreats temporarily, regroups, and returns better fortified. Similarly, incomplete deliverance addresses symptoms but not roots, manifestations but not sources, present struggles but not generational patterns.

Common Forms of Incomplete Deliverance:

- **Symptom-Focused:** Addressing the addiction but not the trauma that triggered it
- **Individual-Focused:** Delivering the person but not addressing familial or territorial strongholds
- **Present-Focused:** Breaking current curses but not ancestral covenants
- **Prayer-Focused:** Engaging in warfare prayer without practical obedience and life change

The "I've Been Delivered" Deception: Many believers experience genuine but partial deliverance, then conclude the work is complete. When symptoms return—often in different forms—they become discouraged or doubt the initial deliverance. In reality, they're experiencing the enemy's counterattack on a partially secured position.

Corporate Incomplete Deliverance: Churches and ministries sometimes engage in corporate deliverance that addresses surface manifestations but not systemic issues. A church might break a spirit of division but not address the leadership pride or theological error that created the opening. The spirit returns, finding the house "empty, swept, and put in order"—ready for repossession.

7. PRIDE: THE UNBOWED WILL

Pride maintains collective captivity by preventing the fundamental posture required for deliverance: humility.

Scripture is unequivocal: "God opposes the proud but gives grace to the humble" (James 4:6; 1 Peter 5:5). The Greek term for "opposes" (*antitassomai*) is a military term meaning to arrange in battle against. Pride literally positions us in battle array against God Himself.

The Many Faces of Spiritual Pride:

- **Doctrinal Pride:** "Our theology is superior"
- **Denominational Pride:** "Our tradition is purer"
- **Ethnic Pride:** "Our people are special"
- **Familial Pride:** "Our family name means something"
- **Personal Pride:** "I don't need help like others do"
- **Religious Pride:** "I'm more spiritual than..."

Pride as Spiritual Blindness: Pride doesn't merely make us arrogant; it makes us blind. The proud person cannot see their own bondage because their self-assessment is distorted. Corporate pride—family pride, church pride, national pride—creates collective spiritual blindness that prevents recognition of corporate captivity.

The Disappointed Bride's Lesson: The woman devastated by her fiancé's rejection illustrates how pride amplifies pain. Had she not invested her identity in "getting married" or "not being rejected," the pain would have been severe but not catastrophic. Her family pride ("Our women don't get rejected!") and personal pride ("How could he choose her over me?") transformed a painful experience into a near-fatal spiritual crisis.

Generational Pride Strongholds: Many families have what I call "pride inheritances"—stories of ancestral greatness that create expectations no one can fulfill, family mantras ("We're survivors!"), or ethnic narratives of superiority. These pride strongholds create vulnerability to specific types of attack and make deliverance difficult because humility feels like betrayal of family identity.

THE INTERCONNECTEDNESS OF THE SEVEN ANCHORS

These seven anchors rarely operate in isolation. They interconnect and reinforce one another:

- Unconfessed sin leads to spiritual starvation
- Spiritual starvation weakens resistance to addiction
- Addiction creates shame that prevents confession
- Shame reinforces pride as a defense mechanism
- Pride prevents seeking help for addiction
- Unaddressed addiction becomes unconfessed sin

This interlocking system creates what addiction specialists call a "self-reinforcing cycle" and what spiritual warriors recognize as a demonic stronghold system. Breaking collective captivity requires addressing not just individual anchors but their interconnections.

THE ESCAPE PATH: BREAKING EACH ANCHOR

For each anchor, there is a biblical escape path:

1. **For Unconfessed Sin:** Radical, specific confession (1 John 1:9) followed by practical repentance
2. **For Unbelief:** Immersion in God's promises (Romans 10:17) and testimonies of His faithfulness
3. **For Unforgiveness:** Decisional forgiveness followed by emotional processing, often requiring spiritual counseling

4. **For Spiritual Starvation:** Reestablishing spiritual disciplines not as duty but as delight
5. **For Addiction:** Combining spiritual warfare with practical strategies (accountability, counseling, support groups)
6. **For Incomplete Deliverance:** Thorough spiritual mapping followed by comprehensive warfare
7. **For Pride:** Cultivating humility through service, confession, and embracing weakness (2 Corinthians 12:9-10)

PRAYER SECTION

A LITURGY OF CORPORATE DELIVERANCE AND GENERATIONAL BREAKTHROUGH

Beloved, we now transition from understanding to engagement, from analysis to warfare. What follows is not a magical incantation but a spiritual legal proceeding where you exercise your authority in Christ to sever every anchor tethering you to collective captivity. Pray these prayers not as a passive recitation but as active spiritual warfare. Engage your will, your faith, and your voice. Remember: you are not pleading from a position of weakness but commanding from a position of authority seated with Christ in heavenly places (Ephesians 2:6).

PREPARATORY CONFESSION AND POSTURING

Before beginning, center yourself with these declarations. Speak them aloud with conviction:

*"I come before the throne of grace as a blood-bought child of God, an heir of Abraham through faith in Christ, a citizen of the Kingdom of Light. My authority is not my own but derived from my union with Jesus Christ, who has disarmed principalities and powers, making a public spectacle of them, triumphing over

them at the cross (Colossians 2:15). I stand not in my righteousness but in His, not in my strength but in His, not in my wisdom but in His. I declare that no weapon formed against me shall prosper, and every tongue that rises against me in judgment I shall condemn (Isaiah 54:17). The blood of Jesus Christ speaks better things than any corporate curse or generational covenant (Hebrews 12:24). I am free indeed!"*

SECTION ONE: ADDRESSING THE SEVEN ANCHORS

1. PRAYERS CONCERNING UNCONFESSED SIN

Comprehensive Repentance Prayer:

Heavenly Father, I come before You in the name of Jesus Christ. I confess that I have sinned against You in thought, word, and deed. I specifically confess [mention any Holy Spirit brings to mind]. I repent of every sin I have committed, every sin I have tolerated, and every sin I have hidden.

I now confess the sins of my ancestors on behalf of my lineage. I confess every idolatry, every occult involvement, every covenant with darkness, every shedding of innocent blood, every sexual immorality, every addiction, every deception, every theft, every violence, and every rebellion against You that has flowed through my family line. I stand in the gap as Ezekiel and Daniel did, repenting for the sins of my fathers.

I apply the blood of Jesus to every confessed sin—mine and my ancestors'. I receive Your complete forgiveness and cleansing. I declare that every legal ground given to the enemy through sin is now nullified by the superior blood of the New Covenant.

Specific Severance Prayer:

In the name of Jesus Christ, I sever every spiritual connection, every legal claim, and every demonic right established through unconfessed sin in my life and lineage. I cancel every contract, every agreement, and every covenant forged in sin. I declare myself and my lineage cleansed by the blood of the Lamb.

2. PRAYERS CONCERNING UNBELIEF AND DOUBLE-MINDEDNESS

Faith Declaration Prayer:

Lord Jesus, I renounce every spirit of unbelief, doubt, and double-mindedness operating in my life or inherited through my lineage. I break every generational stronghold of skepticism, cynicism, and faithlessness. I command every spirit of doubt to loose its grip on my mind and emotions.

I now choose to believe Your Word above all contradictory evidence. I align my thoughts with Your promises. I receive the gift of faith and declare that I believe that You are and that You reward those who diligently seek You (Hebrews 11:6). I plant my feet on the rock of Your faithfulness when everything around me shakes.

Renunciation of Generational Unbelief:

In the name of Jesus, I renounce and break every generational pattern of unbelief, failure expectation, and negative confession in my family line. I cancel every curse of "bad luck," "always failing," or "never succeeding" spoken over my lineage. I declare that I am a believer, not a doubter; an overcomer, not a victim; more than a conqueror through Christ who loves me.

3. PRAYERS CONCERNING UNFORGIVENESS

The Great Release Prayer:

Heavenly Father, in obedience to Your command and following the example of Christ who forgave from the cross, I now release all who have hurt, harmed, or offended me. I specifically forgive [name individuals the Holy Spirit brings to mind]. I release them from the debt I have held against them. I cancel their obligation to make things right. I surrender my right to revenge, retaliation, or resentment.

I ask You to forgive me for holding unforgiveness, bitterness, and resentment in my heart. Cleanse me from all poison of unforgiveness. Heal the wounds caused by others' offenses. Restore what has been damaged.

Breaking Generational Unforgiveness:

In the name of Jesus, I break every generational stronghold of unforgiveness, bitterness, and vengeance in my family line. I renounce every family feud, ethnic hatred, or ancestral grudge that has flowed through my lineage. I declare the cycle of offense and counter-offense ends with me. I choose to be a pipeline of mercy, not a reservoir of bitterness.

4. PRAYERS CONCERNING SPIRITUAL STARVATION

Covenant of Renewal Prayer:

Lord Jesus, I confess that I have neglected spiritual disciplines and allowed my spiritual life to become malnourished. I repent for every time I chose entertainment over prayer, busyness over Scripture, isolation over fellowship, and consumption over worship.

I now make a fresh covenant with You. I commit to daily prayer, regular Scripture meditation, consistent fellowship, and authentic worship. I ask for a fresh hunger for spiritual things. Restore to me the joy of Your salvation. Renew a right spirit within me.

Breaking Generational Spiritual Neglect:

In the name of Jesus, I break every generational pattern of spiritual neglect, religious formalism without power, and cultural Christianity without conversion in my lineage. I command every spirit of lethargy, complacency, and spiritual boredom to loose its grip on me and my household. I declare that from this day forward, my family will serve the Lord in spirit and in truth.

5. PRAYERS CONCERNING ADDICTION

Declaration of Freedom from Addiction:

Lord Jesus, I confess every addiction, bondage, and compulsive behavior in my life. I specifically renounce [mention specific addictions]. I acknowledge that these have had mastery over me, but today I declare that Jesus is my only Master.

I break every soul tie, every neural pathway, every demonic stronghold, and every generational pattern associated with these addictions. I command every spirit of addiction, dependency, and compulsion to loose me now in Jesus' name. I receive my God-given self-control as a fruit of the Spirit.

Severing Generational Addiction Patterns:

In the name of Jesus, I break every generational curse, covenant, and pattern of addiction in my family line. I renounce every ancestral involvement with substances, behaviors, or relationships that created dependency. I declare that the cycle of addiction ends with me. My body is a temple of the Holy Spirit, and I will honor God with it.

6. PRAYERS CONCERNING INCOMPLETE DELIVERANCE

Prayer for Thorough Deliverance:

Heavenly Father, I ask for revelation of any areas of incomplete deliverance in my life. Show me roots I haven't addressed, doors I haven't closed, or strongholds I haven't fully demolished. I don't want partial freedom; I want complete liberation.

I now renounce every compromise, every half-measure, and every incomplete break with the past. I commit to following through on every aspect of deliverance, regardless of cost or inconvenience. I will not rest until every enemy stronghold in my life is fully dismantled.

Closing Every Door Prayer:

In the name of Jesus, I close every door, every window, and every portal that I or my ancestors have opened to demonic influence. I seal every entry point with the blood of Jesus. I post angelic guards at every potential re-entry point. I declare my life a no-fly zone for demonic activity.

7. PRAYERS CONCERNING PRIDE

The Humility Prayer:

Lord Jesus, I confess every form of pride in my life: spiritual pride, intellectual pride, ethnic pride, familial pride, and personal pride. I specifically repent of [mention areas of pride the Holy Spirit reveals]. I choose the low place. I embrace weakness that Your strength might be perfected in me.

I break every agreement with spirits of pride, arrogance, and superiority. I renounce every generational pattern of elitism, racism, classism, or spiritual arrogance in my lineage. I put on the apron of humility and choose to serve rather than be served.

Generational Humility Declaration:

In the name of Jesus, I break every generational stronghold of pride in my family line. I renounce every family narrative of superiority, every ethnic story of exceptionalism, every ancestral claim of privilege. I declare that my family will be known for humility, service, and Christlike character, not for prideful attainment or arrogant distinction.

SECTION TWO: BREAKING CORPORATE AND COLLECTIVE CAPTIVITIES

Now we address the corporate dimensions directly:

1. BREAKING COLLECTIVE CURSES

Comprehensive Curse-Breaking Prayer:

In the name of Jesus Christ, I break every curse, hex, spell, jinx, bewitchment, or evil pronouncement ever spoken against me, my family, my ministry, my possessions, or my destiny. I break curses of death, poverty, failure, divorce, sickness, insanity, addiction, loneliness, rejection, and every other form of destruction.

I specifically break [mention any known curses]. I break curses spoken intentionally and unintentionally, curses spoken recently and generations ago, curses I know about and curses unknown to me. I declare every curse nullified, neutralized, and reversed by the blessing of Abraham that comes through faith in Christ.

Applying the Blood to Generational Curses:

I plead the blood of Jesus over every generational curse operating in my lineage. I apply the blood to my genetic code, my family memory, and my ancestral spiritual inheritance. I declare that the blood of Jesus speaks better things than the blood of animals, sacrifices, or covenants that established these curses. Every curse is broken now!

2. SEVERING FROM COLLECTIVE COVENANTS

Renunciation of Corporate Covenants:

In the name of Jesus, I renounce, revoke, and declare null and void every corporate, collective, or group covenant that my ancestors or I have entered into with any spirit, power, or entity other than the living God. This includes:

- Covenants with family idols or deities
- Covenants with territorial or village spirits
- Covenants through secret society initiations
- Covenants through cultural or traditional rituals
- Covenants through religious systems contrary to Christ
- Covenants through national or ethnic allegiance that supersedes Christ

I specifically renounce [mention any known corporate covenants]. I sever every spiritual connection, every legal obligation, and every demonic claim established through these covenants.

Declaration of Allegiance to Christ Alone:

I declare that I have one covenant: the New Covenant in the blood of Jesus Christ. I have one allegiance: to King Jesus. I have one identity: child of God. All other covenants are broken, all other allegiances are severed, all other identities are surrendered.

3. COMING OUT FROM UNDER DEMONIC UMBRELLAS

The Umbrella Escape Prayer:

In the name of Jesus, I remove myself from under every demonic umbrella, every corporate covering of darkness, every generational spiritual climate that does not reflect God's kingdom. I step out from under umbrellas of:

- Poverty and financial struggle
- Sickness and infirmity
- Marital failure and relational dysfunction
- Vocational limitation and professional frustration
- Spiritual oppression and religious bondage
- Ethnic limitation and cultural captivity
- Geographic curse and territorial stronghold

I declare that I am now under the covering of the Most High, abiding under the shadow of the Almighty (Psalm 91:1). The blood of Jesus is my covering, the Holy Spirit is my climate, and the favor of God is my atmosphere.

4. CUTTING OFF RIVERS OF INIQUITY

Severing Polluted Streams Prayer:

In the name of Jesus, I identify and cut off every polluted spiritual stream, every river of iniquity, every generational flow of sin, dysfunction, or bondage that has flowed from my ancestors to me. I build a spiritual dam at this generation. The pollution stops here. The curse ends with me.

I specifically cut off streams of [mention known patterns: addiction, abuse, poverty, etc.]. I redirect the flow of my lineage toward purity, blessing, and righteousness. From this day forward, my life and my descendants will be sources of living water, not polluted streams.

5. BREAKING TERRITORIAL AND GEOGRAPHIC STRONGHOLDS

Land and Location Cleansing Prayer:

In the name of Jesus, I break every territorial curse, geographic stronghold, and location-based bondage affecting me. I renounce every covenant my ancestors or I have made with spirits of the land, territorial deities, or location-based powers.

I cleanse my home, my property, my workplace, and every location I frequent with the blood of Jesus. I drive out every spirit that claims legal right through previous occupation, ritual dedication, or bloodshed. I reclaim every inch of ground for the Kingdom of God.

Declaration of Kingdom Territory:

I declare that wherever I live, work, or minister becomes Kingdom territory. The ground is holy because I am there as a temple of the Holy Spirit. Angels encamp around my dwelling. The glory of God fills my spaces.

SECTION THREE: PROACTIVE DECLARATIONS AND BLESSINGS

Having broken the negative, now establish the positive:

1. DECLARATION OF NEW COVENANT BLESSINGS

I now receive and declare the blessings of the New Covenant over my life:

- The blessing of Abraham comes upon me through Christ (Galatians 3:14)
- Every spiritual blessing in heavenly places is mine in Christ (Ephesians 1:3)
- The Lord blesses me and keeps me (Numbers 6:24)
- The Lord makes His face shine upon me and is gracious to me (Numbers 6:25)
- The Lord turns His face toward me and gives me peace (Numbers 6:26)
- I am blessed in the city and blessed in the country (Deuteronomy 28:3)
- The fruit of my body, ground, and livestock is blessed (Deuteronomy 28:4)
- My basket and kneading trough are blessed (Deuteronomy 28:5)
- I am blessed when I come in and when I go out (Deuteronomy 28:6)

2. ESTABLISHING GODLY GENERATIONAL PATTERNS

Covenant for Future Generations:
Heavenly Father, I establish a new covenant for my lineage today. I declare that from this generation forward:

- My family will serve the Lord

- My descendants will walk in truth and righteousness
- The blessing of God will flow to the third and fourth generation of those who love Him
- My lineage will be known for faith, not fear; for blessing, not bondage; for freedom, not captivity

I plant my life as a seed of righteousness that will produce a harvest of godliness for generations to come.

3. SEALING PRAYER

Prayer of Protection and Preservation:
Lord Jesus, I ask You to seal this work of deliverance by Your Holy Spirit. Place a hedge of protection around me and my household. Post angels to guard every entrance to my life. Baptize me afresh in the Holy Spirit and fire.

I put on the full armor of God: the belt of truth, the breastplate of righteousness, the shoes of the gospel of peace, the shield of faith, the helmet of salvation, and the sword of the Spirit. I am ready for battle and secure in victory.

SECTION FOUR: WARFARE AGAINST SPECIFIC ROOTS OF COLLECTIVE CAPTIVITY

Now pray aggressively against each root mentioned in the text. As you name each one, declare: "Every effect of [ROOT] upon my life, come out with all your roots, in the name of Jesus!"

1. **Evil physical design** - Every genetic inheritance, bodily weakness, or physical predisposition contrary to God's design
2. **Parental curses** - Every curse spoken by parents or ancestors

3. **Envious rivalry** - Every spirit of jealousy, competition, or comparison operating in your lineage
4. **Demonic incisions** - Every cut, mark, or scar with spiritual significance
5. **Dream pollution** - Every negative spiritual activity in your dream life
6. **Demonic initiations** - Every formal or informal initiation into darkness
7. **Demonic blood transfusion** - Every mixing of blood with demonic intent
8. **Demonic alteration of destiny** - Every assignment to change your God-given purpose
9. **Evil dedication** - Every dedication of you or ancestors to idols or spirits
10. **Demonic marriage** - Every spiritual marriage to demonic entities
11. **Demonic sacrifice** - Every sacrifice made on your behalf to dark powers
12. **Inherited infirmity** - Every sickness or weakness passed through generations
13. **Evil laying on of hands** - Every negative impartation through touch
14. **Wrong exposure to sex** - Every premature, abusive, or perverted sexual experience
15. **Exposure to evil diviners** - Every consultation with psychics, mediums, or fortune-tellers
16. **Fellowship with local idols** - Every interaction with territorial deities
17. **Fellowship with family idols** - Every family god or ancestral spirit
18. **Fellowship with demonic consultants** - Every seeking of guidance from dark sources

19. **Unscriptural manner of conception** - Every conception through rape, adultery, or occult means
20. **Destructive effect of polygamy** - Every negative consequence of multiple marriage relationships

FINAL DECLARATION

I now stand complete in Christ, free from every collective captivity, delivered from every corporate covenant, liberated from every generational stronghold. I am who God says I am. I have what God says I have. I can do what God says I can do. The old has passed away; behold, all things have become new!

I declare that from this moment forward, my life will be a testimony of deliverance, my family will be a lineage of blessing, and my destiny will be a demonstration of God's power to break every chain.

In the mighty, matchless, magnificent name of Jesus Christ, my Lord and Liberator, I pray and declare all these things.

AMEN AND AMEN!

POST-PRAYER INSTRUCTIONS

1. **Give Thanks Immediately:** Spend at least 15 minutes thanking God for your freedom. Praise establishes the victory.
2. **Be Alert to Counterattack:** The enemy may test your declaration in coming days through thoughts, circumstances, or symptoms. Stand firm in your faith. When negative thoughts come, declare: "I am free in Jesus' name!"

3. **Take Practical Steps:** If the Holy Spirit prompts you to destroy objects, change relationships, or make restitution, obey promptly.
4. **Immerse in Scripture:** Read Galatians, Ephesians, and Colossians daily for the next 30 days to renew your mind with your new identity.
5. **Share Your Testimony Wisely:** Your testimony has power, but share with discernment. Some victories need to be secured before they're proclaimed.
6. **Join Christian Community:** Don't stand alone. Connect with other believers who will support your new freedom.
7. **Keep Your Deliverance:** "Therefore let him who thinks he stands take heed lest he fall" (1 Corinthians 10:12). Walk humbly, pray continually, and stay submitted to godly authority.

You have engaged in powerful spiritual warfare. Now walk in your hard-won freedom. The same power that raised Christ from the dead lives in you and will sustain your victory. Go in peace, power, and glorious liberty!

CHAPTER 03

RELEASE FROM CURSES ATTACHED TO EVIL COVENANTS

"Christ hath redeemed us from the curse of the law, being made a curse for us: for it is written, Cursed is everyone that hangeth on a tree: That the blessing of Abraham might come on the Gentiles through Jesus Christ; that we might receive the promise of the Spirit through faith." **— Galatians 3:13–14**

INTRODUCTION: THE REALITY OF CURSES IN A COVENANTAL WORLD

Beloved, if there is one truth that the enemy does not want you to grasp, it is this: **curses are real, and they are often the hidden chains attached to broken or evil covenants.** Many believers walk through life carrying invisible burdens—recurring failures, unexplained sicknesses, financial leakages, relational breakdowns—without ever tracing them back to their spiritual root. They pray, fast, confess the Word, yet find themselves hitting an invisible ceiling. Why? Because a curse, once activated, functions like a spiritual law—a force that opposes the blessing until it is legally revoked by a higher authority.

A curse is not merely a bad word spoken in anger. In the biblical sense, a curse is a **spiritual sentence**, a decree of misfortune or bondage invoked upon a person, family, or lineage, often as a penalty for breaking a covenant or violating divine or moral law. It is the direct opposite of a blessing. While a blessing releases life, favor, and increase, a curse invokes death, limitation, and decay.

When you understand covenants—as we have explored in previous chapters—you realize that every covenant carries with it either blessings for obedience or curses for disobedience (Deuteronomy 28). This is true of God's covenants with His people, and it is tragically true of the evil covenants people make ignorantly or willingly with dark powers. When such covenants are broken—whether consciously or unconsciously—the attached curses are activated, and they begin to exert their oppressive influence.

Today, we are going to delve deeply into the nature of curses, how they operate, where they come from, and most importantly—how you can be **completely and permanently released** from every curse attached to any evil covenant in your life or lineage. This is not a message of fear, but of deliverance. For the Scripture declares clearly: **Christ has redeemed us from the curse of the law!** Your freedom is not a future hope—it is a finished work. But you must appropriate it.

I. THE NATURE AND OPERATION OF CURSES

WHAT IS A CURSE?

Let me break this down for you, not in a distant, theological tone, but as someone who has walked with people through these valleys and seen the chains break. A curse is **not** just a bad day or a run of bad luck. It is a *spiritual reality* with tangible consequences. Think of it like this:

- **A curse is a spoken or spiritual decree of evil**—a word, a wish, a prayer of harm, charged with negative spiritual power. It's like taking a spiritual arrow, dipping it in poison, and firing it at a person's life with the intention to wound, bind, or cripple their destiny.
- **It is a legal claim in the spirit realm.** Think of it as a malicious lawsuit filed against you in a spiritual court. If there is evidence—sin, a broken vow, a violated covenant—that "lawsuit" can be approved, giving demonic forces a perceived *right* or license to enforce suffering, lack, or failure in your life. The Bible speaks of this in Daniel 10, where a prince of Persia (a demonic power) *withstood* the angel bringing Daniel's answer. Why? There was a legal territorial claim. Curses work similarly on a personal level.
- **It is an invisible barrier.** It's like driving with the parking brake on. You press the accelerator of prayer, hard work, and faith, but something is holding you back just short of the breakthrough. Proverbs 26:2 says a curse without cause does not alight—meaning it needs a landing place, a hook. Once it lands, it becomes that barrier.
- **It is the "fine print" of an evil covenant.** This is crucial. When someone—maybe an ancestor, maybe even a younger you—enters an agreement with dark powers (through secret societies, idol worship, occult rituals), that covenant always has terms. The "blessings" might be temporary power or provision, but the *fine print* says:

> "Break this covenant, and the consequence is a curse of X, Y, or Z." Violate the terms, and the curse clause activates automatically.

You see, beloved, in the spiritual realm, words are not just sounds. They are **containers of power**. When God spoke, worlds came into being (Genesis 1). When Jesus spoke to the fig tree, it withered (Mark 11:21). Our words have creative or destructive power (Proverbs 18:21). When a curse is uttered—especially with the weight of a covenant, the backing of a sacrifice (which gives it blood-level seriousness), or spoken by someone in a position of perceived spiritual authority (a parent, a witch doctor, an elder)—it's like signing a dark contract. It sets a process in motion. Demonic forces are dispatched as enforcement officers. Circumstances begin to align, almost supernaturally, to fulfill its terms. And unless a higher authority—a greater power, a superior blood, a more binding covenant—intervenes, that curse will run its grueling course, sometimes for generations, just as the iniquity of the fathers can visit the children (Exodus 20:5).

HOW DO CURSES OPERATE?

Let me paint a picture you might recognize. A person living under a curse often feels like they're in a spiritual nightmare. They are running with all their might on the treadmill of life—praying, believing, working hard—but they never seem to get to the destination. There's sweat, but no forward movement. Or they are like a farmer in the parable of the sower (Matthew 13), faithfully sowing good seed on what appears to be good ground, but the harvest is consistently stolen, choked, or withered. They can't understand why. "God, I'm sowing! Why am I not reaping?"

Curses operate through **spiritual legalities**. They exploit spiritual law. Galatians 3:10 says, "Cursed is everyone who does not continue in *all* things which are written in the book of the law, to do them." The Law pronounced a curse for disobedience. That's a legal principle. The enemy is a legalist. He looks for *grounds*—a place where God's law has been violated, a covenant broken, a door left open through sin—and he slaps a lien on your life. He gets a "right" to harass, to block, to afflict. He's not all-powerful; he's a squatter who needs legal permission to stay.

Let's get practical with examples from the very lives sitting in this room:

- **The Curse of Leaking Finances:** It's not just being broke. It's when money *comes in* but never *stays*. You get a bonus, and the car breaks down. You pay off a debt, and a medical bill arrives. It's a consistent, baffling pattern of "one step forward, two steps back." It's like carrying water in a sieve. That's not just bad economy; that can be the operation of a curse of poverty (Haggai 1:6 - "You earn wages, only to put them in a purse with holes in it").
- **The Curse of Sickness Without Root:** It's not just catching a flu. It's a cycle of unexplained illnesses, one after another. Doctors are puzzled. Tests are inconclusive. You get prayer and feel better, then it returns or morphs into something else. It's a "perpetual infirmity" (Luke 13:11) that doesn't respond to normal treatment. That's often a curse at work, attacking the body.
- **The Curse of Aborted Breakthroughs:** This is the most painful. You see the promotion, the contract, the marriage proposal—it's right there! You can taste it. Then, at the last second, it collapses. The phone call

doesn't come. The offer is withdrawn. The relationship inexplicably ends. It's a pattern of "almost, but not quite." That's the curse of failure erecting a barrier at the edge of your miracle.

But here's the key you must understand: **Curses have demonic reinforcement.** A curse is not a free-floating, impersonal force. Behind every persistent, stubborn curse is a **demonic entity assigned to ensure its fulfillment**. It's a spiritual bounty hunter tasked with making sure you don't escape the sentence. This is why "positive thinking" or sheer willpower can never break a deep curse. You can affirm "I am rich" all day, but if a demon of poverty has a legal right to your finances because of an ancestral covenant with a spirit of greed, your affirmations are just noise to it. You must deal with the *spiritual power* enforcing the curse.

This is why Jesus' ministry wasn't just about teaching; it was about ***confrontation and deliverance***. He didn't just tell the bent-over woman to think positively; He said, "Woman, you are loosed from your infirmity!" and a spirit of infirmity had to leave (Luke 13:12). He dealt with the legal right (18 years under bondage) and the enforcing power (the spirit) simultaneously.

Beloved, this is not to make you fearful, but to make you **wise and armed**. You are not a victim at the mercy of vague curses. You are a believer with authority over all the power of the enemy (Luke 10:19). But you must understand what you're fighting. You're not fighting a mood; you're fighting a legal sentence backed by a demonic enforcer. And praise God, we know the One who has "wiped out the handwriting of requirements that was against us, which was contrary to us. And He has taken it out of the way, having nailed it to the cross. Having disarmed principalities and powers, He made a public spectacle of them, triumphing over them in it" (Colossians 2:14-15).

The curse was nailed to His cross. The legal claim was satisfied. The enforcer was disarmed. Your job is to walk in that truth, enforce that victory, and evict every squatter that doesn't know the lease has been terminated. Let's pray from that position of victory.

II. THE EFFECTS OF CURSES: THE FRUITS YOU MUST RECOGNIZE

Beloved, let me speak to you plainly today. Curses don't announce themselves with flashing neon signs saying "Curse at Work Here!" No—they produce fruits. Visible, tangible fruits in a person's life. And I want you to understand something crucial: **These aren't coincidences. They're patterns.** When you see the same tree producing the same bitter fruit year after year, generation after generation, you're not looking at "bad luck"—you're looking at a spiritual root system that needs to be dealt with.

Let me walk you through what these fruits look like, so you can recognize them—not just in others, but honestly, in your own life. The Holy Spirit is our teacher, and He wants to bring truth that sets us free (John 8:32).

1. LONG-LASTING AND GENERATIONAL EFFECTS

Listen to me carefully. A curse doesn't have an expiration date. It doesn't just wear out over time like an old pair of shoes. It's not like milk that spoils after a week. No—curses can span **generations** until someone in the bloodline has enough spiritual discernment to identify them and enough authority in Christ to break them.

Let me show you from Scripture. In Joshua 6:26, after the walls of Jericho fell, Joshua pronounced this curse: "Cursed before the LORD be the man who rises up and rebuilds this city, Jericho. At the cost of his firstborn shall he lay its foundation, and at the cost of his youngest son shall he set up its gates."

Now fast forward—not just a few years, but **hundreds of years**—to 1 Kings 16:34. "In his days Hiel of Bethel built Jericho. He laid its foundation at the cost of Abiram his firstborn, and set up its gates at the cost of his youngest son Segub, according to the word of the LORD, which he spoke by Joshua the son of Nun."

Did you catch that? A curse spoken in one generation manifested **five hundred years later** with terrifying precision. It didn't fade. It didn't weaken. It waited. It lingered. It was like a spiritual landmine buried in that family line, just waiting for someone to step on it.

Now let me ask you—and I want you to be brutally honest with yourself: What patterns do you see in your family? I'm not talking about genetics—blue eyes or curly hair. I'm talking about **spiritual patterns**:

- Does every generation seem to have marriages that end in divorce or severe dysfunction?
- Do men in your family consistently die young from heart attacks, accidents, or mysterious illnesses?
- Is there a pattern of addiction—alcohol, drugs, gambling, pornography—that keeps showing up?
- Does financial struggle seem to be your family's "normal," no matter how hard people work?
- Are there recurring mental health issues—depression, anxiety, breakdowns—that doctors can't fully explain?

These aren't just "family traits." They're **fruits**. They're the visible evidence of spiritual roots that may have been planted generations ago through idolatry, through occult involvement, through blood covenants, through unrepentant sin. The Bible is clear about this principle: "I, the LORD your God, am a jealous God, visiting the iniquity of the fathers on the children to the third and fourth generations of those who hate me" (Exodus 20:5).

But—and hear this, because this is your hope—that same verse continues: "...but showing steadfast love to thousands of those who love me and keep my commandments." There's a breaking point! There's a place where the generational curse stops and God's mercy begins. That place is at the cross of Jesus Christ.

2. CATASTROPHIC AND SUDDEN REVERSALS

Let me describe another fruit you need to recognize. A life under a curse is often marked by **sudden, catastrophic reversals** that make no natural sense.

You know what I'm talking about. Everything seems fine. You're walking in blessing. Your business is growing. Your family is healthy. Your relationships are strong. Then—seemingly out of nowhere—the bottom falls out.

- The contract you were sure of gets canceled at the last minute.
- The medical report comes back with devastating news.
- The betrayal comes from the person you trusted most.
- The financial collapse happens overnight.

It's like building a house for years, and in one storm, it all comes crashing down. The Book of Job gives us a perfect picture of this. In one day—**one day**—Job lost his oxen, his donkeys, his sheep, his camels, and all ten of his children (Job 1:13-19). Was that just "bad luck"? No! There was a spiritual conversation happening in heaven that Job knew nothing about. There was a **legal ground** that had been given to the enemy.

Listen to what Satan said to God: "Have you not put a hedge around him and his house and all that he has, on every side?" (Job 1:10). There was a protective blessing hedge—and Satan needed permission to get through it. But when that hedge was temporarily lifted (within God's sovereign purposes), sudden catastrophe struck.

Now, I'm not saying every tragedy is a curse. We live in a fallen world, and sometimes terrible things happen. But I am saying that when you see a **pattern** of catastrophic reversals—when it's not just one bad season but repeated, sudden collapses at the edge of breakthrough—you need to ask the Holy Spirit: "Is there a curse at work here?"

Proverbs 6:15 warns about the wicked man: "Therefore calamity will come upon him suddenly; in a moment he will be broken beyond healing." Sudden calamity can be the fruit of covenant-breaking with God.

3. A SHIELD THAT PROTECTS DEMONIC ACTIVITY

This third fruit is the most spiritually significant, and it's why many people pray and pray but see no change. A curse doesn't just produce bad circumstances—it creates a **spiritual environment** where darkness can operate with impunity.

Think of a curse as a **spiritual shield** or a **legal barrier**. It's like spiritual Kevlar that demons wear, making them resistant to normal spiritual warfare. It's like a "No Trespassing" sign in the spirit realm that says to angels: "You can't intervene here—there's a legal claim."

Let me show you this from Daniel's life. In Daniel 10, Daniel had been praying and fasting for 21 days, seeking understanding about a vision. Finally, an angel appears to him and says: "Do not fear, Daniel, for from the first day that you set your heart to understand and to humble yourself before your God, your words were heard; and I have come because of your words. But the prince of the kingdom of Persia withstood me twenty-one days" (Daniel 10:12-13).

What was happening? Daniel's prayers were heard immediately in heaven, but there was a **demonic prince**—a territorial spirit over Persia—that withstood the angel carrying the answer. This demon had some kind of legal right, some territorial claim, that allowed him to resist heaven's messenger for three weeks! It wasn't until Michael, the archangel, came to help that the breakthrough came.

This is exactly what happens when a curse is in place. Your prayers are heard—God isn't ignoring you!—but there's a demonic "prince" that has been given legal ground through that curse. It creates a **spiritual traffic jam**. The blessings, the answers, the healing—they're all dispatched from heaven, but they get held up in transit because there's a curse blocking the delivery route.

This is why some people can receive prayer from every minister in town, read every faith book, claim every promise—and still see no lasting change. It's not that God isn't faithful. It's not that prayer doesn't work. It's that **the curse must be broken first**.

It's like trying to pour clean water into a cup that has a lid on it. You can pour all day, but the water just runs off. You have to remove the lid first. The curse is that lid.

Jesus dealt with this principle when he encountered the Syrophoenician woman in Mark 7. At first, he told her, "Let the children be filled first, for it is not good to take the children's bread and throw it to the little dogs" (Mark 7:27). There was a **covenantal order**—the Jews first, then the Gentiles. But when she responded in faith—"Yes, Lord, yet even the little dogs under the table eat from the children's crumbs"—Jesus said, "For this saying go your way; the demon has gone out of your daughter" (Mark 7:29).

Her faith and humility overcame the covenantal barrier. She accessed what seemed legally unavailable to her.

Beloved, here's your hope: **Jesus became a curse for us** (Galatians 3:13). He was nailed to the cross, and with Him, every curse that was against us. Every legal claim the enemy had was canceled. Every demonic shield was shattered. Every barrier was broken down.

But you have to **appropriate** this truth. You have to **enforce** this victory. You have to look at those generational patterns, those sudden reversals, those prayer-resistant situations, and declare: "No more! The curse is broken by the blood of Jesus! Every legal ground is canceled! Every demonic shield is shattered! I am free!"

Don't just pray about the symptoms. Deal with the root. Break the curse. Then watch as prayers that seemed stuck for years suddenly find their mark. Watch as blessings that were held up in transit finally arrive. Watch as the patterns that plagued your family for generations end with you.

You're not just breaking a curse for yourself. You're breaking it for your children. For your grandchildren. For generations yet unborn. You're changing your family's spiritual DNA. You're rewriting your family's story from curse to blessing.

That's the power of the cross. That's the authority you carry. That's the fruit of freedom you're called to walk in.

III. SOURCES OF CURSES: WHERE DO THEY ORIGINATE?

Beloved, gather close and listen. This might be one of the most important sessions we'll have. Because you can't dismantle what you don't understand, and you can't close doors you don't know are open. Curses don't just materialize out of thin air like morning fog. They have **sources**. They have **points of entry**. They have **legal gateways**.

If there's demonic oppression in your life, I want you to stop asking "Why me, God?" and start asking the Holy Spirit: "Show me the entry point. Reveal the source." Let's walk through these sources systematically, with the Word of God as our guide and the Spirit as our teacher.

1. CURSES FROM GOD: THE JUDICIAL DECREES

Now this might surprise some of you, but we have to start here because it's foundational. Yes—**God Himself pronounces curses**. But before you get a wrong picture of God, understand this: God's curses are never capricious, never arbitrary, never the temper tantrum of a distant deity. They are **judicial**. They are the natural, spiritual consequences of deliberate, unrepentant rebellion against His holy character and covenant.

Think of it like this: If you jump off a ten-story building, you don't curse gravity when you hit the ground. Gravity isn't mean—it's just consistent. It's the law. God's moral and spiritual laws have consequences built into them.

Let's look at Scripture:

Genesis 3:14-19—After Adam and Eve's disobedience, God pronounces curses: on the serpent, on the ground, on childbearing, on work. This wasn't God being petty. This was the cosmos responding to the introduction of sin. The perfect harmony was broken, and **curse was the consequence**.

Deuteronomy 28:15-68—This is the most extensive list in Scripture. God through Moses lays out the blessings for obedience (verses 1-14) and then says: "But it shall come to pass, if you do not obey the voice of the LORD your God... all these curses will come upon you and overtake you." And then He lists them—sickness, drought, defeat, madness, oppression. Sixty-eight verses of consequences!

Why? Because God had entered into a covenant with Israel at Sinai (Exodus 19-24). A covenant always has terms. Blessings for faithfulness, curses for unfaithfulness. This isn't unique to God—it's how covenants work. Even our human contracts have penalty clauses.

But here's what you need to understand about God's curses: They're **reversible** through repentance and redemption! God says in **2 Chronicles 7:14**: "If My people who are called by My name will humble themselves, and pray and seek My face, and turn from their wicked ways, then I will hear from heaven, and will forgive their sin and heal their land."

The prophet Jonah preached coming judgment to Nineveh, and when they repented, "God relented from the disaster that He had said He would bring upon them" (Jonah 3:10).

So, if you're under God's corrective hand, there's a clear pathway: **Humble repentance → Genuine turning → Divine restoration**.

But here's the glorious New Covenant truth: **Galatians 3:13**—"Christ has redeemed us from the curse of the law, having become a curse for us." Jesus took the full judicial curse of Deuteronomy 28 upon Himself on the cross! Every curse God ever pronounced against sin fell on Him, so it could never fall on you if you're in Christ!

But—and this is crucial—you must be *in Christ*. You must be under the New Covenant through faith in His blood. If you're living in deliberate, unrepentant sin while claiming to be a Christian, you're essentially stepping out from under the covering of His blood and exposing yourself to the consequences of broken covenant.

2. CURSES FROM SATANIC AGENTS AND OCCULT PRACTITIONERS

Now we move into the realm of deliberate, malicious spiritual warfare. This is where curses are **engineered** by human agents in league with demonic powers.

Throughout Scripture, we see this reality:

Balaam in Numbers 22-24 was hired by Balak, king of Moab, to curse Israel. He was a professional curser—a mercenary prophet who used divination. But every time he opened his mouth to curse, God turned it to blessing. Why? Because Israel was under God's covenant protection. Balaam later taught Balak how to entice Israel into sexual immorality and idolatry (Numbers 31:16, Revelation 2:14), which would **invite God's curse** upon them.

That's important—sometimes satanic agents can't curse you directly if you're under God's protection, so they tempt you into sin that gives God's curses legal ground.

The witch of Endor in 1 Samuel 28 is another example. King Saul, who had expelled mediums and spiritists from Israel, went in disguise to consult her to summon Samuel's spirit. This was direct engagement with the occult, and it contributed to Saul's tragic end.

In Acts 13:6-12, we meet Elymas the sorcerer who opposed Paul and Barnabas. Paul, filled with the Holy Spirit, said: "O full of all deceit and all fraud, you son of the devil, you enemy of all righteousness, will you not cease perverting the straight ways of the Lord? And now, indeed, the hand of the Lord is upon you, and you shall be blind, not seeing the sun for a time." Notice—Paul didn't curse him; he pronounced God's judgment on his occult practices.

Now, in our context today, this includes:

- **Witchdoctors and native doctors** who perform rituals
- **Babalawos and Ifa priests** who consult oracles
- **Sangomas and traditional healers** who work with ancestral spirits
- **Spiritualists and mediums** who claim to contact the dead
- **Overseas "prophets"** who mix Christianity with divination
- **Freemasons, Rosicrucians, and other secret societies** that involve occult oaths

These practitioners operate in the demonic realm. When they pronounce curses, they're not just saying words. They're:

1. Making sacrifices (animal or sometimes worse) that give their words demonic power
2. Calling upon specific demons by name or function
3. Creating spiritual "documents" or "contracts" in the unseen realm
4. Assigning demons to enforce the curse

I've had people come to me with physical evidence—buried concoctions found in their yards, figurines with their names on them, animals killed at their doorsteps. This is real, beloved. But hear me: **Greater is He who is in you than he who is in the world** (1 John 4:4).

3. PARENTAL AND ANCESTRAL CURSES

This might be the most common source of bondage I encounter. It's what the Bible calls "the iniquity of the fathers" affecting the children.

Exodus 20:5—"I, the LORD your God, am a jealous God, visiting the iniquity of the fathers on the children to the third and fourth generations of those who hate Me."

Exodus 34:6-7—God describes Himself as "keeping mercy for thousands, forgiving iniquity and transgression and sin, but by no means clearing the guilty, visiting the iniquity of the fathers upon the children and the children's children to the third and the fourth generation."

This isn't God being unfair. This is the principle of **spiritual inheritance**. Just as you can inherit genetic traits, you can inherit spiritual conditions. When a parent or ancestor:

- **Engages in idolatry** (worshipping Sango, Ogun, Oya, ancestors, etc.)
- **Enters blood covenants** (with secret societies, occult groups)
- **Commits serious moral sins** (murder, adultery, incest)
- **Dedicates children to idols** (sometimes at naming ceremonies)
- **Aborts children** (shedding innocent blood)

...they open spiritual doors that can affect their descendants.

Let me give you a biblical example: **Achan's sin in Joshua 7**. After the battle of Jericho, Achan took devoted things God had said not to take. When Israel next fought Ai, they were defeated. Joshua cried out to God, and God said: "Israel has sinned, and they have also transgressed My covenant which I commanded them... Therefore, the children of Israel could not stand before their enemies" (Joshua 7:11-12).

One man's sin affected the entire nation! And not just Achan died—his sons and daughters were stoned with him (Joshua 7:24-25). His entire family line was cut off because of his covenant-breaking.

In 2 Samuel 21:1-14, there was a three-year famine in David's time. When David inquired of God, He said: "It is because of Saul and his bloodthirsty house, because he killed the Gibeonites." Saul had broken a covenant Joshua made with the Gibeonites 400 years earlier (Joshua 9), and the curse affected a generation that wasn't even born when the covenant was broken!

Now, here's your hope: **Ezekiel 18:19-20**—"Yet you say, 'Why should the son not bear the guilt of the father?' Because the son has done what is lawful and right, and has kept all My statutes and observed them, he shall surely live. The soul who sins shall die. The son shall not bear the guilt of the father, nor the father bear the guilt of the son."

In the New Covenant, you have the right as a believer to **renounce, reject, and break** every ancestral curse. You're not helplessly bound by your family's past. You can say: "In Jesus' name, I break every curse coming from my father's line. I break every curse from my mother's line. I apply the blood of Jesus to my genealogy."

4. SELF-IMPOSED CURSES

This one breaks my heart because so many believers do this without realizing it. You're cursing yourself with your own mouth!

Proverbs 18:21—"Death and life are in the power of the tongue, and those who love it will eat its fruit."

James 3:5-6—"The tongue is a little member and boasts great things. See how great a forest a little fire kindles! And the tongue is a fire, a world of iniquity. The tongue is so set among our members that it defiles the whole body, and sets on fire the course of nature; and it is set on fire by hell."

Your words are **containers of spiritual power**. When you consistently say:

- "I'm so stupid"
- "Nothing ever works out for me"
- "I'll never get married"
- "I'll always be poor"
- "This sickness is going to kill me"

- "Bad luck follows me everywhere"

...you're not just expressing feelings. You're making **decrees**. You're issuing **self-fulfilling prophecies**. You're giving demons legal ground to manifest what you're speaking.

In **Numbers 13-14**, when the twelve spies returned from Canaan, ten gave a negative report: "We are not able to go up against the people, for they are stronger than we... The land through which we have gone as spies is a land that devours its inhabitants" (Numbers 13:31-32).

The people believed this report and said: "If only we had died in the land of Egypt! Or if only we had died in this wilderness!... Would it not be better for us to return to Egypt?" (Numbers 14:2-3).

God responded to their words: "Say to them, 'As I live,' says the LORD, 'just as you have spoken in My hearing, so I will do to you: Your carcasses shall fall in this wilderness'" (Numbers 14:28-29).

They spoke death over themselves, and God said, "Okay, have it your way." Their words became their reality.

Beloved, monitor your mouth! Don't partner with the enemy against yourself. Don't curse what God has blessed. Don't speak death over what God wants to bring life to.

5. CURSES FROM UNLAWFUL ACTS

Finally, there are specific actions the Bible explicitly says attract curses. These aren't suggestions—they're **spiritual laws**.

In **Deuteronomy 27**, Moses instructs the Israelites that when they cross into Canaan, they're to set up stones, plaster them, and write the law on them. Then the Levites are to proclaim curses for specific violations, and the people are to say "Amen" (so be it).

Let's look at some of these:

Verse 16: "Cursed is the one who treats his father or his mother with contempt." Dishonoring parents brings a curse. This is why some people struggle no matter what they do—they've dishonored their parents, maybe even cursed them in anger.

Verse 17: "Cursed is the one who moves his neighbor's landmark." This is property fraud—cheating people out of what's rightfully theirs. If you've acquired land or property through deception, there's a curse on it.

Verse 18: "Cursed is the one who makes the blind to wander off the road." Taking advantage of vulnerable people.

Verse 19: "Cursed is the one who perverts the justice due the stranger, the fatherless, and widow." Unfair treatment of the defenseless.

Verses 20-23: Curses for various sexual sins—incest, bestiality.

Verse 24: "Cursed is the one who attacks his neighbor secretly." This includes gossip, slander, backbiting.

Verse 25: "Cursed is the one who takes a bribe to slay an innocent person." Perverting justice for money.

Verse 26: "Cursed is the one who does not confirm all the words of this law by observing them." A comprehensive curse for covenant-breaking.

These are spiritual laws, beloved. Just as jumping off a building violates the law of gravity with consequences, violating these moral laws violates spiritual reality with consequences.

But here's the beautiful thread through all of this: **JESUS.**

Jesus became the curse for dishonoring parents—He honored His Father perfectly.

Jesus became the curse for stealing—He owned nothing but gave everything.

Jesus became the curse for injustice—He received the ultimate injustice at His trial.

Jesus became the curse for all sexual sin—He was tempted in every way yet without sin.

Jesus became the curse for covenant-breaking—He kept the whole law perfectly.

And He did it so that "the blessing of Abraham might come upon the Gentiles in Christ Jesus, that we might receive the promise of the Spirit through faith" (Galatians 3:14).

So, when you identify the source of a curse in your life, you don't have to live in fear or condemnation. You have a remedy! You have an advocate! You have a Redeemer who specializes in turning curses into blessings, bondage into freedom, death into life.

But you must cooperate with the Holy Spirit. You must be willing to:

1. **Repent** where you've opened doors

2. **Renounce** what needs breaking
3. **Restore** what needs restoring (like with Zacchaeus in Luke 19:8)
4. **Receive** your freedom by faith
5. **Resist** ever opening those doors again

The blood of Jesus is sufficient for every curse from every source. But you must apply it specifically to each entry point. You must close each door. You must cancel each legal claim.

That's what we're going to learn to do. Not in our strength, but in His. Not by our wisdom, but by His Word. Not by our authority, but in His mighty name.

IV. THE TEN LAWS GOVERNING CURSES

Beloved, listen to me carefully. Understanding curses isn't just about knowing they exist—it's about understanding *how* they operate. You see, the spiritual realm operates by laws, just like the natural realm. Gravity is a law—drop something, it falls. Fire is a law—touch it, you get burned. In the same way, there are **spiritual laws** that govern how curses work, how they're activated, how they're sustained, and how they're broken.

If you want to dismantle curses effectively, you can't just shout at them. You have to understand the principles that govern them. Let me walk you through these ten spiritual laws—these governing principles that determine whether a curse has power in your life or not.

1. A CURSE DOES NOT COME WITHOUT A CAUSE (Proverbs 26:2)

Let's start with the foundational law: "As the bird by wandering, as the swallow by flying, so the curse causeless shall not come."

Think about that imagery. A bird doesn't just land anywhere. It looks for a branch, a wire, a ledge—a *landing place*. A swallow in flight doesn't suddenly drop from the sky for no reason. It lands where there's something to land on.

A curse is the same. It needs a **landing place**. It needs a **cause**. It needs *legal ground*.

If a curse is trying to operate in your life, I want you to ask the Holy Spirit: "What is the landing place? What gave this curse permission to land here?"

The landing places are always spiritual violations:

- **Sin** (unconfessed, unrepented)
- **Covenant-breaking** (with God or with people)
- **Injustice** (especially against the vulnerable)
- **Idolatry** (giving God's place to something else)
- **Unforgiveness** (holding bitterness in your heart)
- **Bloodshed** (abortion, murder, violence)

Look at Israel in the Old Testament. When they experienced curses—defeat, famine, captivity—God would send prophets to explain *why*. "You have forsaken the covenant... you have worshipped idols... you have shed innocent blood." There was always a *cause*.

Remove the landing place, and the curse has nowhere to land. It wanders like that bird, looking for somewhere to perch, and if it can't find it in your life, it moves on.

2. A CURSE, UNLESS BROKEN, CONTINUES TO OPERATE

Here's a sobering truth: Curses don't have expiration dates. They don't just wear out over time. They're not like medicine that loses potency after a few years.

If a curse is not deliberately, intentionally, and authoritatively broken, it will continue its operation. It will pass from generation to generation. It will persist through seasons and circumstances.

Remember the curse on Jericho? Joshua pronounced it in Joshua 6:26. It was still active **five hundred years later** when Hiel rebuilt Jericho and lost his sons exactly as the curse specified (1 Kings 16:34). The curse didn't fade. It didn't weaken. It waited.

Or consider the Amalekites. In Exodus 17:14-16, God told Moses: "Write this for a memorial in the book and recount it in the hearing of Joshua, that I will utterly blot out the remembrance of Amalek from under heaven... The LORD will have war with Amalek from generation to generation."

Generations later, in 1 Samuel 15, God commands Saul through Samuel to completely destroy the Amalekites. Why? Because the judgment was still in effect. Saul's disobedience in sparing Agag meant the curse continued, and Agag's descendant Haman nearly destroyed the Jews in Esther's time!

A curse is like a spiritual computer program. Once it's installed, it will keep running until someone with administrator privileges uninstalls it. It doesn't just stop because you ignore it or because time has passed.

3. CURSES ARE SPIRITUAL AND MUST BE DEALT WITH SPIRITUALLY

You cannot break a spiritual problem with natural solutions alone. You can't heal a curse with medicine alone. You can't break a poverty curse with financial advice alone. You can't break a relational curse with counseling alone.

Now, am I saying don't go to doctors? Don't get financial advice? Don't get counseling? No! Use all the natural means God provides. But understand: if there's a spiritual root—a curse—then the natural solutions will only provide temporary relief at best.

The Apostle Paul makes this clear in **2 Corinthians 10:3-4**: "For though we walk in the flesh, we do not war according to the flesh. For the weapons of our warfare are not carnal but mighty in God for pulling down strongholds."

Our weapons are spiritual:

- **Prayer** (especially aggressive, faith-filled prayer)
- **The Word of God** (spoken in authority)
- **The Name of Jesus** (the name above every name)
- **The Blood of Jesus** (that cleanses from all sin)
- **The Holy Spirit** (our Helper and Empowerer)

When Jesus delivered people, He didn't give them medicine for demonic oppression. He didn't counsel the man with the legion of demons. He spoke with spiritual authority: "Come out of the man, unclean spirit!" (Mark 5:8).

When Peter confronted Simon the sorcerer in Acts 8, he didn't argue philosophy. He said: "Repent therefore of this your wickedness, and pray God if perhaps the thought of your heart may be forgiven you. For I see that you are poisoned by bitterness and bound by iniquity" (Acts 8:22-23). He dealt with the spiritual root.

4. SIN GIVES CURSES THE RIGHT TO REMAIN

This is directly connected to Law #1, but it's important enough to stand on its own. Even after a curse has been initially broken, if the sin that invited it remains unconfessed, unrepented, and unchanged, that curse will find its way back.

Jesus taught this in **Matthew 12:43-45**: "When an unclean spirit goes out of a man, he goes through dry places, seeking rest, and finds none. Then he says, 'I will return to my house from which I came.' And when he comes, he finds it empty, swept, and put in order. Then he goes and takes with him seven other spirits more wicked than himself, and they enter and dwell there; and the last state of that man is worse than the first."

Notice: the house was "empty." The demon was cast out (the curse was broken), but nothing filled the space. No repentance. No filling of the Holy Spirit. No renewal of the mind. So the demon came back with reinforcements.

Unconfessed sin is like leaving the door unlocked after you've chased a thief out. Unforgiveness is like posting a sign saying "Welcome back!" to spirits of bitterness. Hidden rebellion is like rolling out the red carpet for demonic oppression.

But repentance—true, heartfelt, turn-from-your-ways repentance—slams the door shut. It changes the locks. It posts "No Trespassing" signs backed by heaven's authority.

5. DEMONS ENFORCE CURSES

This is where many believers miss it. They try to break curses with declarations alone, but they don't deal with the enforcers.

Behind every persistent curse is a **demonic entity assigned to ensure its fulfillment**. This isn't superstition—it's biblical reality.

Look at **Daniel 10**. Daniel had been praying and fasting for 21 days. Finally, an angel appears and says: "From the first day that you set your heart to understand and to humble yourself before your God, your words were heard; and I have come because of your words. But the prince of the kingdom of Persia withstood me twenty-one days" (Daniel 10:12-13).

There was a demonic "prince" over Persia that resisted the angel bringing Daniel's answer. This demon had territorial authority, and it exercised it.

When a curse is spoken, demons are often assigned as "enforcement officers." Their job is to:

- Create circumstances that fulfill the curse
- Resist prayers and interventions against the curse
- Reinforce the curse through temptation, accusation, and oppression

This is why Jesus' deliverance ministry was so central to His mission. He didn't just teach people how to cope with their problems—He cast out the demons causing them!

When you break a curse, you must also address the demonic enforcers: "In Jesus' name, I command every demon assigned to enforce this curse to be bound and cast out! You have no legal right here—the curse is broken by the blood of Jesus!"

6. CHRIST HAS REDEEMED US FROM EVERY CURSE BY SUBSTITUTION (Galatians 3:13)

Now here's the game-changer. This isn't just a law about curses—it's the law of redemption that overrides all curse laws!

"Christ has redeemed us from the curse of the law, having become a curse for us (for it is written, 'Cursed is everyone who hangs on a tree')."

Let me break this down:

Under the Old Covenant, if you broke the law, you came under the curse of the law (Deuteronomy 27-28). There was no way out. The law demanded perfect obedience, and everyone failed.

But Jesus—perfect, sinless, obedient Jesus—took our place. He who knew no sin became sin for us (2 Corinthians 5:21). More specifically for our discussion: He became a *curse* for us.

When Jesus hung on the cross, He wasn't just dying a physical death. He was absorbing in His body the full judicial curse of God against sin. Every curse from Deuteronomy 28 fell on Him:

- The curse of sickness? He bore our infirmities (Isaiah 53:4).
- The curse of poverty? He became poor that we might become rich (2 Corinthians 8:9).
- The curse of shame? He endured the cross, despising the shame (Hebrews 12:2).
- The curse of separation from God? "My God, My God, why have You forsaken Me?" (Matthew 27:46).

This is a **finished legal work**. In heaven's court, the case is closed. The curse has been fully adjudicated at Calvary. When you accept Christ, you're not just getting your sins forgiven—you're getting transferred from the kingdom of darkness into the kingdom of light (Colossians 1:13), from under curse to under blessing.

But—and this is crucial—you must *appropriate* this truth. You must enforce this finished work in your life. The check has been written, but you have to cash it.

7. AN UNJUST CURSE RETURNS TO ITS SENDER (Proverbs 26:2b)

The second part of Proverbs 26:2 says: "So the curse without cause shall not alight."

If someone curses you *without cause*—out of pure malice, jealousy, or wickedness—and you're walking in righteousness, covered by the blood of Jesus, that curse cannot land on you. Instead, it boomerangs back to the sender.

We see this principle in Scripture:

When **Balaam** was hired to curse Israel, every time he opened his mouth, blessings came out instead. He finally told Balak: "How shall I curse whom God has not cursed? And how shall I denounce whom the LORD has not denounced?" (Numbers 23:8). The unjust curses couldn't land.

In **Nehemiah's** time, when Sanballat and Tobiah opposed the rebuilding of Jerusalem's walls and mocked Nehemiah, he prayed: "Hear, O our God, for we are despised; turn their reproach on their own heads, and give them as plunder to a land of captivity!" (Nehemiah 4:4). And God did exactly that.

Now, this doesn't mean you should focus on cursing your enemies. Jesus taught us to love our enemies and pray for those who persecute us (Matthew 5:44). But it does mean you can have confidence that if you're walking righteously, unjust curses have no power over you.

The key phrase is "without cause." If there's sin in your life giving the curse a cause, this protection isn't automatic. But if you're covered by the blood and walking in obedience, you're like a Teflon pan—curses slide right off.

8. YOU CANNOT BLESS WHOM GOD HAS CURSED, NOR CURSE WHOM GOD HAS BLESSED (Numbers 23:8)

This law comes straight from Balaam's mouth when he was trying to curse Israel: "How shall I curse whom God has not cursed? And how shall I denounce whom the LORD has not denounced?"

There's a divine sovereignty at work here. When God has blessed someone, no human or demonic curse can override it. When God has cursed someone (judicially, for unrepentant sin), no human blessing can reverse it.

This is why it's so important to be in right standing with God. If God is for you, who can be against you? (Romans 8:31). If God has blessed you, who can curse you?

But the converse is also true: if you're living in deliberate rebellion against God, no amount of positive confession, no "blessing" from a prophet, can override God's judicial hand.

This is why David prayed after his sin with Bathsheba: "Create in me a clean heart, O God, and renew a steadfast spirit within me. Do not cast me away from Your presence, and do not take Your Holy Spirit from me" (Psalm 51:10-11). He knew that being in right relationship with God was his only true protection and blessing.

9. A CURSE CANNOT HOLD A CHILD OF GOD WHO WALKS IN OBEDIENCE

This is the practical outworking of our position in Christ. Yes, we're redeemed from the curse (Law #6). But there's a condition to walking in that redemption: obedience.

Think of it like citizenship. When you become a citizen of a country, you gain certain rights and protections. But if you break that country's laws, you can still end up in prison despite your citizenship.

In the same way, when you're born again, you become a citizen of heaven (Philippians 3:20). You're under Christ's protection. But if you willfully, persistently disobey God's laws, you're essentially stepping out from under that protection.

Psalm 91 is the great chapter of protection, but notice the conditions:

- "He who dwells in the secret place of the Most High shall abide under the shadow of the Almighty" (verse 1). Dwelling implies abiding, remaining.

- "Because he has set his love upon Me, therefore I will deliver him" (verse 14). Love demonstrated by obedience.

Jesus said in **John 15:7**: "If you abide in Me, and My words abide in you, you will ask what you desire, and it shall be done for you." Abiding brings authority in prayer.

Walking in obedience is like staying inside the fortress. The walls are high, the gates are strong, and you're protected from every curse launched against you. Willful disobedience is like wandering outside the walls where you're exposed.

10. CURSES CAN BE ACQUIRED UNCONSCIOUSLY

This final law is so important because it destroys the "I didn't know" excuse. Ignorance does not grant immunity in the spirit realm.

You can inherit a curse from ancestors without knowing anything about what they did. You can pick up a curse through unknowing involvement in something occultic. You can even speak a curse over yourself without realizing the power of your words.

The Bible addresses this:

In **Joshua 9**, the Gibeonites deceived Israel into making a covenant with them. Israel didn't consult God (verse 14), and they made the covenant based on false information. But guess what? It was still binding! Generations later, in **2 Samuel 21**, there was a famine because Saul had broken that covenant by attacking the Gibeonites. Israel was still bound by a covenant their ancestors made, even though they made it in ignorance initially.

Or consider **Hosea 4:6**: "My people are destroyed for lack of knowledge." Ignorance leads to destruction.

This is why we need the Holy Spirit to reveal hidden things. This is why we need to prayerfully examine our lives and our family histories. This is why we need to break curses proactively, not just reactively.

But here's the good news: even curses acquired unconsciously can be broken consciously! You don't need to know every detail of how a curse entered. You just need to know that if it's there, you have authority in Jesus' name to break it.

These ten laws aren't meant to frighten you—they're meant to empower you. When you understand how curses operate, you know exactly how to dismantle them. You know:

- To remove the landing places (repentance)
- To use spiritual weapons (prayer, the Word, the Blood)
- To deal with demonic enforcers (binding and casting out)
- To stand on your redemption in Christ (appropriating Calvary)
- To walk in obedience (staying under protection)
- To break even what you didn't know was there (proactive spiritual warfare)

You're not a victim of mysterious spiritual forces. You're a blood-bought, Spirit-filled believer who has been given authority over all the power of the enemy (Luke 10:19). These laws don't control you—they're tools for your liberation.

V. HOW HIDDEN CURSES ENTER A LIFE

Beloved, I want you to lean in and listen with your spiritual ears today. Many of you are dealing with things you didn't start. You're fighting battles you didn't initiate. You're carrying burdens you didn't create. That's because curses often enter our lives not through our personal sins, but through **open doors**—specific entry points that give the enemy legal access.

Let me walk you through these doors carefully. We need to examine each one, because you can't close a door you don't know is open. You can't secure a house when you don't know where the breach is. This is about spiritual housekeeping—identifying every point of entry so we can shut it, lock it, and seal it with the blood of Jesus.

1. BREAKING MARRIAGE COVENANTS

Marriage isn't just a contract—it's a **divine covenant** witnessed by God Himself. When God joins a man and woman together, He's not just signing a certificate; He's establishing a spiritual union that reflects Christ and the Church (Ephesians 5:31-32).

But what happens when that covenant is broken?

Adultery—when a married person sleeps with someone not their spouse—isn't just a "mistake." It's covenant-breaking of the highest order. Proverbs 6:32-33 says: "Whoever commits adultery with a woman lacks understanding; he who does so destroys his own soul. Wounds and dishonor he will get, and his reproach will not be wiped away."

Divorce without biblical grounds—Jesus said in Matthew 19:9: "And I say to you, whoever divorces his wife, except for sexual immorality, and marries another, commits adultery." When you divorce for unbiblical reasons and remarry, you're breaking covenants and entering adultery.

Abandonment—when a spouse walks away without cause, leaving their covenant partner to fend for themselves.

Here's the spiritual reality: When you break a marriage covenant, you activate spiritual consequences:

- **Curses of relational strife**—future relationships become battlegrounds
- **Curses of loneliness**—even in a crowd, you feel profoundly alone
- **Curses of betrayal**—you become either the betrayer or the betrayed in relationships
- **Curses on children**—the innocent suffer the consequences of broken covenants

Look at **Malachi 2:13-16**: "And this is the second thing you do: You cover the altar of the LORD with tears, with weeping and crying... Yet you say, 'For what reason?' Because the LORD has been witness between you and the wife of your youth, with whom you have dealt treacherously... Therefore, take heed to your spirit, and let none deal treacherously with the wife of his youth. 'For the LORD God of Israel says that He hates divorce.'"

God takes covenant-breaking so seriously that He says He **hates** divorce. Why? Because it destroys the very picture of His faithful love for His people.

But hear me—if this is your story, there's mercy at the cross. There's healing. There's restoration. But it starts with repentance and the breaking of every curse that entered through that broken door.

2. UNFAIR TREATMENT OF OTHERS

Beloved, how you treat people matters eternally. Especially how you treat:

- **The poor**—those who can't repay you
- **The vulnerable**—widows, orphans, foreigners
- **Those who trusted you**—employees, partners, friends
- **The defenseless**—those who can't fight back

Proverbs 22:22-23 warns: "Do not rob the poor because he is poor, nor oppress the afflicted at the gate; for the LORD will plead their cause and plunder the soul of those who plunder them."

When you cheat someone, exploit someone, or bring unnecessary suffering to another human being, you're not just committing a moral failure—you're opening yourself up to a **curse of reversal and justice**.

Remember the story of **Jacob and Laban** in Genesis 29-31? Jacob served Laban for seven years for Rachel, but Laban deceived him and gave him Leah instead. Then he made Jacob work another seven years for Rachel. Laban also changed Jacob's wages ten times (Genesis 31:7). Laban cheated and exploited Jacob repeatedly.

But what happened? God blessed Jacob despite Laban's cheating, and Laban's household suffered. In fact, God told Laban in a dream: "Be careful that you speak to Jacob neither good nor bad" (Genesis 31:24). Laban's exploitation opened him up to divine intervention against him.

Or consider **Zacchaeus** in Luke 19. He was a tax collector who had cheated people. When Jesus came to his house, he didn't just say "I'm sorry." He said: "Look, Lord, I give half of my goods to the poor; and if I have taken anything from anyone by false accusation, I restore fourfold" (Luke 19:8). Why fourfold? Because that's what the Law required for stealing (Exodus 22:1). Zacchaeus knew that his unjust gains carried a curse that needed to be broken through restitution.

When you mistreat people, especially those who can't defend themselves, you're essentially praying this prayer: "God, do to me what I've done to them." And God often answers that prayer.

3. SEXUAL IMMORALITY

This is one of the most powerful doors for curses to enter. Why? Because sexual union isn't just physical—it's **spiritual**. It creates **soul ties** and, in a very real sense, **blood covenants**.

1 Corinthians 6:15-18 says: "Do you not know that your bodies are members of Christ? Shall I then take the members of Christ and make them members of a harlot? Certainly not! Or do you not know that he who is joined to a harlot is one body with her? For 'the two,' He says, 'shall become one flesh.' But he who is joined to the Lord is one spirit with Him. Flee sexual immorality. Every sin that a man does is outside the body, but he who commits sexual immorality sins against his own body."

When you have sex with someone, you become "one flesh" with them. This isn't just poetry—it's spiritual reality. You're exchanging spiritual DNA. You're connecting your spirit to theirs.

Now think about what this means:

- **Fornication**—premarital sex creates ungodly soul ties that affect future marriage
- **Adultery**—mixes your spouse's spiritual DNA with someone else's
- **Incest**—creates perverted connections within family lines
- **Pornography**—creates soul ties with images and with the people involved
- **Sexual abuse**—forces a connection that damages the victim's soul

These doors allow in:

- **Curses of guilt and shame** that won't lift
- **Curses on reproductive organs**—infertility, miscarriages, sexual dysfunction
- **Curses of marital failure**—future marriages carry the baggage of past connections
- **Demonic oppression**—spirits of lust, perversion, and shame gain entry

Look at the Corinthian church. They had a man sleeping with his father's wife (1 Corinthians 5:1). Paul didn't just say "Stop that." He said: "Deliver such a one to Satan for the destruction of the flesh, that his spirit may be saved in the day of the Lord Jesus" (1 Corinthians 5:5). Why such severe discipline? Because sexual sin opens devastating spiritual doors.

But there's cleansing! There's breaking of soul ties! There's restoration through the blood of Jesus that breaks every ungodly connection!

4. WEALTH OBTAINED UNJUSTLY

Proverbs 10:22 says: "The blessing of the LORD makes rich, and He adds no sorrow with it."

There's a difference between **wealth** and **riches**. Wealth is what God gives—it comes with peace, joy, and the ability to be a blessing. Riches can be obtained many ways, but if they're obtained unjustly, they come with **sorrow attached**.

How is wealth obtained unjustly?

- **Fraud**—lying, deception, false advertising
- **Bribery**—paying for favorable treatment
- **Theft**—taking what isn't yours
- **Exploitation**—underpaying workers, price gouging
- **Oppression**—using power to take advantage

Proverbs 13:11 says: "Wealth gained by dishonesty will be diminished, but he who gathers by labor will increase."

Proverbs 20:17 says: "Bread gained by deceit is sweet to a man, but afterward his mouth will be filled with gravel."

The curse on unjust wealth is that:

- It **never satisfies**—you always want more
- It **brings trouble**—lawsuits, thieves, disasters
- It **disappears**—vanishes as mysteriously as it came
- It **corrupts**—turns your heart from God

Remember **Achan** in Joshua 7? After Jericho fell, God said everything was to be devoted to Him. But Achan took a Babylonian garment, silver, and gold and hid them. What happened? Israel lost the next battle, and Achan and his whole family were stoned. The unjust gain brought a curse on him and everyone connected to him.

Or consider **Judas**. He was the treasurer for Jesus' ministry, and he stole from the money bag (John 12:6). He also betrayed Jesus for thirty pieces of silver. What happened? The money brought him no joy—he tried to return it, then hanged himself. The money was used to buy a field that became known as the Field of Blood (Matthew 27:3-8).

If you have wealth obtained unjustly, the only way to break the curse is **restitution**. Give it back. Make it right. Like Zacchaeus did. The sorrow won't lift until the injustice is corrected.

5. PARENTAL AND ANCESTRAL SINS

This door is so wide, many entire families walk through it generation after generation. **Exodus 20:5** makes it clear: God visits "the iniquity of the fathers on the children to the third and fourth generations of those who hate Me."

What sins of ancestors open these doors?

- **Idolatry**—worshipping other gods, ancestors, spirits
- **Witchcraft**—consulting mediums, using charms, casting spells
- **Secret societies**—taking oaths in Masonic lodges, Rosicrucians, etc.
- **Bloodshed**—murder, violence, shedding innocent blood
- **Sexual perversion**—incest, adultery, prostitution

These create **generational curses** that affect:

- **Health**—same diseases recurring in the family
- **Finances**—poverty, debt, business failures
- **Relationships**—divorce, abuse, loneliness
- **Destiny**—unfulfilled potential, early death

Look at the **kings of Israel**. Jeroboam set up golden calves at Bethel and Dan (1 Kings 12:28-30). This sin became known as "the sins of Jeroboam." Generation after generation, the evaluation of kings included: "He did not depart from the sins of Jeroboam." The idolatry pattern persisted for generations.

But here's the hope: **Ezekiel 18** gives us the principle of individual responsibility. Verse 20 says: "The soul who sins shall die. The son shall not bear the guilt of the father, nor the father bear the guilt of the son."

You can break generational curses! You don't have to live under what your ancestors did. But you must consciously, deliberately renounce their sins and break the curses they invited.

6. SHEDDING OF INNOCENT BLOOD

Blood is sacred. Life is in the blood (Leviticus 17:11). When innocent blood is shed, it **cries out from the ground**.

Genesis 4:10—After Cain killed Abel, God said: "What have you done? The voice of your brother's blood cries out to Me from the ground."

Numbers 35:33 says: "So you shall not pollute the land where you are; for blood defiles the land, and no atonement can be made for the land, for the blood that is shed on it, except by the blood of him who shed it."

What sheds innocent blood?

- **Murder**—taking a human life
- **Abortion**—terminating a pregnancy
- **Violence**—assault that causes bloodshed
- **Ritual killing**—human sacrifice

- **Negligence**—causing death through carelessness

The curse of innocent blood is severe:

- The land becomes defiled
- Restlessness and guilt plague the shedder
- Premature death often follows
- Generations can be affected

Look at **King David** after he had Uriah killed to cover his adultery with Bathsheba (2 Samuel 11). The prophet Nathan told him: "Now therefore, the sword shall never depart from your house... Thus says the LORD: 'Behold, I will raise up adversity against you from your own house'" (2 Samuel 12:10-11). And it happened—Amnon raped Tamar, Absalom killed Amnon, Absalom led a rebellion against David... the sword never departed.

Or consider **Pilate** who washed his hands and said "I am innocent of the blood of this just Person" (Matthew 27:24). The people answered: "His blood be on us and on our children" (Matthew 27:25). And for generations, the Jewish people suffered.

But the blood of Jesus speaks better things than the blood of Abel (Hebrews 12:24)! His blood cleanses from all sin, including bloodguiltiness.

7. HANDLING CURSED OBJECTS

Objects can carry spiritual contamination. Things dedicated to demons, used in occult practices, or connected with sin can transfer curses to those who possess them.

Deuteronomy 7:25-26 warns about idols: "You shall burn the carved images of their gods with fire; you shall not covet the silver or gold that is on them, nor take it for yourselves, lest you be snared by it; for it is an abomination to the LORD your God. Nor shall you bring an abomination into your house, lest you be doomed to destruction like it."

What objects can carry curses?

- **Idols and images**—statues of gods, goddesses
- **Occult objects**—ouija boards, tarot cards, charms
- **Stolen goods**—property taken from others
- **Property of atrocities**—land where murders occurred, houses with dark histories
- **Inherited items**—family heirlooms connected to idolatry

Acts 19:19 shows new believers dealing with this: "Also, many of those who had practiced magic brought their books together and burned them in the sight of all. And they counted up the value of them, and it totaled fifty thousand pieces of silver." They didn't sell them—they destroyed them!

I've prayed with people who had:

- Family idols passed down for generations
- Jewelry with occult symbols
- Art with demonic imagery
- Property purchased from ritual murderers

The objects carried spiritual baggage that affected their lives until they were destroyed or cleansed by the blood of Jesus.

8. OCCULT INVOLVEMENT

Any involvement with the occult—even "just curiosity"—opens doors to curses.

Deuteronomy 18:10-12 lists occult practices God hates: "There shall not be found among you anyone who... practices witchcraft, or a soothsayer, or one who interprets omens, or a sorcerer, or one who conjures spells, or a medium, or a spiritist, or one who calls up the dead. For all who do these things are an abomination to the LORD."

What constitutes occult involvement?

- **Consulting diviners**—fortune tellers, palm readers, astrologers
- **Using charms**—amulets, talismans, "protection" objects
- **Participating in rituals**—initiations, ceremonies
- **Playing with occult games**—ouija boards, séances
- **Reading occult materials**—horoscopes, witchcraft books

These invite:

- **Curses of confusion**—can't think clearly
- **Curses of fear**—anxiety, panic attacks
- **Demonic attachment**—oppression, obsession
- **Spiritual blindness**—can't discern truth

King Saul started well but ended consulting the witch of Endor (1 Samuel 28). His occult involvement contributed to his tragic end.

But there's deliverance! The early Church saw magicians like **Simon** (Acts 8) and **Bar-Jesus** (Acts 13) confronted and defeated by the power of the Holy Spirit.

9. NEGATIVE SELF-TALK AND VOWS

Your mouth is either building your life or tearing it down. **Proverbs 18:21** says: "Death and life are in the power of the tongue."

When you consistently say:

- "I'm cursed"
- "Nothing good ever happens to me"
- "I'll never succeed"
- "This sickness will kill me"
- "I'm so stupid"

...you're not just expressing feelings. You're making **decrees**. You're issuing **self-fulfilling prophecies**. You're giving demons legal ground to manifest what you're speaking.

James 3:5-6 warns: "The tongue is a little member and boasts great things. See how great a forest a little fire kindles! And the tongue is a fire, a world of iniquity. The tongue is so set among our members that it defiles the whole body, and sets on fire the course of nature; and it is set on fire by hell."

Even **vows** made in moments of emotion can become curses:

- "I'll never trust a man again"
- "I'll never let anyone get close"
- "I'd rather die than go through that again"

These aren't just words—they're spiritual commitments that shape your reality.

But you can break them! You can renounce every negative word you've spoken over yourself. You can replace curses with blessings.

10. TOUCHING THE UNCLEAN

2 Corinthians 6:17 says: "Therefore 'Come out from among them and be separate, says the Lord. Do not touch what is unclean, and I will receive you.'"

What is "unclean" in Scripture?

- **Certain foods** (in the Old Testament)
- **Dead bodies** (spiritual contamination)
- **Lepers** (in the ceremonial law)
- **Things dedicated to idols**

But in the New Testament, "unclean" also includes:

- **Ungodly associations**—friendships that pull you from God
- **Immorality**—pornography, illicit relationships
- **Occult practices**—even as an observer
- **Compromising situations**—places that dishonor God

When you touch the unclean, you get contaminated. It's like touching a corpse—you need cleansing.

But praise God—**Jesus touches the unclean and makes them clean**! The leper in Matthew 8:2-3 said: "Lord, if You are willing, You can make me clean." Jesus touched him and said: "I am willing; be cleansed." Jesus' touch doesn't contaminate Him—it cleanses us!

The key is to come to Jesus for cleansing from all contamination, then stay clean by walking in holiness.

Beloved, these ten doors aren't meant to condemn you—they're meant to show you where the enemy may have gained access. Now that you know the doors, you can close them. You can lock them. You can seal them with the blood of Jesus.

The next step is learning how to actually shut these doors and keep them shut. That's where our victory lies—not in ignorance, but in knowledge applied through the power of the Holy Spirit.

VI. THE PATH TO FREEDOM: STEPS TO BREAK HIDDEN CURSES

Beloved, gather around. We've been through much together in this study. We've identified what curses are. We've seen their effects. We've traced their sources. We've understood the laws that govern them. We've examined how they enter our lives. But all of this knowledge—as vital as it is—is useless if we don't know **what to do with it**.

Knowledge without application is like having a map to buried treasure but never digging. It's like having medicine on the shelf but never taking it. It's like having the keys to your chains but never unlocking them.

So today, I want to give you more than information—I want to give you **implementation**. I want to walk you through the actual, practical, step-by-step process of breaking free from every hidden curse. This isn't theory. This isn't abstract theology. This is battlefield strategy. This is spiritual warfare methodology.

STEP 1: DEAL WITH THE CURSE DIRECTLY

You cannot break what you will not acknowledge. You cannot dismantle what you refuse to confront. You cannot be delivered from what you won't admit has you bound.

A. IDENTIFICATION THROUGH REVELATION

The first step is **identification**. You must ask the Holy Spirit—the Spirit of truth who searches all things, even the deep things of God (1 Corinthians 2:10)—to reveal to you any curses operating in your life.

Psalm 139:23-24 gives us the perfect prayer for this: "Search me, O God, and know my heart; try me, and know my anxieties; and see if there is any wicked way in me, and lead me in the way everlasting."

You need to pray with sincere humility: "Holy Spirit, You are the revealer of hidden things. Show me. Illuminate what I cannot see. Reveal to me any curses that have gained access to my life. Show me their source. Show me their legal ground. I give You permission to search the deepest recesses of my heart, my history, and my heritage."

B. EXAMINING THE PATTERNS

While waiting on the Holy Spirit's revelation, you should also examine the **patterns** in your life. As we discussed earlier, curses produce consistent, identifiable fruits. Look for:

- **Generational patterns**—What keeps happening in your family line?
- **Repetitive failures**—Where do you consistently fall short?

- **Unexplained obstacles**—What blocks your progress repeatedly?
- **Persistent struggles**—What won't lift despite prayer and effort?

Remember **Nehemiah's** approach in Nehemiah 1. When he heard about Jerusalem's broken walls, he didn't just start rebuilding. He first sat down, wept, mourned, fasted, and prayed. He examined the situation. He acknowledged the problem. He traced it back to disobedience: "Both my father's house and I have sinned. We have acted very corruptly against You, and have not kept the commandments, the statutes, nor the ordinances which You commanded Your servant Moses" (Nehemiah 1:6-7).

C. SPECIFICITY IN IDENTIFICATION

Don't be vague. Curses thrive in vagueness. You can't break "bad luck" or "hard times." You need to be specific.

Is it a curse of poverty? Identify it as such.
Is it a curse of sickness? Name it specifically.
Is it a curse of relational failure? Call it what it is.
Is it a curse of barrenness? Don't hide behind euphemisms.

The more specific your identification, the more targeted your deliverance can be.

D. TRACING THE SOURCE AND LEGAL GROUND

Once you've identified the curse, ask the Holy Spirit to show you:

1. **When** it entered—Was it through a specific event? Through a generational line?

2. **How** it entered—Which of the ten doors did it come through?
3. **The legal ground**—What sin, covenant, or action gave it right of entry?

This is spiritual detective work. You're gathering evidence not to condemn yourself, but to prosecute the case against the curse in the court of heaven.

E. THE COURAGE TO CONFRONT

Finally, you need courage to confront what has been revealed. This isn't the time for denial. This isn't the time for excuses. This is the time for brutal, holy honesty.

Like **David** after his sin with Bathsheba, when Nathan the prophet confronted him, David didn't make excuses. He said: "I have sinned against the LORD" (2 Samuel 12:13). Short. Direct. Honest.

Or like the **Prodigal Son** in Luke 15 who "came to himself" and said: "I will arise and go to my father, and will say to him, 'Father, I have sinned against heaven and before you'" (Luke 15:18).

Confrontation precedes liberation. Acknowledgement precedes deliverance.

STEP 2: DEAL WITH THE POWER BEHIND THE CURSE

Beloved, this is where many well-meaning believers stop short. They identify the curse. They repent of whatever gave it access. They claim their freedom. But they don't deal with **the enforcers**.

Curses aren't free-floating, impersonal forces. They're enforced by demonic entities assigned to ensure their fulfillment. You must deal with these spiritual enforcers.

A. UNDERSTANDING DEMONIC ENFORCEMENT

Every persistent curse has demonic backup. These demons are like spiritual police officers enforcing a court order. Their job is to:

- Create circumstances that fulfill the curse
- Resist prayers and interventions against the curse
- Reinforce the curse through temptation and accusation
- Report back to higher demonic authorities about their progress

Look at **Daniel 10** again. When Daniel prayed, an angel was dispatched with the answer immediately. But "the prince of the kingdom of Persia" (a demonic territorial spirit) withstood him for 21 days. Michael the archangel had to come help. There was a demonic enforcer resisting the answer to prayer.

Or consider **Zechariah 3**, where Joshua the high priest is standing before the angel of the LORD, and Satan is standing at his right hand to oppose him. The enemy was there as an accuser, a legal opponent.

B. THE AUTHORITY OF THE BELIEVER

But here's your victory: **You have authority over all demonic power!**

Luke 10:19: "Behold, I give you the authority to trample on serpents and scorpions, and over all the power of the enemy, and nothing shall by any means hurt you."

Mark 16:17: "And these signs will follow those who believe: In My name they will cast out demons..."

James 4:7: "Therefore submit to God. Resist the devil and he will flee from you."

You don't have to live in fear of demonic enforcers. You have been given authority to bind them, cast them out, and render them powerless.

C. BINDING THE STRONG MAN

Matthew 12:29 gives us Jesus' strategy: "Or how can one enter a strong man's house and plunder his goods, unless he first binds the strong man? And then he will plunder his house."

The "strong man" here represents the demonic power in control. Before you can reclaim what's been stolen (plunder his house), you must first bind the strong man.

How do you bind demonic enforcers?

1. **Use the Name of Jesus**—There's power in that name! Philippians 2:9-11 says God has given Jesus the name above every name, that at the name of Jesus every knee should bow, of things in heaven, earth, and under the earth.
2. **Use the Word of God**—When Jesus was tempted, He responded with "It is written..." (Matthew 4:4, 7, 10). The Word is your sword (Ephesians 6:17).
3. **Use the Blood of Jesus**—Revelation 12:11 says believers overcome "by the blood of the Lamb and by the word of their testimony."

D. SPECIFIC COMMANDS AGAINST DEMONIC ENFORCERS

You need to be specific and authoritative in your commands:

"In the name of Jesus Christ, I bind every demonic spirit assigned to enforce the curse of _______ in my life. I command you to be paralyzed, silenced, and rendered powerless right now."

"I break your assignment over my life. I cancel your authority. I revoke your legal right to operate here."

"I command you to loose me and my family from your grip. I command you to go where Jesus sends you. You cannot stay here any longer."

E. CASTING THEM OUT

After binding them, cast them out:

"In the mighty name of Jesus, I cast you out, spirit of _______. Go now! You have no right to remain. I expel you from my life, my family, my home, my finances, my health, my destiny."

Remember, demons recognize authority. They recognized Jesus' authority immediately (Mark 1:24). They must recognize yours when you operate in Jesus' name and under His authority.

F. DEALING WITH THE SPIRIT BEHIND THE CURSE

Often, specific types of curses have specific types of demonic enforcers:

- Poverty curses often have spirits of poverty, lack, or mammon
- Sickness curses often have spirits of infirmity, death, or affliction

- Relational curses often have spirits of strife, division, or jealousy
- Failure curses often have spirits of sabotage, delay, or obstruction

You need to address not just the generic "demonic enforcer" but the specific type of spirit. The more specific your warfare, the more complete your victory.

G. CLOSING DOORS PERMANENTLY

After casting out demonic enforcers, you must close the doors they used to enter. This is why Step 1 (repentance, renunciation) is so important. If you cast out demons but don't close the door, they'll come back with reinforcements (Matthew 12:43-45).

STEP 3: REVERSE THE CURSE

Beloved, this third step is what separates temporary relief from permanent freedom. Many people stop at Step 2. They break the curse. They cast out demons. But they leave a vacuum. And nature—including spiritual nature—abhors a vacuum.

You must **replace** the curse with blessing. You must **displace** darkness with light. You must **exchange** death for life.

This is the law of displacement in the spirit realm.

A. THE PRINCIPLE OF REPLACEMENT

Isaiah 61:3 gives us God's replacement principle: He gives "beauty for ashes, the oil of joy for mourning, the garment of praise for the spirit of heaviness."

God doesn't just remove the negative; He replaces it with something positive. He doesn't just take away ashes (what's left after destruction); He gives beauty. He doesn't just stop the mourning; He gives joy. He doesn't just remove heaviness; He gives praise.

When you break a curse, you must consciously, deliberately replace it with God's blessing.

B. SPEAKING BLESSINGS TO REPLACE CURSES

Your words have creative power. After breaking a curse, you need to speak blessings over that same area.

If you broke a poverty curse, speak: "The blessing of the LORD makes rich, and He adds no sorrow with it (Proverbs 10:22). I declare that I am blessed to be a blessing. Wealth and riches are in my house (Psalm 112:3)."

If you broke a sickness curse, speak: "By His stripes I am healed (Isaiah 53:5). Jesus Himself took my infirmities and bore my sicknesses (Matthew 8:17). I declare divine health over my body."

If you broke a failure curse, speak: "I am more than a conqueror through Christ (Romans 8:37). I can do all things through Christ who strengthens me (Philippians 4:13). Whatever I do shall prosper (Psalm 1:3)."

C. USING SCRIPTURE TO CANCEL EVIL DECREES

The Word of God is your legal document to cancel every evil decree. When Satan brings accusations or when curses try to reassert themselves, you respond with Scripture.

This is what Jesus did in the wilderness (Matthew 4). Three times Satan tempted Him, and three times Jesus responded with "It is written..."

When a poverty curse tries to reassert itself, declare: "My God shall supply all my need according to His riches in glory by Christ Jesus" (Philippians 4:19).

When a sickness curse tries to return, declare: "He forgives all my iniquities, He heals all my diseases" (Psalm 103:3).

When a failure curse tries to resurface, declare: "No weapon formed against me shall prosper" (Isaiah 54:17).

D. THE BLESSINGS OF ABRAHAM

Galatians 3:13-14 ties everything together: "Christ has redeemed us from the curse of the law, having become a curse for us... that the blessing of Abraham might come upon the Gentiles in Christ Jesus, that we might receive the promise of the Spirit through faith."

When Jesus broke the curse, He didn't just leave us curse-free; He made us eligible for **the blessing of Abraham**. What is the blessing of Abraham?

Genesis 12:2-3: "I will make you a great nation; I will bless you and make your name great; and you shall be a blessing. I will bless those who bless you, and I will curse him who curses you; and in you all the families of the earth shall be blessed."

Genesis 13:2: "Abram was very rich in livestock, in silver, and in gold."

Genesis 24:1: "Now Abraham was old, well advanced in age; and the LORD had blessed Abraham in all things."

The blessing of Abraham includes:

- Divine prosperity
- Protection from curses
- Becoming a blessing to others
- Favor with God and man
- Success in all things

After breaking curses, consciously appropriate the blessing of Abraham over your life.

E. FILLING THE VACUUM WITH THE HOLY SPIRIT

After casting out demonic spirits, invite the Holy Spirit to fill every area they vacated.

Luke 11:24-26 warns about the empty house. Don't leave any area of your life empty. Consciously surrender every area to the Lordship of Jesus and the filling of the Holy Spirit.

Pray: "Holy Spirit, I invite You to fill every area of my life that has been cleansed. Be Lord over my finances, my health, my relationships, my mind, my emotions. I will not leave any room empty for the enemy to return."

F. MAINTAINING YOUR FREEDOM

Freedom isn't just obtained; it's maintained. After going through these three steps, you need to:

1. **Walk in obedience**—Stay under God's protection by obeying His Word.

2. **Guard your tongue**—Speak life, not death; blessing, not cursing.
3. **Put on the armor daily**—Ephesians 6:10-18.
4. **Stay in fellowship**—Hebrews 10:25.
5. **Continue in prayer**—1 Thessalonians 5:17.

G. TESTIFYING TO YOUR FREEDOM

Revelation 12:11: "They overcame him by the blood of the Lamb and by the word of their testimony."

Your testimony is a weapon. When you testify to what God has done in breaking curses in your life:

- It glorifies God
- It encourages others
- It establishes your victory
- It prevents the enemy from convincing you the curse is still there

Don't be silent about your deliverance. Your testimony is part of maintaining your freedom.

Beloved, these three steps aren't magical formulas. They're biblical principles applied through faith in the finished work of Jesus Christ. They work because Jesus already won the victory. You're simply enforcing what He already accomplished.

You're not trying to convince God to free you—He already did at Calvary.

You're not trying to earn your deliverance—it's already purchased by the blood.

You're simply walking in what's already yours.

But you must walk. You must apply. You must enforce.

These steps require:

- **Honesty** to face what's there
- **Courage** to confront spiritual forces
- **Faith** to believe God's Word over your circumstances
- **Persistence** to maintain your freedom
- **Obedience** to stay under God's covering

The path to freedom isn't always easy, but it's always available. The door isn't always comfortable to walk through, but it's always open. The process isn't always quick, but it's always effective.

You don't have to live under curses any longer. You don't have to accept generational patterns. You don't have to resign yourself to repetitive failures.

The blood of Jesus has broken every curse.

The name of Jesus has authority over every demon.

The Word of Jesus has power to create new realities.

Now walk in it. Apply it. Live in the freedom that is already yours in Christ Jesus.

VII. THE TEN-STEP PROCESS FOR PERSONAL RELEASE

Beloved, gather close now. We're about to move from understanding to application. From theology to therapy. From principle to practice. This is where the rubber meets the road.

This is where you take everything we've been learning and actually **do something** with it.

I'm going to walk you through a ten-step process for personal release. This isn't theory. This isn't religious ritual. This is spiritual surgery. This is the careful, deliberate, biblical process of removing every curse from your life.

Take your time with each step. Don't rush. Don't skip. The enemy has had years, maybe generations, to build strongholds. You need to systematically dismantle them. Let's begin.

STEP 1: REPENT OF ALL KNOWN AND UNKNOWN SIN

Beloved, we must start here because repentance removes the **legal ground** that curses stand on. You cannot break curses while still living in the sin that invited them. That's like trying to heal an infection while still pouring poison into the wound.

The Biblical Foundation of Repentance

Acts 3:19 says: "Repent therefore and be converted, that your sins may be blotted out, so that times of refreshing may come from the presence of the Lord."

1 John 1:9 gives us the promise: "If we confess our sins, He is faithful and just to forgive us our sins and to cleanse us from all unrighteousness."

But I want to show you a powerful example of comprehensive repentance from **Daniel 9**. Daniel was a righteous man—the Bible calls him "greatly beloved" (Daniel 9:23). Yet when he prayed for Israel's restoration, he didn't say "They have sinned."

He said: "We have sinned and committed iniquity, we have done wickedly and rebelled" (Daniel 9:5). He included himself in the corporate confession.

A. Personal Sins

Start with what you know. The Holy Spirit will bring things to mind. Don't rationalize. Don't minimize. Don't compare ("At least I'm not as bad as...").

Be specific:

- "Lord, I confess the sin of lying to my employer about my hours."
- "I confess the sin of gossiping about my sister in the church."
- "I confess the sin of unforgiveness toward my father for abandoning us."
- "I confess the sin of sexual immorality with my former partner."
- "I confess the sin of stealing office supplies from my workplace."
- "I confess the sin of idolizing my career above You."

Write them down if you need to. There's something powerful about seeing your sins on paper, then watching as you apply the blood of Jesus to each one.

B. Ancestral Sins

This is where Daniel's prayer becomes our model. In verses 4-20, Daniel confesses the sins of his ancestors: "We have sinned against You... To us belongs shame of face... because we have sinned against You" (Daniel 9:8).

You need to confess the sins of your family line:

- "Lord, I confess the sins of my ancestors who practiced idolatry, worshipping [name local deities]."
- "I confess the sins of my forefathers who joined secret societies like [name them]."
- "I confess the sins of my family who consulted witch doctors and diviners."
- "I confess the sins of my lineage who shed innocent blood through [abortion, murder, violence]."
- "I confess the sins of my parents who broke their marriage covenants."

You're not taking responsibility for their guilt—you're acknowledging the spiritual reality that their sins opened doors that affect you.

C. Sins of Ignorance

Leviticus 4 describes the sin offering for unintentional sins. Just because you didn't know something was sin doesn't mean it wasn't sinful.

Psalm 19:12 says: "Who can understand his errors? Cleanse me from secret faults."

Pray: "Lord, I confess any sins I've committed in ignorance. Any involvement with things I didn't know were sinful. Any participation in customs or traditions that dishonor You. Cleanse me from these secret faults."

D. The Quality of True Repentance

Repentance isn't just saying "I'm sorry." The Greek word is *metanoia*—a change of mind that leads to a change of direction.

True repentance involves:

1. **Acknowledgement**—Naming the sin specifically
2. **Remorse**—Godly sorrow (2 Corinthians 7:10), not just regret for getting caught
3. **Confession**—Speaking it out to God
4. **Repudiation**—Renouncing the sin
5. **Restitution**—Making it right where possible (like Zacchaeus in Luke 19:8)
6. **Change**—Turning from the sin

When you repent this way, you're pulling up the legal stakes that curses have been tied to. You're removing their right to remain.

STEP 2: RENOUNCE THE SINS OF YOUR FOREFATHERS

Beloved, this is different from confession. Confession is acknowledging. Renunciation is **cutting ties**. It's declaring: "I am no longer connected to this. I am no longer bound by this. I am no longer party to this."

Biblical Precedent for Renunciation

Joshua 24:14-15 gives us a powerful example. Joshua tells Israel: "Put away the gods which your fathers served on the other side of the River and in Egypt. Serve the LORD!... Choose for yourselves this day whom you will serve... But as for me and my house, we will serve the LORD."

He didn't just say "Stop worshipping idols." He said "Put them away." Remove them. Renounce them.

Nehemiah 9:2 shows the returned exiles: "Then those of Israelite lineage separated themselves from all foreigners; and they stood and confessed their sins and the iniquities of their fathers."

They separated themselves. They drew a line. They said: "This is where it stops. This is where the connection ends."

How to Renounce Specifically

You need to be verbal. You need to be specific. You need to be authoritative.

Say out loud:

- "In the name of Jesus, I renounce every covenant, pact, or agreement my ancestors made with demonic powers through idol worship."
- "I renounce all involvement my family has had with secret societies like Freemasonry, Rosicrucians, Ogboni, etc."
- "I renounce all dedications of myself or my ancestors to any god, spirit, or power other than Jehovah."
- "I renounce all curses spoken by or against my ancestors."
- "I renounce all blood covenants my forefathers entered into."
- "I renounce all witchcraft, divination, or occult practices in my family line."
- "I renounce every sinful pattern—addiction, divorce, poverty, sickness—that has run in my family."

The Legal Power of Renunciation

When you renounce, you're doing several things spiritually:

1. **You're revoking power of attorney**—You're telling the enemy: "You no longer have any legal claim through my ancestors."
2. **You're breaking continuity**—You're declaring the generational chain is broken.
3. **You're establishing a new lineage**—You're now establishing your spiritual genealogy in Christ.

Ezekiel 18: The Principle of Individual Responsibility

Ezekiel 18:19-20 is your biblical right to renounce: "Yet you say, 'Why should the son not bear the guilt of the father?' Because the son has done what is lawful and right, and has kept all My statutes and observed them, he shall surely live. The soul who sins shall die. The son shall not bear the guilt of the father, nor the father bear the guilt of the son."

You're exercising your right as a new creation in Christ to not bear the guilt of your fathers.

STEP 3: ACCEPT GOD'S FORGIVENESS AND FORGIVE YOURSELF

Beloved, this step trips up more people than any other. They can believe God forgives them, but they can't forgive themselves. They live in self-condemnation, which becomes a prison more secure than any demonic curse.

The Problem of Self-Condemnation

1 John 3:20 addresses this: "For if our heart condemns us, God is greater than our heart, and knows all things."

Your heart—your own conscience—may condemn you. But God is greater! His forgiveness is greater than your guilt!

Romans 8:1 declares: "There is therefore now no condemnation to those who are in Christ Jesus."

If you're in Christ, the court of heaven has declared you "Not guilty!" Why would you hold yourself to a higher standard than God does?

Receiving God's Forgiveness

Psalm 103:11-12 gives us the measure of God's forgiveness: "For as the heavens are high above the earth, so great is His mercy toward those who fear Him; as far as the east is from the west, so far has He removed our transgressions from us."

God doesn't just forgive—He forgets! **Hebrews 8:12** quotes God saying: "For I will be merciful to their unrighteousness, and their sins and their lawless deeds I will remember no more."

When God forgets, why do you remember? When God removes it as far as east from west, why do you keep bringing it back?

The Process of Forgiving Yourself

1. **Acknowledge that self-condemnation is pride**—It's saying your standards are higher than God's. It's saying your judgment matters more than His.
2. **Accept that if God forgives you, you must forgive yourself**—To refuse to forgive yourself is to call God a liar about His forgiveness.
3. **Speak it out loud**: "I accept God's complete forgiveness for [name the sin]. I forgive myself as God has forgiven

me. I release myself from self-condemnation. I break agreement with every accusing voice—internal or external—that says I'm still guilty."

4. **When memories return, respond with Scripture**: When the enemy brings up your past, respond with: "That is under the blood of Jesus. God remembers it no more. I choose to walk in His forgiveness, not my condemnation."

The Woman Caught in Adultery

Remember **John 8:1-11**? The religious leaders brought a woman caught in adultery to Jesus. They wanted to stone her. Jesus said: "He who is without sin among you, let him throw a stone at her first." They all left.

Then Jesus asked: "Woman, where are those accusers of yours? Has no one condemned you?" She said, "No one, Lord." Jesus said: "Neither do I condemn you; go and sin no more."

If Jesus doesn't condemn you, why do you condemn yourself? Receive His "Neither do I condemn you" today.

STEP 4: FORGIVE ALL WHO HAVE OFFENDED YOU

Beloved, this is non-negotiable. Unforgiveness is spiritual poison. It's drinking poison and hoping the other person dies. It's giving the enemy legal right to torment you.

Jesus on Forgiveness

Matthew 6:14-15: "For if you forgive men their trespasses, your heavenly Father will also forgive you. But if you do not forgive men their trespasses, neither will your Father forgive your trespasses."

Matthew 18:21-35 gives us the parable of the unforgiving servant. A servant owed his master 10,000 talents (millions of dollars). The master forgave the debt. That same servant then refused to forgive a fellow servant who owed him 100 denarii (a few dollars). The master reinstated the original debt and delivered him to torturers.

Jesus concludes: "So My heavenly Father also will do to you if each of you, from his heart, does not forgive his brother his trespasses" (Matthew 18:35).

Unforgiveness puts you back under debt—spiritual debt—and opens you to tormentors (demonic oppression).

The Process of Forgiveness

Forgiveness isn't:

- Saying what happened was okay
- Trusting the person again (that's reconciliation, which requires repentance)
- Forgetting (only God can choose to forget)

Forgiveness is:

- Releasing the debt—they don't owe you anymore
- Releasing the right to revenge
- Releasing the offense to God

How to Forgive Specifically

1. **Make a list**—Write down every person who has hurt you. Every betrayal. Every offense.
2. **Pray for each one**: "Lord, I choose to forgive [name] for [specific offense]. I release them from the debt they owe me. I release my right to revenge. I bless them in Jesus' name."
3. **Forgive from the heart**—Don't just say words. Mean it. You may need to pray it multiple times until your heart catches up.
4. **Forgive God**—Some people are angry at God for allowing pain. Say: "Lord, I forgive You for not intervening when... I trust that You are good even when I don't understand."
5. **Forgive yourself**—We already covered this, but it bears repeating.

Jesus' Example on the Cross

Luke 23:34: "Then Jesus said, 'Father, forgive them, for they do not know what they do.'"

While being crucified, Jesus forgave His executioners. If He can forgive that, you can forgive what was done to you.

The Freedom of Forgiveness

When you forgive, you're not just freeing them—you're freeing yourself. You're cutting the chain that binds you to the offense. You're closing a legal door the enemy was using to torment you.

STEP 5: RENOUNCE ALL CONTACT WITH FALSE RELIGION AND THE OCCULT

Beloved, you cannot serve two masters (Matthew 6:24). You cannot drink the cup of the Lord and the cup of demons (1 Corinthians 10:21). You need to make a clean break.

Biblical Commands to Separate

2 Corinthians 6:14-17: "Do not be unequally yoked together with unbelievers. For what fellowship has righteousness with lawlessness? And what communion has light with darkness? ... Therefore 'Come out from among them and be separate, says the Lord. Do not touch what is unclean, and I will receive you.'"

Deuteronomy 18:9-13 lists occult practices and says: "You shall be blameless before the LORD your God."

What Constitutes False Religion and Occult?

1. **Traditional idol worship**—Sango, Ogun, Oya, Amadioha, etc.
2. **Ancestor worship**—Praying to or through dead ancestors
3. **Secret societies**—Freemasonry, Rosicrucians, Ogboni, etc.
4. **Divination**—Ifa, palm reading, astrology, numerology
5. **Spiritism**—Consulting mediums, séances
6. **Witchcraft**—Charms, potions, spells
7. **Syncretistic Christianity**—Mixing Christianity with occult practices
8. **New Age practices**—Reiki, transcendental meditation, yoga with spiritual components

How to Renounce Specifically

Say out loud:

- "I renounce all involvement with [name specific practice or group]."
- "I break all soul ties with spirits associated with these practices."
- "I revoke all dedications made through these practices."
- "I close every door opened through these involvements."
- "I declare that I serve Jehovah alone. Jesus Christ is my only Lord."

The Ephesian Believers' Example

Acts 19:18-20: "And many who had believed came confessing and telling their deeds. Also, many of those who had practiced magic brought their books together and burned them in the sight of all. And they counted up the value of them, and it totaled fifty thousand pieces of silver. So the word of the Lord grew mightily and prevailed."

They didn't just stop practicing—they destroyed the materials! They made a public break.

STEP 6: DESTROY ALL EVIL AND POLLUTED MATERIALS

Beloved, objects carry spiritual history. Things dedicated to demons, used in sin, or connected to your past bondage can be points of contact for curses to reactivate.

Biblical Precedent for Destruction

Deuteronomy 7:5: "But thus you shall deal with them: you shall destroy their altars, and break down their sacred pillars, and cut down their wooden images, and burn their carved images with fire."

2 Kings 23:24: King Josiah "put away the mediums and the spiritists, the household idols and the idols, all the abominations that were seen in the land of Judah and Jerusalem."

What to Destroy

1. **Idols and images**—Statues, pictures, carvings of false gods
2. **Occult objects**—Charms, amulets, talismans, ouija boards
3. **Ritual objects**—Items used in traditional ceremonies
4. **Immoral materials**—Pornography, sensual music/movies
5. **Stolen property**—Things not rightfully yours
6. **Objects of addiction**—Drug paraphernalia, gambling tools
7. **Objects with demonic symbolism**—Certain jewelry, art, decor

How to Destroy Them

1. **Don't sell them**—That transfers the curse to someone else.
2. **Don't give them away**—Same problem.
3. **Burn them** if safe—Fire often represents God's cleansing.
4. **Break them** into pieces.
5. **Bury them** if burning isn't possible.
6. **Pray over them first**: "In Jesus' name, I break all demonic attachment to these objects. I cleanse them with the blood of Jesus. I render them spiritually neutral."

The Importance of Complete Obedience

1 Samuel 15 shows Saul's partial obedience with the Amalekites. God said destroy everything. Saul kept the best sheep and oxen. Samuel told him: "To obey is better than sacrifice, and to heed than the fat of rams. For rebellion is as the sin of witchcraft, and stubbornness is as iniquity and idolatry" (1 Samuel 15:22-23).

Partial obedience is disobedience. Destroy everything connected to your past bondage.

STEP 7: RELEASE YOURSELF FROM CURSES WITH AGGRESSIVE PRAYER

Now we get to the direct confrontation. You've prepared the ground. You've removed legal obstacles. Now you face the curses directly.

The Nature of Aggressive Prayer

Matthew 11:12: "And from the days of John the Baptist until now the kingdom of heaven suffers violence, and the violent take it by force."

The Greek word for "violence" here is *biazo*—to force, to seize. This isn't gentle, passive prayer. This is taking what's yours by force!

James 5:16: "The effective, fervent prayer of a righteous man avails much."

"Fervent" means energetic, intense. This is prayer with passion!

How to Pray Aggressively

1. **Use the name of Jesus**—There's power in that name! (Philippians 2:9-11)
2. **Be specific**—Name the curse you're breaking
3. **Be authoritative**—You're not begging God; you're enforcing what Jesus already accomplished
4. **Be persistent**—Don't quit until you feel release in your spirit
5. **Be vocal**—There's power in speaking out loud

Sample Aggressive Prayers

"In the name of Jesus Christ, I break the curse of poverty over my life and my family! I command every financial limitation to be shattered now!"

"I break the curse of sickness and infirmity! By the stripes of Jesus, I am healed! I command every spirit of infirmity to loose me now!"

"I break the curse of failure and sabotage! I decree that I will finish what I start! I will succeed where my ancestors failed!"

"I break the curse of marital strife and divorce! I declare my marriage is blessed! My home is a place of peace and love!"

"I break every generational curse coming from my father's line and my mother's line! I am free in Jesus' name!"

The Blood of Jesus as Your Weapon

Revelation 12:11: "And they overcame him by the blood of the Lamb and by the word of their testimony."

Apply the blood verbally: "I plead the blood of Jesus over my life. The blood breaks every curse. The blood cancels every legal claim. The blood cleanses every defilement."

STEP 8: CAST OUT THE DEMONS BEHIND THE CURSES

Beloved, breaking curses without casting out demons is like evicting squatters but leaving them in your yard. They'll find a way back in.

Jesus' Ministry of Deliverance

Mark 16:17: "And these signs will follow those who believe: In My name they will cast out demons..."

Luke 10:19: "Behold, I give you the authority to trample on serpents and scorpions, and over all the power of the enemy, and nothing shall by any means hurt you."

Identifying Demonic Enforcers

Behind curses are often specific demonic types:

- Poverty curses—spirits of poverty, lack, debt
- Sickness curses—spirits of infirmity, death, affliction
- Failure curses—spirits of sabotage, delay, obstruction
- Relational curses—spirits of strife, division, jealousy
- Mental curses—spirits of confusion, depression, anxiety

How to Cast Them Out

1. **Bind them first** (Matthew 12:29): "I bind you, spirit of [name], in Jesus' name. You are paralyzed, silenced, and rendered powerless."
2. **Command them to leave**: "I cast you out, spirit of [name]! Go now in Jesus' name! You cannot stay here any longer!"
3. **Send them to where Jesus sends them**—Don't send them to someone else!
4. **Forbid return**: "I forbid you to return or send any other spirits. I seal this eviction with the blood of Jesus."

Dealing with Resistance

Sometimes demons resist. They may:

- Cause physical manifestations (coughing, shaking)
- Speak through the person (don't engage in conversation!)
- Cause emotional outbursts

Stand firm! Use Scripture:

"It is written: 'He who is in you is greater than he who is in the world'" (1 John 4:4).

"Jesus has disarmed principalities and powers, making a public spectacle of them" (Colossians 2:15).

After Casting Out

Pray for the person to be filled with the Holy Spirit (Luke 11:24-26). An empty house invites worse problems.

STEP 9: CLAIM BLESSINGS TO REPLACE THE CURSES

Beloved, nature abhors a vacuum—including spiritual nature. You can't just remove curses; you must replace them with blessings.

The Law of Displacement

Isaiah 61:3: "To give them beauty for ashes, the oil of joy for mourning, the garment of praise for the spirit of heaviness."

God doesn't just take away—He gives something better in its place.

Speaking Blessings

Proverbs 18:21: "Death and life are in the power of the tongue."

Your words create reality. After breaking curses, speak blessings over every area:

Over your finances: "The LORD is my shepherd; I shall not want" (Psalm 23:1). "The blessing of the LORD makes rich, and He adds no sorrow with it" (Proverbs 10:22).

Over your health: "He Himself took our infirmities and bore our sicknesses" (Matthew 8:17). "By His stripes I am healed" (Isaiah 53:5).

Over your mind: "I have the mind of Christ" (1 Corinthians 2:16). "God has not given me a spirit of fear, but of power, love, and a sound mind" (2 Timothy 1:7).

Over your relationships: "My home is blessed. My marriage is blessed. My children are taught of the LORD, and great is their peace" (Isaiah 54:13).

Over your destiny: "I am more than a conqueror through Christ" (Romans 8:37). "I can do all things through Christ who strengthens me" (Philippians 4:13).

The Blessing of Abraham

Galatians 3:13-14 tells us Christ redeemed us from the curse "that the blessing of Abraham might come upon the Gentiles in Christ Jesus."

Claim Abraham's blessing:

- Divine prosperity (Genesis 13:2)
- Divine protection (Genesis 12:3)
- Becoming a blessing to others (Genesis 12:2)
- Success in all things (Genesis 24:1)

Creating a Blessing Environment

Fill your life with:

- God's Word—read it, speak it, meditate on it
- Anointed music—worship drives out darkness
- Godly fellowship—iron sharpens iron (Proverbs 27:17)
- Positive declarations—speak what God says about you

STEP 10: GIVE THANKS TO GOD FOR YOUR FREEDOM

Beloved, this final step seals everything. Thanksgiving isn't just good manners—it's spiritual warfare. It's faith in action.

Thanksgiving as Warfare

2 Chronicles 20 gives us the story of King Jehoshaphat facing overwhelming armies. God told him: "You will not need to fight in this battle. Position yourselves, stand still and see the salvation of the LORD" (2 Chronicles 20:17).

Jehoshaphat's response? He appointed singers to go before the army, praising God: "Praise the LORD, for His mercy endures forever" (2 Chronicles 20:21).

When they began to sing and praise, God set ambushes against their enemies, and they were defeated!

Thanksgiving as Faith

Philippians 4:6: "Be anxious for nothing, but in everything by prayer and supplication, with thanksgiving, let your requests be made known to God."

Thanksgiving demonstrates that you believe God has answered before you see the manifestation.

1 Thessalonians 5:18: "In everything give thanks; for this is the will of God in Christ Jesus for you."

How to Give Thanks Specifically

Thank God for:

- Breaking every curse over your life
- Setting you free from generational bondage
- Healing your body from sickness
- Prospering you financially
- Restoring your relationships

- Fulfilling your destiny

Thank Him by faith—even if you don't feel different yet. Thank Him because His Word says it's done.

Testimony as Thanksgiving

Revelation 12:11: "They overcame him by the blood of the Lamb and by the word of their testimony."

Start testifying:

- Tell someone what God is doing
- Share your freedom with your family
- Write it down as a memorial
- Praise God publicly

Maintaining a Thankful Heart

Make thanksgiving a lifestyle, not just a one-time event:

- Start each day with thanksgiving
- Thank God in the middle of challenges
- Thank Him for what He's doing, not just what He's done
- Let thanksgiving be your atmosphere

Beloved, these ten steps are your pathway to complete freedom. They're not magic. They're not formulas. They're biblical principles applied through faith in the finished work of Jesus Christ.

You don't have to do this alone. The Holy Spirit is your Helper. Jesus is your Advocate. The Father is waiting with open arms.

But you must take the steps. You must walk the path. You must apply the blood.

Freedom is already yours in Christ. Now walk in it. Live in it. And never go back to bondage again.

The chains are broken. The prison doors are open. The curse is reversed.

Now walk out into the glorious liberty of the children of God!

VIII. THE MINISTRY OF THE BLOOD AND THE SALT: DIVINE CLEANSING AND PRESERVATION

Beloved, lean in close. We've walked through much together—identifying curses, understanding their operation, tracing their sources, and learning the steps to break them. But now I want to give you two of the most powerful spiritual realities you will ever apply in your walk to freedom: **the Blood of Jesus** and **the Salt of the Covenant**.

These aren't just religious concepts. These aren't theological abstractions. These are divine substances with supernatural properties. They're God's cleansing agents. His preserving power. His covenant enforcers.

THE ELSHA ENCOUNTER: WHEN SALT HEALED THE WATERS

Let me take you to a powerful story in **2 Kings 2:19-22**. The setting is important. Elijah has just been taken to heaven in a chariot of fire. Elisha has taken up his mantle—literally and spiritually. He's now the prophet in Israel. And the men of Jericho come to him with a problem.

"Look," they said, "the situation of this city is pleasant, as my lord sees; but the water is bad, and the ground barren."

Think about that statement. From the outside, everything looked good. Pleasant situation. But there was a hidden problem: **the source was polluted**. The water was bad. And because the water—the source of life—was poisoned, the ground was barren. Nothing could grow. Nothing could thrive. Death and barrenness were the fruits of a poisoned source.

This, beloved, is exactly the condition of many lives, many families, many destinies today. The exterior looks fine. The person seems successful. The family appears stable. But internally, the source is poisoned. The spiritual waters are bitter. And as a result, there's barrenness—in relationships, in finances, in health, in spiritual fruitfulness.

Now watch what Elisha does. He doesn't pray a long prayer. He doesn't perform a dramatic ceremony. He asks for a **new bowl** with **salt** in it.

Why a *new* bowl? Because the old vessels were contaminated. You can't put a new solution in an old contaminated vessel. You need a new vessel—a renewed mind, a transformed heart.

Why *salt*? Because in the ancient world, salt was:

1. **A purifier**—It killed bacteria, preserved food from decay
2. **A preserver**—It kept things from spoiling
3. **A seasoning**—It brought out flavor, made things palatable
4. **A covenant symbol**—"Covenant of salt" meant an everlasting covenant (Numbers 18:19)

Elisha took the salt, went to the **source** of the waters—the spring—and threw the salt in. He didn't treat the symptoms downstream. He went to the source. And he declared: "Thus says the LORD: 'I have healed this water; from it there shall be no more death or barrenness.'"

And Scripture says: "So the waters remain healed to this day, according to the word of Elisha which he spoke."

The healing was permanent! The cure went to the source! The barrenness ended!

THE BLOOD OF JESUS: YOUR SPIRITUAL SALT

Beloved, the blood of Jesus is your spiritual salt. It does everything natural salt does—but at a spiritual level.

1. THE BLOOD PURIFIES

1 John 1:7 declares: "But if we walk in the light as He is in the light, we have fellowship with one another, and the blood of Jesus Christ His Son cleanses us from all sin."

The Greek word for "cleanses" is *katharizō*—it means to purify, to make clean, to free from defilement. It's present tense—continually cleanses. Not just once, but constantly.

Hebrews 9:14 says: "How much more shall the blood of Christ, who through the eternal Spirit offered Himself without spot to God, cleanse your conscience from dead works to serve the living God?"

The blood doesn't just clean your record in heaven; it cleanses your conscience here on earth! It removes guilt, shame, and condemnation.

When curses have defiled your life—when sexual sin, occult involvement, generational idolatry, or personal rebellion have polluted your spiritual waters—the blood of Jesus is your purifying salt. It doesn't just cover the defilement; it removes it!

2. THE BLOOD PRESERVES

In Egypt, during the Passover, the blood on the doorposts preserved the firstborn from death (**Exodus 12:13**): "Now the blood shall be a sign for you on the houses where you are. And when I see the blood, I will pass over you; and the plague shall not be on you to destroy you when I strike the land of Egypt."

The blood created a **zone of preservation** in the midst of judgment. While death visited every Egyptian household, the blood-marked houses were preserved.

Today, the blood of Jesus preserves you from:

- The curse of the law (Galatians 3:13)
- The wrath of God (Romans 5:9)
- The attacks of the enemy (Revelation 12:11)
- The corruption of this world (2 Peter 1:4)

When you apply the blood over your life, your family, your home, you're creating a spiritual preservation zone. You're saying: "Death and destruction cannot enter here. Curses cannot operate here. This territory is marked with covenant blood."

3. THE BLOOD SEASONES AND MAKES PALATABLE

Colossians 4:6 says: "Let your speech always be with grace, seasoned with salt, that you may know how you ought to answer each one."

The blood of Jesus seasons your life with grace. It makes you "palatable" to God. Sin made us repulsive to a holy God. But the blood makes us acceptable, pleasing, fragrant.

Ephesians 5:2 says: "And walk in love, as Christ also has loved us and given Himself for us, an offering and a sacrifice to God for a sweet-smelling aroma."

Because of the blood, when God looks at you, He doesn't smell the stench of your sin; He smells the sweet fragrance of His Son's sacrifice!

4. THE BLOOD ESTABLISHES COVENANT

Matthew 26:28: "For this is My blood of the new covenant, which is shed for many for the remission of sins."

Hebrews 13:20: "Now may the God of peace who brought up our Lord Jesus from the dead, that great Shepherd of the sheep, through the blood of the everlasting covenant..."

The blood of Jesus isn't just cleansing fluid; it's **covenant blood**. It establishes the New Covenant. And covenants have terms. Blessings for faithfulness. Protection for obedience. Inheritance for sonship.

When you're under the blood, you're under covenant. You're not a spiritual orphan trying to survive; you're a covenant child with covenant rights and covenant protection.

HOW TO APPLY THE BLOOD PRACTICALLY

Beloved, this isn't just theology to agree with; it's substance to apply. Let me show you how.

A. APPLY THE BLOOD VERBALLY

There's power in speaking the blood. Your words release spiritual realities.

Revelation 12:11: "And they overcame him by the blood of the Lamb and by the word of their testimony."

Your testimony about the blood is a weapon! Speak it:

- "I apply the blood of Jesus over my mind. Every curse of mental illness, confusion, or depression is broken."
- "I apply the blood of Jesus over my body. Every curse of sickness, infirmity, or genetic disease is healed."
- "I apply the blood of Jesus over my finances. Every curse of poverty, debt, or lack is reversed."
- "I apply the blood of Jesus over my marriage and family. Every curse of divorce, strife, or barrenness is cancelled."
- "I apply the blood of Jesus over my past. Every defilement from sin is cleansed."
- "I apply the blood of Jesus over my future. Every curse aimed at my destiny is neutralized."

B. APPLY THE BLOOD BY FAITH

Hebrews 11:28: "By faith he [Moses] kept the Passover and the sprinkling of blood, lest he who destroyed the firstborn should touch them."

The Israelites didn't just paint blood; they painted it **by faith**. They believed that blood would protect them.

You must believe the blood works. It's not magic paint. It's faith in a finished work.

When you say "I apply the blood," believe that:

1. Every demonic accusation against you loses its power
2. Every legal claim of curses is cancelled
3. Every defilement is cleansed
4. Every doorway is sealed
5. Every attack is diverted

C. APPLY THE BLOOD SPECIFICALLY

Be specific in your application:

- Over doorways of your home
- Over your vehicles
- Over your workplace
- Over your children's schools
- Over your bank accounts
- Over your medical reports
- Over legal documents
- Over your marriage bed
- Over your thought life

The blood isn't limited. Apply it everywhere!

THE SALT OF THE COVENANT: DIVINE PRESERVATION

Now let's talk about salt specifically. The Bible speaks repeatedly of the "covenant of salt."

1. SALT AS AN EVERLASTING COVENANT

Numbers 18:19: "All the heave offerings of the holy things, which the children of Israel offer to the LORD, I have given to you and your sons and daughters with you as an ordinance forever; it is a **covenant of salt** forever before the LORD with you and your descendants with you."

2 Chronicles 13:5: "Should you not know that the LORD God of Israel gave the dominion over Israel to David forever, to him and his sons, by a **covenant of salt**?"

A "covenant of salt" was considered **permanent, unbreakable, and enduring**. Salt doesn't spoil. It doesn't decay. It lasts. So a covenant sealed with salt was understood to be everlasting.

2. SALT AS A PURIFYING AGENT

As we saw with Elisha, salt purifies. It kills what causes decay.

In your life, you need God to send His **heavenly salt** into:

Your Spiritual Foundations—The core beliefs that shape your life. If the foundation is polluted (with lies, with false doctrine, with worldly philosophy), the whole structure is unstable. Pray: "Lord, send Your salt into my spiritual foundations. Purify what I believe about You, about myself, about others. Heal the waters of my theology."

Your Emotional Foundations—The deep wounds, traumas, and memories that shape your reactions. Emotional wounds are like poisoned springs—they produce bitter reactions. Pray: "Lord, send Your salt into my emotional foundations. Heal the wounds from my past. Purify my memories. Let the waters of my emotions be healed so they no longer produce death and barrenness."

Your Generational Foundations—The family patterns, inherited tendencies, and ancestral doors. Pray: "Lord, send Your salt into my generational foundations. Go back through my family line and heal every poisoned spring. Break every pattern of addiction, sickness, poverty, and failure. Let Your salt neutralize every curse at its source."

3. SALT AS A PRESERVATIVE AGAINST CORRUPTION

Matthew 5:13: "You are the salt of the earth; but if the salt loses its flavor, how shall it be seasoned? It is then good for nothing but to be thrown out and trampled underfoot by men."

Jesus says **YOU** are the salt! Your presence in your family, your workplace, your community is meant to be preservative. You're there to:

- Prevent moral decay
- Stop the spread of corruption
- Preserve righteousness
- Resist the encroachment of darkness

But salt can lose its savor. How? By compromise. By dilution. By becoming so mixed with the world that you lose your distinctiveness.

You need to pray: "Lord, keep me salty! Don't let me lose my preserving power. Don't let me blend in so much that I lose my effectiveness."

4. SALT AS A SEASONING OF GRACE

Colossians 4:6 again: "Let your speech always be with grace, seasoned with salt, that you may know how you ought to answer each one."

Your words should be:

- Graceful—full of undeserved favor

- Salty—preserving, purifying, preventing decay
- Wise—knowing how to answer each person

When you speak to your children, season your words with salt.

When you correct someone, season it with salt.

When you confront sin, season it with salt.

When you share the gospel, season it with salt.

COMBINING THE BLOOD AND THE SALT

Beloved, the most powerful spiritual applications happen when we combine the blood and the salt.

THE PATTERN OF THE TABERNACLE

In the Old Testament tabernacle, we see both blood and salt:

The Altar of Burnt Offering—Blood was sprinkled, poured, and smeared on the altar (Leviticus 1-7).

The Grain Offerings—"And every offering of your grain offering you shall season with salt; you shall not allow the salt of the covenant of your God to be lacking from your grain offering. With all your offerings you shall offer salt" (Leviticus 2:13).

Every offering—representing our worship, our service, our lives—was to be seasoned with salt. And the blood made the sacrifice acceptable.

Today, your life is a living sacrifice (Romans 12:1). Apply the blood to make it acceptable to God. Apply the salt to preserve it from corruption and to establish it in covenant.

PRAYING WITH BLOOD AND SALT

Let me lead you in a powerful prayer that combines both:

"Heavenly Father, I come before You in the mighty name of Jesus. I thank You for the precious blood of Your Son that was shed for me. Right now, I apply that blood over every area of my life.

I plead the blood of Jesus over my spirit, soul, and body. Over my past, present, and future. Over my thoughts, emotions, and will. Over my family—living and deceased. Over my possessions, my calling, my destiny.

Lord, just as Elisha took salt and healed the waters, I ask You to take Your heavenly salt and throw it into every poisoned spring in my life. Send Your salt into:

My spiritual foundations—heal my understanding of who You are.
My emotional foundations—heal every wound, every trauma.
My generational foundations—heal my family line back to Adam.
My mental foundations—heal every pattern of thinking.
My relational foundations—heal how I see and relate to others.

Where there has been death, let there be life. Where there has been barrenness, let there be fruitfulness. Where the waters have been bitter, make them sweet.

I declare that the blood of Jesus cleanses me from every curse, and the salt of Your covenant preserves me from every corruption. I am under a covenant of salt—an everlasting covenant that cannot be broken.

I am marked by blood and seasoned with salt. I am cleansed and preserved. I am healed and made whole.

Just as the waters in Jericho remained healed according to Elisha's word, let my life remain healed according to Your Word. Let this healing be permanent. Let this freedom be lasting.

In Jesus' mighty name, amen."

MAINTAINING THE CLEANSING AND PRESERVATION

Beloved, this isn't a one-time prayer. This is a lifestyle. You need to:

1. DAILY APPLY THE BLOOD

Make it part of your morning routine. Before you face the day, cover yourself and your family in the blood of Jesus.

2. REGULARLY RENEW THE SALT

Just as natural salt needs to be replenished, so does your spiritual saltiness. Through:

- Regular prayer and fasting
- Consistent Word intake
- Obedience to the Holy Spirit
- Fellowship with other believers

3. GUARD AGAINST CONTAMINATION

1 Corinthians 15:33: "Do not be deceived: 'Evil company corrupts good habits.'"

Be careful what and who you allow into your life. Some relationships, some entertainments, some environments will dilute your saltiness and contaminate what the blood has cleansed.

4. TESTIFY CONTINUALLY

Revelation 12:11 again: They overcame by the blood AND the word of their testimony.

Keep testifying to what the blood has done and what the salt is doing. Your testimony isn't just for others; it's for you. It reinforces your faith. It reminds the enemy of his defeat.

THE EVIDENCE OF HEALED WATERS

When Elisha healed the waters, the evidence was immediate and lasting: "So the waters remain healed to this day, according to the word of Elisha which he spoke" (2 Kings 2:22).

When the blood cleanses and the salt heals your spiritual waters, you'll see evidence:

1. **Life instead of death**—Where there was spiritual death, there will be vitality. Where relationships were dying, they'll come alive. Where dreams were dead, they'll be resurrected.
2. **Fruitfulness instead of barrenness**—You'll bear fruit: the fruit of the Spirit (Galatians 5:22-23), the fruit of ministry, the fruit of increase. Barren areas will become productive.
3. **Sweetness instead of bitterness**—The bitter waters of resentment, anger, and hurt will become sweet waters of forgiveness, joy, and peace.
4. **Permanence instead of temporary relief**—This won't be a temporary emotional high. It will be a lasting

transformation, "to this day"—enduring through trials, persisting through challenges.

Beloved, your life doesn't have to be like Jericho—pleasant on the outside but poisoned at the source. You don't have to live with hidden pollution that produces death and barrenness.

The blood of Jesus is available. The salt of God's covenant is ready.

Apply the blood to cleanse every curse.

Ask for the salt to heal every poisoned spring.

Then watch as death turns to life. Watch as barrenness turns to fruitfulness. Watch as what was poisoned becomes pure. Watch as your life becomes what God always intended—a well of living water, springing up into eternal life (John 4:14).

The ministry of the blood and the salt isn't just for your freedom—it's for your flourishing. It's not just for your survival—it's for your supernatural living.

Receive it. Apply it. Live in it. And let the healing remain to this day, according to the word of the Lord.

IX. PRAYER SECTION: AGGRESSIVE DECLARATIONS FOR IMMEDIATE RELEASE

Beloved, listen to me. The time for theory is over. The time for analysis is past. We've studied, we've learned, we've understood. But now we must **do**. We must **war**. We must **confront**. We must **overcome**.

This prayer section is not a gentle, contemplative moment of quiet reflection. This is spiritual warfare. This is hand-to-hand combat in the heavenly places. This is the enforcement of Calvary's victory in your personal territory. The Bible says in **Matthew 11:12**, "And from the days of John the Baptist until now the kingdom of heaven suffers violence, and the violent take it by force."

The Greek word for "violence" here is *biazo*—to force, to seize, to lay hold of with determination. That's the spirit in which we must pray now. We're not asking politely. We're not hoping vaguely. We're **taking by force** what Jesus already purchased with His blood.

Before we begin, I want to give you some critical understanding about why we pray this way:

THE NATURE OF AGGRESSIVE PRAYER

In **Ephesians 6:12**, Paul tells us: "For we do not wrestle against flesh and blood, but against principalities, against powers, against the rulers of the darkness of this age, against spiritual hosts of wickedness in the heavenly places."

The word "wrestle" is *palē*—it means to wrestle, to hand-to-hand combat, to struggle. This isn't a distant, polite exchange. This is close-quarters combat!

When Jesus confronted demons, He didn't negotiate. He didn't have a discussion. He **commanded**. In **Mark 1:25**, He said: "Be quiet, and come out of him!" In **Mark 9:25**, He said: "You deaf and dumb spirit, I command you, come out of him and enter him no more!"

There's authority in His voice. There's power in His command. And He has given us that same authority! **Luke 10:19** says: "Behold, I give you the authority to trample on serpents and scorpions, and over all the power of the enemy, and nothing shall by any means hurt you."

So as we pray, we're not begging God to do something. We're enforcing what He has already done. We're using the authority He has already given. We're applying the victory He has already won.

Now, find your voice. Find your spiritual backbone. Find your holy anger against what the enemy has done to you, your family, your destiny. And let's pray with fire, with faith, and with violent determination.

---

1. I REFUSE TO DRINK FROM THE FOUNTAIN OF SORROW, IN JESUS' NAME.

Beloved, there are two fountains available to every human being: the fountain of sorrow and the fountain of salvation. The fountain of sorrow is fed by the broken cisterns of this world—by sin, by disappointment, by betrayal, by loss. The fountain of salvation is fed by the living waters of Jesus Christ.

Jeremiah 2:13 says: "For My people have committed two evils: They have forsaken Me, the fountain of living waters, and hewn themselves cisterns—broken cisterns that can hold no water."

The enemy wants you drinking from broken cisterns—from relationships that drain you, from pursuits that empty you, from habits that poison you. He wants you constantly returning to the fountain of sorrow, drinking deeply of grief, pain, and mourning until it becomes your normal.

But today, you're declaring: "Enough! I'm changing fountains!"

Psalm 36:9 says: "For with You is the fountain of life; in Your light we see light."

John 4:14 says: "But whoever drinks of the water that I shall give him will never thirst. But the water that I shall give him will become in him a fountain of water springing up into everlasting life."

So pray with me:

"Lord Jesus, I come to You as the only true fountain of living water. Right now, I deliberately, consciously, and violently turn away from every fountain of sorrow that I've been drinking from. I reject the bitter waters of my family's history of grief. I spit out the poisoned waters of past disappointments. I refuse to drink again from the well of my own failures and regrets.

I disconnect my spiritual pipes from every source of sorrow, pain, and mourning that has fed my soul. I sever every attachment to cycles of depression, anxiety, and despair. I renounce every agreement I've made with a spirit of heaviness.

Instead, I plunge myself into the fountain of Your salvation! I drink deeply from the well of Your goodness! I immerse myself in the river of Your joy! Let Your living waters flush out every residue of bitterness, every memory of pain, every expectation of sorrow.

From this day forward, my thirst will be satisfied in You alone. My soul will be refreshed by Your Spirit alone. My life will be sustained by Your grace alone. I drink from the fountain of life, and I shall never thirst again. In Jesus' mighty name!"

---

2. I TAKE AUTHORITY OVER ALL CURSES ISSUED AGAINST MY LIFE, IN THE NAME OF JESUS.

Beloved, authority isn't given to the passive. Authority isn't given to the timid. Authority is taken by those who know who they are in Christ and what belongs to them.

Ephesians 1:19-22 tells us about the authority of Christ: "And what is the exceeding greatness of His power toward us who believe, according to the working of His mighty power which He worked in Christ when He raised Him from the dead and seated Him at His right hand in the heavenly places, far above all principality and power and might and dominion, and every name that is named, not only in this age but also in that which is to come. And He put all things under His feet..."

Did you hear that? **ALL THINGS** are under His feet! Every curse, every demon, every principality, every power! And **Ephesians 2:6** says God has "raised us up together, and made us sit together in the heavenly places in Christ Jesus."

You're seated with Him in that place of authority! So when you speak, you're not speaking from beneath the curse; you're speaking from above it! You're not speaking as a victim; you're speaking as a victor!

Now pray with that authority:

"By the supreme authority of the Lord Jesus Christ, the name that is above every name, before whom every knee must bow in heaven, on earth, and under the earth—I now exercise my legal right as a blood-bought child of God to cancel, revoke, and nullify every curse that has been issued against my life!

I cancel every curse spoken over me in secret chambers by witchdoctors and diviners. I revoke every curse written against me in demonic ledgers and occult records. I nullify every curse decreed upon my destiny by envious lips and malicious hearts.

I declare that every parchment, every scroll, every document in the spirit realm that bears my name with curses attached is now shredded by the angels of God! Every demonic court ruling against me is overturned by the Supreme Court of Heaven! Every spiritual sentence passed against me is commuted by the blood of Jesus!

According to **Colossians 2:14-15**, Jesus has 'wiped out the handwriting of requirements that was against us, which was contrary to us. And He has taken it out of the way, having nailed it to the cross. Having disarmed principalities and powers, He made a public spectacle of them, triumphing over them in it.'

I stand on that finished work! I enforce that complete victory! Every curse is null and void! Every accusation is without legal standing! Every demonic claim is rejected by heaven's court!

In the name that causes demons to tremble—the name of Jesus Christ of Nazareth—I take authority and I declare: IT IS FINISHED over every curse against my life!"

---

3. ASK GOD TO REMOVE ANY CURSE HE HAS PLACED ON YOUR LIFE AS A RESULT OF DISOBEDIENCE.

Beloved, we must be humble enough to acknowledge that sometimes our suffering isn't from the devil; it's from the hand of a loving Father who disciplines His children. **Hebrews 12:6** says: "For whom the LORD loves He chastens, and scourges every son whom He receives."

God's curses in Scripture are always judicial—they're the consequences of covenant-breaking. **Deuteronomy 28** makes it clear: blessings for obedience, curses for disobedience.

If you're living in deliberate, unrepentant sin while claiming to be a Christian, you may be under God's corrective hand. The solution isn't to bind a demon; it's to repent!

2 Chronicles 7:14 gives us the pattern: "If My people who are called by My name will humble themselves, and pray and seek My face, and turn from their wicked ways, then I will hear from heaven, and will forgive their sin and heal their land."

So let's pray with humility:

"Righteous and holy Father, I come before You with the humility that Your majesty demands. I bow before Your throne of grace, not with excuses, not with justification, but with naked honesty.

Search me, O God, and know my heart; try me, and know my anxieties; and see if there is any wicked way in me (**Psalm 139:23-24**). Show me any area of deliberate disobedience, any pocket of rebellion, any secret sin that has invited Your corrective hand.

I repent right now for [name specific areas of disobedience the Holy Spirit brings to mind]. I turn from these ways. I renounce these patterns. I choose obedience over convenience, holiness over compromise, Your will over my own.

Father, I appeal to the mercy seat, not the judgment seat. I appeal to the blood of Jesus that speaks better things than the blood of Abel (**Hebrews 12:24**). I appeal to the cross where Jesus bore the curse for me (**Galatians 3:13**).

Let every corrective curse—every disciplinary measure, every consequence of my disobedience—be lifted now by the authority of that precious blood. Let the chastening accomplish its purpose in my heart, but let its external manifestations cease.

As You did with Nineveh when they repented (**Jonah 3:10**), relent from the disaster You said You would bring. As You did with Hezekiah when he wept (**2 Kings 20:1-6**), add years to my life. As You did with the prodigal when he returned (**Luke 15:20-24**), restore me fully to sonship.

I receive Your forgiveness. I walk in Your cleansing. I embrace Your restoration. In Jesus' merciful name."

---

4. I COMMAND ANY DEMON ATTACHED TO ANY CURSE TO DEPART FROM ME NOW, IN THE MIGHTY NAME OF OUR LORD JESUS CHRIST.

Beloved, understand this spiritual reality: Curses have demonic enforcement. When a curse is spoken, demons are often assigned to ensure its fulfillment. They're like spiritual bounty hunters with a warrant for your bondage.

But you have authority over them! **Luke 10:19** says you have authority over ALL the power of the enemy. **James 4:7** says: "Resist the devil and he will flee from you."

Notice it doesn't say "ask God to resist the devil for you." It says YOU resist him! How? With the authority Jesus gave you!

When Jesus sent out the seventy, they returned rejoicing that demons were subject to them in His name. Jesus responded: "Behold, I give you the authority to trample on serpents and scorpions, and over all the power of the enemy" (**Luke 10:19**).

That authority is yours today! So let's use it:

"Listen to me, you demonic forces assigned to enforce curses in my life! I address you directly now with the full authority of the Lord Jesus Christ!

I bind you, spirit of infirmity enforcing sickness curses! I bind you, spirit of poverty enforcing lack curses! I bind you, spirit of failure enforcing sabotage curses! I bind you, spirit of strife enforcing relational curses! I bind you, spirit of confusion enforcing mental curses!

I bind every principality, every power, every ruler of darkness, every spiritual wickedness in heavenly places that has been assigned to ensure curses are fulfilled in my life! I bind you with chains that cannot be broken, with fetters forged in the fires of heaven!

Now I command you: LOOSE ME AND MY FAMILY FROM YOUR GRIP! Release your hold on my health! Release your claim on my finances! Release your sabotage of my relationships! Release your obstruction of my destiny!

You have no legal right here! The blood of Jesus has cancelled every legal claim! The name of Jesus has broken every chain! The Word of Jesus has shattered every curse!

I command you to GO NOW! Leave my body! Leave my mind! Leave my home! Leave my family! Leave my finances! Leave my destiny! Go where Jesus sends you! You cannot stay here any longer!

And I forbid you to return or to send any other spirits in your place! I seal this eviction with the blood of Jesus! I post angelic guards at every entry point! I declare this territory cleansed and occupied by the Holy Spirit!

In the mighty, matchless, magnificent name of Jesus Christ—the name at which you must bow—I command you to FLEE NOW!"

---

5. LET ALL CURSES ISSUED AGAINST ME BE CONVERTED TO BLESSINGS, IN THE NAME OF JESUS.

Beloved, this is one of the most powerful prayers you can pray. You're not just asking for curses to be removed; you're asking for them to be reversed into blessings! You're asking for what the enemy meant for evil to be turned for your good!

This isn't a new concept. It's a biblical pattern:

Genesis 50:20: Joseph said to his brothers who sold him into slavery: "But as for you, you meant evil against me; but God meant it for good, in order to bring it about as it is this day, to save many people alive."

Romans 8:28: "And we know that all things work together for good to those who love God, to those who are the called according to His purpose."

But there's a specific example of curses being turned to blessings: **Balaam in Numbers 22-24**. King Balak hired Balaam to curse Israel. But every time Balaam opened his mouth, blessings came out! He finally said: "How shall I curse whom God has not cursed? And how shall I denounce whom the LORD has not denounced?" (**Numbers 23:8**).

God turned the intended curses into blessings! And He can do the same for you!

So pray with expectation:

"Almighty God, Creator of heaven and earth, Master of turning darkness into light and curses into blessings—I stand before You today asking for divine reversal!

Just as You did for Israel with Balaam, turn every curse that has been spoken against me into a blessing! Transform every word meant for harm into a testimony of Your goodness!

Let the curse of poverty become a testimony of supernatural provision! Let the curse of sickness become a testimony of divine healing! Let the curse of failure become a testimony of unprecedented success! Let the curse of relational strife become a testimony of restored harmony! Let the curse of barrenness become a testimony of supernatural fruitfulness!

Father, You specialize in reversal! You turned the cross—an instrument of curse and shame—into the means of salvation and glory! You turned Joseph's prison into a pathway to palace! You turned the disciples' fear into apostolic boldness! You turned Saul the persecutor into Paul the apostle!

Now do it for me! Reverse what the enemy has done! Convert his weapons into my testimonies! Transform his attacks into my advancements!

I declare that every curse is now raw material for blessing! Every attack is now fertilizer for growth! Every obstacle is now a platform for miracle!

And just as Balaam finally declared about Israel: 'How lovely are your tents, O Jacob! Your dwellings, O Israel!' (**Numbers 24:5**), let those who once cursed me now say: 'God is with them! Blessing follows them! Favor surrounds them!'

I receive this divine conversion now! I expect to see curses transformed into blessings before my eyes! In Jesus' powerful name!"

---

6. NOW, AGGRESSIVELY ADDRESS EACH SPECIFIC CURSE.

Beloved, now we get specific. General prayers have general results. Specific prayers have specific victories. You need to name each curse and break it specifically.

The Bible says in **Mark 11:23**: "For assuredly, I say to you, whoever says to this mountain, 'Be removed and be cast into the sea,' and does not doubt in his heart, but believes that those things he says will be done, he will have whatever he says."

You have to speak to the specific mountain! So let's do that now. As I name each curse, I want you to pray with violent determination:

"BE BROKEN, BE BROKEN, BE BROKEN, IN THE NAME OF JESUS! I RELEASE MYSELF FROM YOU!"

- **EVERY CURSE OF MENTAL AND PHYSICAL SICKNESS**

"By the stripes of Jesus, I am healed! (**Isaiah 53:5**). Jesus Himself took my infirmities and bore my sicknesses! (**Matthew 8:17**). I break every curse of cancer, diabetes, hypertension, autoimmune diseases, mental illness, depression, anxiety, and every named and unnamed sickness! My body is the temple of the Holy Spirit, and sickness has no right in God's temple!"

- **EVERY CURSE OF FAILURE AND DEFEAT**

"I am more than a conqueror through Christ! (**Romans 8:37**). Thanks be to God who always leads me in triumph in Christ! (**2 Corinthians 2:14**). I break every curse of sabotage, of almost-but-not-quite, of collapse at the edge of breakthrough! I shall succeed! I shall finish! I shall overcome!"

• **EVERY CURSE OF POVERTY AND LACK**

"The LORD is my shepherd; I shall not want! (**Psalm 23:1**). My God shall supply all my need according to His riches in glory by Christ Jesus! (**Philippians 4:19**). I break every curse of debt, of financial leakage, of unexplained lack, of business failure, of unemployment! Wealth and riches are in my house! (**Psalm 112:3**)."

• **EVERY CURSE OF FAMILY BREAK-UP AND DIVORCE**

"As for me and my house, we will serve the LORD! (**Joshua 24:15**). God sets the solitary in families! (**Psalm 68:6**). I break every curse of divorce, separation, estrangement, conflict, and dysfunction! My marriage is blessed! My children are taught of the LORD! (**Isaiah 54:13**). My home is a place of peace!"

• **EVERY CURSE OF OPPRESSION AND SUPPRESSION**

"The Spirit of the LORD is upon me, because He has anointed me to preach good news to the poor; He has sent me to heal the brokenhearted, to proclaim liberty to the captives and recovery of sight to the blind, to set at liberty those who are oppressed! (**Luke 4:18**). I break every curse that has held me down, held me back, silenced my voice, limited my potential! I am free to rise! Free to speak! Free to become!"

• **EVERY CURSE OF BAD REPUTATION AND SLANDER**

"No weapon formed against me shall prosper, and every tongue which rises against me in judgment I shall condemn! (**Isaiah 54:17**). Let the lying lips be put to silence, which speak insolent things proudly and contemptuously against the righteous! (**Psalm 31:18**). I break every curse of false accusation, gossip, slander, and damaged reputation! My name is being restored! My character is being vindicated!"

- **EVERY CURSE OF PERSONAL DESTRUCTION OR SUICIDE**

"I shall not die, but live, and declare the works of the LORD! (**Psalm 118:17**). God has not given me a spirit of fear, but of power and love and a sound mind! (**2 Timothy 1:7**). I break every curse of premature death, of suicidal thoughts, of self-destructive patterns, of accident-proneness! I have a future and a hope! (**Jeremiah 29:11**)."

- **EVERY CURSE OF CHRONIC SICKNESS AND INFIRMITY**

"Beloved, I pray that you may prosper in all things and be in health, just as your soul prospers! (**3 John 1:2**). He forgives all my iniquities, He heals all my diseases! (**Psalm 103:3**). I break every curse of chronic pain, of lifelong conditions, of incurable diagnoses, of generational illnesses! By His stripes, I AM HEALED!"

- **EVERY CURSE OF CORRUPTION OF THE REPRODUCTIVE ORGANS**

"Children are a heritage from the LORD, the fruit of the womb is His reward! (**Psalm 127:3**). There shall be no barren one in Israel! I break every curse of infertility, miscarriage, stillbirth, fibroids, endometriosis, PCOS, erectile dysfunction, prostate issues, and every reproductive disorder! My body is fruitful! My womb is blessed! My seed is ordained!"

• **EVERY CURSE OF FAMILY STRIFE AND DISCORD**

"Behold, how good and how pleasant it is for brethren to dwell together in unity! (**Psalm 133:1**). Love suffers long and is kind; love does not envy; love does not parade itself, is not puffed up! (**1 Corinthians 13:4**). I break every curse of arguments, bitterness, jealousy, competition, and division in my family! Peace rules in our hearts! (**Colossians 3:15**)."

• **EVERY CURSE OF PROFITLESS HARD WORK**

"You shall eat the fruit of the labor of your hands; you shall be happy, and it shall be well with you! (**Psalm 128:2**). The sleep of a laboring man is sweet, whether he eats little or much! (**Ecclesiastes 5:12**). I break every curse of laboring without profit, of working hard without advancement, of sowing without reaping, of investment without return! My labor is blessed! My work is productive! My efforts yield harvest!"

• **EVERY CURSE OF EVIL DEDICATION AND OCCULT BONDAGE**

"Therefore, if the Son makes you free, you shall be free indeed! (**John 8:36**). You are of God, little children, and have overcome them, because He who is in you is greater than he who is in the world! (**1 John 4:4**). I break every curse from ancestral dedications, from occult initiations, from secret society oaths, from pagan rituals! I am dedicated to Jesus alone! I serve Jehovah only!"

• **EVERY CURSE OF WITCHCRAFT AND SORCERY**

"Then many who had believed came confessing and telling their deeds. Also, many of those who had practiced magic brought their books together and burned them in the sight of all! (**Acts 19:18-19**). No sorcery can prevail against Israel! I break every curse of witchcraft, of jinxes, of hexes, of spells, of psychic attacks, of remote control! I am protected by the blood! I am shielded by the name! I am covered by the covenant!"

---

7. NOW, SPEAK BLESSINGS OVER YOURSELF.

Beloved, you cannot leave a vacuum. When you break curses, you must replace them with blessings. When you cast out darkness, you must fill the space with light. When you uproot the negative, you must plant the positive.

Deuteronomy 30:19 says: "I call heaven and earth as witnesses today against you, that I have set before you life and death, blessing and cursing; therefore choose life, that both you and your descendants may live."

You've chosen to reject the curses. Now choose to embrace the blessings! Speak them with faith! Decree them with authority!

"Today, I choose blessing! I choose life! I speak God's promises over every area of my existence!

There shall be no more poverty in my life! The blessing of the LORD makes rich, and He adds no sorrow with it! (**Proverbs 10:22**). The LORD will command the blessing on me in my storehouses and in all to which I set my hand! (**Deuteronomy 28:8**). I am blessed to be a blessing! My needs are met according to His riches in glory! I have more than enough to do everything God has called me to do!

No more sickness! He Himself bore my sins in His own body on the tree, that I, having died to sins, might live for righteousness—by whose stripes I was healed! (**1 Peter 2:24**).

Healing is my bread! Health is my portion! My body functions as God designed it to function! Every cell, every organ, every system operates in divine order!

No more failure! I can do all things through Christ who strengthens me! (**Philippians 4:13**). Whatever I do shall prosper! (**Psalm 1:3**). I am the head and not the tail! I am above only and not beneath! (**Deuteronomy 28:13**). Success is my portion! Achievement is my destiny! Completion is my testimony!

No more shame! Instead of your shame you shall have double honor! (**Isaiah 61:7**). I am not ashamed, for I know whom I have believed and am persuaded that He is able to keep what I have committed to Him until that Day! (**2 Timothy 1:12**). My past is redeemed! My present is purposeful! My future is glorious!

I AM BLESSED! Blessed coming in and blessed going out! (**Deuteronomy 28:6**). My basket and my kneading bowl are blessed! My offspring are blessed! All who see me shall acknowledge that I am the seed whom the LORD has blessed! (**Isaiah 61:9**).

I AM HEALED! He sent His word and healed me! (**Psalm 107:20**). With long life He satisfies me and shows me His salvation! (**Psalm 91:16**). I walk in divine health all the days of my life!

I AM PROSPEROUS! Let the LORD be magnified, who has pleasure in the prosperity of His servant! (**Psalm 35:27**). I meditate in His word day and night, and whatever I do prospers! (**Psalm 1:2-3**). Abundance is my portion! Overflow is my experience!

I AM FAVORED! For His anger is but for a moment, His favor is for life! (**Psalm 30:5**). You, O LORD, will bless the righteous; with favor You will surround him as with a shield! (**Psalm 5:12**). I walk in supernatural favor with God and with man!

I AM FREE! Therefore, if the Son makes you free, you shall be free indeed! (**John 8:36**). Where the Spirit of the Lord is, there is liberty! (**2 Corinthians 3:17**). I am free from every curse! Free from every bondage! Free from every limitation! Free to be all God created me to be!

This is my declaration! This is my testimony! This is my reality—IN JESUS' NAME!"

Beloved, you have prayed with power. You have declared with authority. You have warred with violence in the spirit. Now stand firm in what you have proclaimed.

Ephesians 6:13 says: "Therefore take up the whole armor of God, that you may be able to withstand in the evil day, and having done all, to stand."

You have done all. Now stand. Stand on the Word. Stand in faith. Stand in your authority. Stand in your freedom.

The curses are broken. The blessings are released. The victory is yours.
Now walk in it. Live in it. And never look back at bondage again.

X. CONTINUING IN FREEDOM: A LIFESTYLE OF BLESSING

Beloved, gather close now. We have come through deep waters together. We have identified curses. We have understood their operation. We have traced their sources. We have prayed with violence and authority. We have broken chains that may have bound families for generations. We have applied the blood and the salt. We have declared our freedom with holy aggression.

But now we come to the most critical part of all: **staying free**.

Breaking curses is not a one-time event. It is not a spiritual vaccination that gives you lifetime immunity. It is the **beginning** of a new life, not the end of an old struggle. It is crossing the Red Sea, not entering the Promised Land. There's still a wilderness to navigate. There are still giants to face. There's still a land to possess.

If you don't learn how to **guard your freedom**, how to **maintain your deliverance**, how to **walk in continual blessing**, then what happened to Israel can happen to you. They were delivered from Egypt—a type of deliverance from bondage, from curse, from slavery. But in the wilderness, they constantly looked back. They murmured. They complained. They disobeyed. And an entire generation died in the wilderness, never entering their promised inheritance.

I don't want that for you. I want you to not only **get out** of Egypt but to **get into** Canaan. I want you to not only be **free from** curses but to be **filled with** blessings. I want you to not only have your chains broken but to have your cup overflowing.

So let me give you the keys to continuing in freedom. This is not optional homework. This is survival manual. This is discipleship 101 for the delivered.

1. WALK IN OBEDIENCE TO GOD'S WORD

Beloved, obedience is not legalism. Obedience is not bondage. Obedience is **the fence that keeps you in the pasture of**

blessing. Obedience is **the umbrella that keeps you dry in the storm of curse**.

Deuteronomy 28 makes it abundantly clear: blessings follow obedience; curses follow disobedience. This isn't Old Testament theology that doesn't apply anymore. This is spiritual principle that transcends covenants. **Galatians 6:7** says: "Do not be deceived, God is not mocked; for whatever a man sows, that he will also reap."

If you sow obedience, you reap blessing. If you sow disobedience, you reap consequences. It's that simple.

But let me make this practical. What does walking in obedience look like daily?

A. Obedience in the Small Things

Many people want to be obedient in the big dramatic things while ignoring the daily, mundane obedience. But Jesus said in **Luke 16:10**: "He who is faithful in what is least is faithful also in much; and he who is unjust in what is least is unjust also in much."

Your obedience in secret—when no one is watching—determines your blessing in public. Your faithfulness with little determines your stewardship with much.

Are you obedient with:

- Your tithes and offerings? (**Malachi 3:10**)
- Your time—giving God the first fruits of your day?
- Your tongue—speaking truth always?
- Your thought life—taking every thought captive? (**2 Corinthians 10:5**)

- Your entertainment choices—not filling your mind with garbage?
- Your relationships—not being unequally yoked? (**2 Corinthians 6:14**)

B. Obedience as Love, Not Duty

John 14:15: "If you love Me, keep My commandments."

John 14:21: "He who has My commandments and keeps them, it is he who loves Me. And he who loves Me will be loved by My Father, and I will love him and manifest Myself to him."

Obedience flows from love, not fear. It's not "I have to" but "I get to." It's not "I must obey or God will punish me" but "I want to obey because I love Him and trust that His ways are best."

When you understand that every command of God is for your protection, your provision, and your prosperity, obedience becomes delight, not drudgery.

C. The Blessing of Obedience

Psalm 1:1-3 gives us the picture of the blessed man: "Blessed is the man who walks not in the counsel of the ungodly, nor stands in the path of sinners, nor sits in the seat of the scornful; but his delight is in the law of the LORD, and in His law he meditates day and night. He shall be like a tree planted by the rivers of water, that brings forth its fruit in its season, whose leaf also shall not wither; and whatever he does shall prosper."

Obedience positions you by the river! Disobedience positions you in the desert!

Make a decision today: I will obey God's Word—not perfectly, but persistently. When I fail, I'll repent quickly. But I will make obedience my lifestyle, not my occasional activity.

2. KEEP SHORT ACCOUNTS WITH GOD—REPENT QUICKLY

Beloved, sin is like spiritual mold. If you don't deal with it immediately, it spreads. It grows in darkness. It contaminates everything around it.

1 John 1:9 is your daily cleansing station: "If we confess our sins, He is faithful and just to forgive us our sins and to cleanse us from all unrighteousness."

But notice: **IF** we confess. The forgiveness is guaranteed, but the confession is required.

A. The Danger of Unconfessed Sin

Psalm 66:18: "If I regard iniquity in my heart, the Lord will not hear."

The word "regard" means to cherish, to hold onto, to refuse to release. Unconfessed sin that you're holding onto—whether because of shame, pride, or love for the sin—creates a barrier between you and God.

It's like having a security breach in your spiritual firewall. The enemy now has a point of entry. The curse now has legal ground.

Remember **Achan** in **Joshua 7**. He took accursed things from Jericho and hid them in his tent. One man's hidden sin caused defeat for the entire nation! When the sin was exposed and dealt with, victory returned.

Your unconfessed sin doesn't just affect you. It can affect your family, your ministry, your community.

B. The Discipline of Daily Examination

Lamentations 3:40: "Let us search out and examine our ways, and turn back to the LORD."

Make it a daily habit—preferably at the end of each day—to ask the Holy Spirit: "Is there anything in me that offends You? Any thought, word, or deed that needs confession?"

Psalm 139:23-24: "Search me, O God, and know my heart; try me, and know my anxieties; and see if there is any wicked way in me, and lead me in the way everlasting."

Don't wait for conviction to become condemnation. Don't wait for the Holy Spirit's gentle whisper to become a prophet's public rebuke. Deal with it quickly.

C. The Difference Between Conviction and Condemnation

Conviction is from the Holy Spirit. It's specific: "That word you spoke was unkind." "That thought was lustful." "That action was dishonest." It leads to repentance and freedom.

Condemnation is from the enemy. It's general: "You're such a failure." "You'll never change." "God is disappointed in you." It leads to shame and bondage.

When you feel conviction, say: "Thank You, Holy Spirit, for showing me that. I confess it as sin. I receive Your forgiveness. I choose to turn from it."

When you feel condemnation, say: "I reject that accusation! I am the righteousness of God in Christ Jesus! (**2 Corinthians 5:21**). There is therefore now no condemnation to those who are in Christ Jesus! (**Romans 8:1**)."

D. The Power of Immediate Repentance

The moment you become aware of sin—whether it's five minutes after or five days after—repent immediately. Don't let the sun go down on your anger (**Ephesians 4:26**), and don't let the day end with unconfessed sin.

This keeps your accounts short. This keeps your conscience clean. This keeps your fellowship with God uninterrupted.

3. GUARD YOUR TONGUE—SPEAK LIFE, NOT DEATH

Beloved, your tongue is either building your future or destroying it. **Proverbs 18:21** is not poetry; it's spiritual law: "Death and life are in the power of the tongue, and those who love it will eat its fruit."

You will eat the fruit of your words. If you speak death—complaint, criticism, negativity, doubt—you'll eat bitter fruit. If you speak life—faith, hope, blessing, praise—you'll eat sweet fruit.

A. The Creative Power of Words

Genesis 1 shows us: God spoke, and creation happened. **Hebrews 11:3** tells us: "By faith we understand that the worlds were framed by the word of God."

Your words are framing your world. Your declarations are shaping your reality.

Mark 11:23: "For assuredly, I say to you, whoever says to this mountain, 'Be removed and be cast into the sea,' and does not doubt in his heart, but believes that those things he says will be done, he will have whatever he says."

Jesus didn't say "whoever thinks" or "whoever hopes." He said "whoever **says**"! There's creative power in your spoken word!

B. Breaking Old Patterns of Speech

Many of us have inherited speech patterns from our families:

- "We never have enough."
- "Nothing good ever happens to us."
- "I'm always sick."
- "Men can't be trusted."
- "Women always leave."

These aren't just phrases; they're **curses in sentence form**! And you've been eating the fruit of them!

Today, identify those patterns. Write them down. Then write the biblical opposite next to each one. And begin to speak the truth instead.

C. Practicing Blessing Speech

Ephesians 4:29: "Let no corrupt word proceed out of your mouth, but what is good for necessary edification, that it may impart grace to the hearers."

Make it your practice to:

1. **Bless your children** when they leave for school: "The LORD bless you and keep you. The LORD make His face

shine upon you and be gracious to you." (**Numbers 6:24-26**)

2. **Bless your spouse** daily: "You are God's gift to me. I thank God for you."
3. **Bless your food**: "Thank You, Lord, for this food. Sanctify it to my body's health and strength."
4. **Bless your home**: "This home is dedicated to God. Peace dwells here. Love abides here. Joy fills here."
5. **Bless your city**: "Peace be within your walls, prosperity within your palaces." (**Psalm 122:7**)

D. The Ministry of Encouragement

1 Thessalonians 5:11: "Therefore comfort each other and edify one another, just as you also are doing."

Make your default speech edifying. Look for what's right, not what's wrong. Speak to people's potential, not their problems. Call out the gold, not the dirt.

Your tongue should be like **Proverbs 25:11**: "A word fitly spoken is like apples of gold in settings of silver."

4. AVOID EVERY FORM OF DEFILEMENT AND COMPROMISE

Beloved, freedom is fragile in the presence of defilement. Holiness is vulnerable in the atmosphere of compromise. You cannot play with fire and not get burned. You cannot touch pitch and not get defiled.

2 Corinthians 6:17: "Therefore 'Come out from among them and be separate, says the Lord. Do not touch what is unclean, and I will receive you.'"

A. Defining Defilement

Defilement is anything that:

- Pollutes your spirit
- Dulls your spiritual sensitivity
- Gives the enemy access
- Weakens your resistance to sin
- Compromises your testimony

It includes:

- **Entertainment**—movies, music, websites that glorify sin
- **Associations**—friendships that pull you away from God
- **Practices**—habits, traditions, or customs with occult roots
- **Environments**—places where sin is celebrated
- **Materials**—books, artifacts, jewelry with demonic connections

B. The Principle of Separation

Separation doesn't mean isolation. Jesus ate with sinners. But He didn't become like them; they became like Him!

Separation means:

- You're in the world but not of it (**John 17:14-16**)
- You're a witness, not a participant
- You're salt and light, not blending in

Romans 12:2: "And do not be conformed to this world, but be transformed by the renewing of your mind, that you may prove what is that good and acceptable and perfect will of God."

C. Practical Boundaries

1. **Media boundaries**—What are you watching? Listening to? Reading?
2. **Relationship boundaries**—Who speaks into your life? Who has access to your heart?
3. **Financial boundaries**—Is your money clean? Are your business practices holy?
4. **Time boundaries**—Are you giving God your best time or your leftovers?
5. **Thought boundaries**—Are you guarding what enters your mind?

D. The Cleansing Power of the Word

John 15:3: "You are already clean because of the word which I have spoken to you."

Ephesians 5:26: "That He might sanctify and cleanse her with the washing of water by the word."

Daily immersion in God's Word is your spiritual shower. It washes off the dust of the world. It cleanses from the contamination of daily living.

Make the Word your filter. Before engaging with anything—a movie, a relationship, a business opportunity—ask: "Does this align with God's Word? Will this draw me closer to Him or pull me away?"

5. PUT ON THE WHOLE ARMOR OF GOD DAILY (EPHESIANS 6:10–18)

Beloved, you're in a war. Whether you acknowledge it or not, whether you feel it or not, you have an enemy who wants to re-enslave you. He wants to put back the chains Jesus broke. He wants to re-activate the curses the blood cancelled.

1 Peter 5:8: "Be sober, be vigilant; because your adversary the devil walks about like a roaring lion, seeking whom he may devour."

Notice: he's seeking whom he **may** devour. Not whom he **will** devour. He can only devour those who are unprotected, unaware, unarmed.

That's why Paul gives us the armor of God in **Ephesians 6:10-18**. This isn't optional equipment for special forces Christians. This is standard issue for every believer!

Let me walk you through putting it on daily:

A. The Belt of Truth (Verse 14)

Truth is your foundation. Lies are the enemy's primary weapon. He's the father of lies (**John 8:44**).

Putting on the belt means:

- Starting your day with God's Word—what is true about Him, about you, about your situation
- Rejecting every lie the enemy whispers
- Walking in honesty and integrity

Pray: "Father, gird me with Your truth today. Let Your Word be the standard by which I measure everything. Expose every lie trying to influence me."

B. The Breastplate of Righteousness (Verse 14)

Righteousness is your protection for vital organs—your heart, your emotions, your will.

This is not self-righteousness; it's the righteousness of Christ imputed to you (**2 Corinthians 5:21**).

Putting on the breastplate means:

- Walking in obedience (practical righteousness)
- Resting in your position in Christ (imputed righteousness)
- Guarding your heart (**Proverbs 4:23**)

Pray: "Lord, cover my heart with the righteousness of Jesus. Let no accusation penetrate. Let no condemnation settle. I am the righteousness of God in Christ."

C. The Shoes of the Gospel of Peace (Verse 15)

Your feet take you places. The gospel of peace determines where you go and how you stand.

Putting on the shoes means:

- Being ready to share the gospel
- Walking in peace with God and others
- Standing firm on the finished work of Christ

Pray: "Father, shod my feet with the preparation of the gospel of peace. Let me walk in places of divine assignment. Let me stand firm when storms come."

D. The Shield of Faith (Verse 16)

Faith is your protection against the enemy's attacks—the "fiery darts."

1 John 5:4: "For whatever is born of God overcomes the world. And this is the victory that has overcome the world—our faith."

Putting up the shield means:

- Believing God's promises despite circumstances
- Trusting His character despite feelings
- Standing on His Word despite contradictions

Pray: "Lord, I lift the shield of faith against every doubt, every fear, every attack. I believe Your Word over what I see, over what I feel, over what others say."

E. The Helmet of Salvation (Verse 17)

Your mind is the battlefield. The helmet protects your thinking.

Romans 12:2 again: "Be transformed by the renewing of your mind."

Putting on the helmet means:

- Taking every thought captive (**2 Corinthians 10:5**)
- Meditating on things that are true, noble, just, pure, lovely, of good report (**Philippians 4:8**)
- Remembering you're saved, sealed, and secure

Pray: "God, place the helmet of salvation on my mind. Guard my thoughts. Renew my thinking. Let the mind of Christ be in me."

F. The Sword of the Spirit (Verse 17)

This is your offensive weapon—the Word of God.

Hebrews 4:12: "For the word of God is living and powerful, and sharper than any two-edged sword."

Wielding the sword means:

- Knowing Scripture so you can use it (like Jesus in the wilderness—Matthew 4)
- Speaking God's Word in prayer
- Declaring God's promises in battle

Pray: "Holy Spirit, make Your Word alive in me. Teach me to wield it skillfully. Let it be fire in my bones and a sword in my mouth."

G. Praying Always (Verse 18)

Prayer is the atmosphere in which the armor functions. It's the communication line with Command Central.

Praying always means:

- Maintaining constant communion with God
- Praying in the Spirit (**Jude 1:20**)
- Being watchful and persistent

Pray: "Lord, teach me to pray without ceasing. Let prayer be my first response, not my last resort. Keep me alert and dependent on You."

6. STAY PLANTED IN A BIBLE-BELIEVING, SPIRIT-FILLED CHURCH

Beloved, you cannot maintain freedom in isolation. You cannot walk in blessing alone. The Christian life is team sports, not solo athletics.

Hebrews 10:24-25: "And let us consider one another in order to stir up love and good works, not forsaking the assembling of ourselves together, as is the manner of some, but exhorting one another, and so much the more as you see the Day approaching."

A. The Danger of Lone Ranger Christianity

Every animal the lion picks off is the one that strayed from the herd. Every believer who falls away is usually one who isolated themselves.

Ecclesiastes 4:9-12: "Two are better than one, because they have a good reward for their labor. For if they fall, one will lift up his companion. But woe to him who is alone when he falls, for he has no one to help him up... Though one may be overpowered by another, two can withstand him. And a threefold cord is not quickly broken."

B. The Purpose of the Local Church

The church is:

1. **A family**—for belonging, support, encouragement
2. **A hospital**—for healing, restoration, recovery
3. **A school**—for teaching, training, equipping
4. **An army**—for warfare, advancement, conquest
5. **A body**—each part needing the others (**1 Corinthians 12**)

C. What to Look for in a Church

1. **Sound doctrine**—Does it teach the whole counsel of God?
2. **Spirit-empowered**—Is the Holy Spirit welcome and active?
3. **Authentic community**—Is there real fellowship, not just Sunday smiles?

4. **Biblical leadership**—Are the pastors shepherd-leaders or CEO-managers?
5. **Outward focus**—Is there evangelism and mission?

D. How to Engage with the Church

Don't just attend; belong. Don't just spectate; participate.

1. **Commit**—Be there consistently, not just when convenient.
2. **Connect**—Build real relationships. Join a small group.
3. **Contribute**—Serve with your gifts. Give of your resources.
4. **Care**—Bear one another's burdens (**Galatians 6:2**).
5. **Celebrate**—Rejoice with those who rejoice, weep with those who weep (**Romans 12:15**).

REMEMBER: CHRIST HAS REDEEMED YOU FROM THE CURSE

Beloved, let this truth be the anchor of your soul, the foundation of your faith, the melody of your heart:

Galatians 3:13-14: "Christ has redeemed us from the curse of the law, having become a curse for us (for it is written, 'Cursed is everyone who hangs on a tree'), that the blessing of Abraham might come upon the Gentiles in Christ Jesus, that we might receive the promise of the Spirit through faith."

A. Redemption is Past Tense

"Christ HAS redeemed us." Not "might redeem." Not "will redeem." HAS redeemed. It's done. Finished. Accomplished.

At the cross, every curse that could ever come against you was laid on Jesus. He absorbed it all. He exhausted it all. He satisfied it all.

B. You Are No Longer Under Jurisdiction

You've been transferred! **Colossians 1:13**: "He has delivered us from the power of darkness and conveyed us into the kingdom of the Son of His love."

You're no longer in the kingdom of darkness where curses have authority. You're in the kingdom of light where blessings reign!

C. You Are a Child of the Blessing

Because of Jesus, you're now Abraham's seed and heirs according to promise (**Galatians 3:29**). The blessing of Abraham—the covenant blessing of prosperity, protection, and purpose—is yours!

Deuteronomy 28:1-14 is your inheritance! Read it regularly. Confess it daily. Expect it continually.

WALK IN THIS TRUTH. ENFORCE THIS REALITY.

Beloved, truth known but not walked in is like food bought but not eaten. It doesn't nourish. It doesn't strengthen.

A. Walk by Faith, Not by Sight

2 Corinthians 5:7: "For we walk by faith, not by sight."

Your circumstances may scream "Curse!" But your faith declares "Blessing!" Your feelings may shout "Defeat!" But your spirit knows "Victory!"

Choose to believe what God says over what you see. Choose to trust His character over your circumstances.

B. Renew Your Mind Daily

Romans 12:2 once more: "Be transformed by the renewing of your mind."

The battle for your freedom will be won or lost in your mind. If you think like a slave, you'll live like a slave. If you think like a son, you'll live like a son.

Fill your mind with God's Word. Meditate on it day and night (**Joshua 1:8**). Let it wash away the slave mentality, the poverty mentality, the sickness mentality, the failure mentality.

C. Celebrate Your Freedom

Don't be quiet about what God has done! **Psalm 107:2**: "Let the redeemed of the LORD say so, whom He has redeemed from the hand of the enemy."

Your testimony is a weapon. Your praise is warfare. Your celebration is declaration.

When you praise, you're saying: "God is good! His deliverance is real! His power is present!"

MAY THE LORD TURN EVERY AREA OF YOUR LIFE INTO A TESTIMONY OF HIS REDEEMING POWER.

This is my prayer for you. This is God's purpose for you. Not just to be free from, but to be a display of. Not just to be delivered, but to be a demonstration.

Isaiah 61:1-3: "The Spirit of the Lord GOD is upon Me, because the LORD has anointed Me to preach good tidings to the poor; He has sent Me to heal the brokenhearted, to proclaim liberty to the captives, and the opening of the prison to those who are bound; to proclaim the acceptable year of the LORD, and the day of vengeance of our God; to comfort all who mourn, to console those who mourn in Zion, to give them beauty for ashes, the oil of joy for mourning, the garment of praise for the spirit of heaviness; that they may be called trees of righteousness, the planting of the LORD, that He may be glorified."

You are that planting! You are that tree of righteousness! You are that display of His glory!

Now go. Walk in your freedom. Live in your blessing. And let every area of your life—your health, your finances, your relationships, your emotions, your mind, your destiny—shout to the world:

"My God redeems! My God delivers! My God transforms curses into blessings! And I am His living proof!"

CHAPTER 04

PRISONER OF LOCAL ALTARS

"Have respect unto the covenant: for the dark places of the earth are full of the habitations of cruelty"
— Psalm 74:20

INTRODUCTION

Beloved, before we dive into this heavy, life-changing chapter, I need you to do something with me. I need you to pray. Not a sleepy, mumbled prayer. Not a religious, going-through-the-motions prayer. I need you to pray with **fire in your spirit**. Because what we're about to confront is not theoretical—it's territorial. It's not philosophical—it's powerfully spiritual. And you cannot face darkness with a dimly lit soul.

So, right where you are—whether you're reading this in your living room, on your bed, in your office, or even in a public place—I need you to pray these prayer points with holy aggression:

1. **"I release my promotion from the hand of the oppressor, in the name of Jesus!"**

   That breakthrough that's been delayed, that elevation that's been blocked, that door that's been shut—I command it released right now!

2. **"I refuse to be intimidated by any evil giant, in the name of Jesus!"**

   That problem that looks bigger than you, that circumstance that seems impossible, that diagnosis that sounds final—I command you to bow to the name of Jesus!

3. **"All my buried virtues, receive resurrection now, in Jesus' name!"**

   Those gifts that have been hidden, that potential that's been suppressed, that calling that's been dormant—I command resurrection power upon them now!

4. **"I refuse to be controlled by any power contrary to that of the Holy Spirit, in the name of Jesus!"**

   Every foreign influence, every strange manipulation, every unclean leading—I break your hold over my life!

Now, let me pray for you:

"Wonderful God, I thank You for every soul reading this book right now. I thank You that You are not distant, You are not disinterested, You are not disconnected from their struggle. I know that as is Your nature, You are already at work to destroy the destroyer. I know that even as these words are being read, You are paralysing every satanic agent assigned against these precious lives.

It is written: **'The Lord is a man of war; the Lord is His name' (Exodus 15:3).** By the authority of that name, by the power in that declaration, I speak to every evil stranger the enemy has gathered against the reader: SCATTER NOW in the name of Jesus! Let there be abundant healing where there has been sickness. Let there be supernatural blessings where there has been lack. Let there be divine restoration where there has been loss.

In Jesus' mighty name I pray. Thank You, heavenly Father. Amen."

Now, beloved, we're diving into a topic that has kept countless believers in invisible chains: **"Prisoners of Local Altars."** I want you to read this chapter with your spiritual antennas up. Read it with full concentration, because I believe God is going to give you breakthroughs through this revelation.

At our ministry, Mountain of Fire and Miracles, we're known for praying aggressively against evil altars. We make declarations like: **"I withdraw my name from the captivity of every evil altar!"** and **"I break every covenant with every evil altar!"** But today, I want you to understand **why** we pray this way. I want you to grasp the spiritual realities behind these prayers.

WHAT IS AN ALTAR?

Let's start with the most basic question: What exactly is an altar?

At its simplest definition: **An altar is a place of slaughter to something that is worshipped.**

But that definition doesn't even begin to capture the spiritual weight of what an altar represents. The Bible mentions altars over **433 times**. That's not coincidence. That's emphasis. That's God saying: "Pay attention! This is important!"

The Biblical Significance of Altars

When you trace altars through Scripture, you discover they're markers of spiritual encounters:

- **Cain and Abel** (Genesis 4)—The first worship recorded in Scripture involved altars. Both brothers brought offerings, but Abel's was accepted while Cain's was rejected. Why? Hebrews 11:4 tells us: "By faith Abel offered to God a more excellent sacrifice than Cain." Faith makes the difference at the altar!
- **Noah** (Genesis 8:20)—After surviving the flood, the first thing Noah did was build an altar to the Lord. After massive deliverance, he prioritized worship.
- **Abraham**—You can practically map Abraham's journey by following the altars he built: Shechem (Genesis 12:7), Bethel (12:8), Hebron (13:18), Moriah (22:9). Every major encounter with God was marked by an altar.
- **Jacob**—At Bethel, he set up a stone as a pillar and poured oil on it (Genesis 28:18). At Mizpah, he and Laban set up

a heap of stones as a witness (31:45-46). Jacob understood: altars memorialize divine encounters.

- **Moses** (Exodus 17:15)—After defeating Amalek, "Moses built an altar and called its name, The-LORD-Is-My-Banner."
- **Gideon** (Judges 6:24)—After his angelic encounter, "Gideon built an altar there to the LORD, and called it The-LORD-Is-Peace."
- **David** (2 Samuel 24:25)—After the plague stopped, "David built there an altar to the LORD, and offered burnt offerings and peace offerings."
- **Elijah** (1 Kings 18)—At Mount Carmel, before calling down fire, Elijah "repaired the altar of the LORD that was broken down." He understood: a broken altar means compromised worship.

Every major move of God in Scripture was connected to an altar. Why? Because **the altar is where heaven and earth connect. The altar is where the spiritual and natural realms intersect. The altar is where covenant is established.**

Therefore, the altar is a very important spiritual material. It is a powerful covenant instrument.

COVENANTS

Many churches today don't understand the power and importance of covenants. We've reduced covenant to a theological concept when it's actually a **spiritual reality with tangible consequences.**

The altar and covenant are inseparable. What happens on an altar is covenant material. As far as the Bible is concerned, the altar is serious business. **Anytime anything is sacrificed on an altar, a powerful covenant comes into being.**

There is the altar, and there is the covenant. It is **on the altar** that covenants are made. Therefore, that place—whether it's a magnificent temple, a simple raised platform, or even ordinary ground—where sacrifice happens **becomes an altar**.

When blood is shed on a piece of ground, that ground is no longer neutral. When life is offered at a particular location, that location is no longer ordinary. It has been consecrated—either to God or to demons—for covenant purposes.

SECRETS ABOUT ALTARS

Now let me unveil some spiritual secrets about altars that many don't understand:

1. AN ALTAR IS A PLACE OF SACRIFICE

1 Corinthians 10:19-20 makes it painfully clear: "What am I saying then? That an idol is anything, or what is offered to idols is anything? Rather, that the things which the Gentiles sacrifice they sacrifice to demons and not to God, and I do not want you to have fellowship with demons."

Beloved, let this sink in: **When people sacrifice to idols, they're not sacrificing to nothing. They're sacrificing to demons.** That "small" chicken killed at the shrine? That "harmless" bottle of gin poured at the crossroads? That "innocent" kola nut broken before the family idol? These are sacrifices establishing covenants with demonic powers.

Anyone who has a background with local deities—whether Sango, Ogun, Oya, Amadioha, or any other—needs to understand: at one time or another, you or your ancestors have been at an altar. You've participated in sacrifice. You've made covenant with demons, whether knowingly or unknowingly.

2. THE LAND OR PLACE WHERE AN ALTAR SITS IS DEDICATED TO THE SPIRITS BEING WORSHIPPED

This is a critical revelation: **Land carries spiritual memory.** When sacrifices are made repeatedly on a piece of land, that land becomes dedicated to the spirits receiving those sacrifices.

It doesn't matter if a shopping mall is built there fifty years later. It doesn't matter if a church building is erected on the spot. If the land was originally dedicated to demonic powers through repeated sacrifices, that dedication remains until it's broken by spiritual authority.

Whether you know it or not, if you live on, work on, or frequent land that has been altar-ground, you're already in covenant relationship with the spirits that own that land. They consider you a tenant on their property. They expect rent. And if you don't pay (through sacrifice or worship), they'll come collecting.

3. ANYTIME A SACRIFICE IS MADE, A BLOOD COVENANT IS FORMED

Blood is not just biological fluid. Blood is **covenant currency**. In the spiritual realm, blood speaks. Blood testifies. Blood establishes agreements.

Hebrews 9:22 tells us: "Without shedding of blood there is no remission." This principle works in both directions: God's covenant with us was sealed with Jesus' blood. Demonic covenants with people are sealed with the blood of animals (or worse).

When someone kills a goat at a shrine, they're not just providing meat. They're saying with their actions: "I enter into covenant with you, O spirit. My blood (represented by the animal's blood) for your power. My allegiance for your assistance."

It doesn't matter if it's a chicken, a goat, or a cow. The size of the animal doesn't determine the strength of the covenant. The **act of bloodshed** establishes the covenant. And covenants are binding in the spirit realm.

4. ANY ALTAR IS A PLACE WHERE BLOOD IS CRYING

Genesis 4:10: "The LORD said, 'What have you done? The voice of your brother's blood cries out to Me from the ground.'"

Blood has a voice. Innocent blood cries for justice. Sacrificed blood cries for covenant enforcement.

Think about this: many hospitals today qualify as altars. Why? Because abortions happen there daily. The blood of innocent babies is crying from those places. Don't be surprised if a clinic that specializes in abortions has strange spiritual atmospheres, unexplained failures, or recurring tragedies. The blood is crying.

The same principle applies to places where ritual murders occurred, where violent crimes happened, where injustice was done. The blood remembers. The blood cries. And that crying creates spiritual atmospheres.

5. AN ALTAR IS A SPIRITUAL DINING TABLE WHERE SPIRITS ARE FED

Demons eat. Not physical food, but spiritual food. What's on their menu? Worship. Sacrifice. Fear. Attention.

Psalm 106:37-38 describes Israel's idolatry: "They even sacrificed their sons and their daughters to demons, and shed innocent blood, the blood of their sons and daughters... the land was polluted with blood."

When people sacrifice to demons, they're feeding them. They're strengthening them. They're inviting them to dinner and saying: "Come eat at my table. I'll provide for you if you provide for me."

Here's the dangerous part: if you've been feeding a demon through sacrifices (or your ancestors have), and you suddenly stop when you get born again, the demon doesn't just say, "Oh well, they found Jesus. I'll move on." No! That demon comes demanding: "Where's my food? We had an agreement! You can't just cancel the catering contract without consequences!"

That's why many new believers face intense attacks. They've stopped feeding demons that were accustomed to regular meals. And hungry demons are angry demons.

6. THE ALTAR IS A PLACE OF SLAUGHTER

At the altar, something always dies. In godly worship, our flesh dies. Our selfish ambitions die. Our sinful desires die. We present ourselves as living sacrifices (Romans 12:1).

But at demonic altars, the slaughter is literal and destructive. Animals die. Sometimes people die. Dreams die. Marriages die. Health dies. Finances die.

Here's another sobering truth: **If there is an evil minister at the altar, his sacrifices are polluted.** This applies in churches too! If a pastor is living in sin, if he's involved in secret societies, if he's compromising morally, the communion he serves, the prayers he prays, the marriages he conducts—all are polluted at the altar.

I've seen it too many times: a couple gets married by a pastor who's in a secret society. Years later, their marriage is in shambles. They pray, they fast, they counsel—but the problem started at the altar. An unclean priest polluted their covenant.

Beloved, more people have been killed on polluted altars in churches than during World War II. I don't say that lightly. Spiritual pollution is more deadly than chemical pollution.

7. AN ALTAR IS A PLACE OF SPIRITUAL EXCHANGE

At the altar, you give something to get something. You shed blood in exchange for something. You offer a life to benefit a life.

The trouble is this: **the exchange rate at demonic altars is always rigged.** You think you're getting a good deal—wealth for a chicken, protection for some palm wine, success for a goat—but the fine print is deadly. What you don't realize is that the initial payment is just a down payment. The full payment will be demanded later, and you have no control over when or how.

Maybe they'll demand your firstborn child. Maybe they'll demand your health. Maybe they'll demand your sanity. The contract says: "Payment due upon our demand." And they always demand payment at the worst possible time.

The only altar where the exchange was perfectly fair was the cross. Jesus paid it all. All to Him I owe. At Calvary, the sacrifice was sufficient, complete, and eternally effective.

8. AN ALTAR IS A PLACE WHERE CONTACT IS MADE WITH THE SPIRIT WORLD

Whenever people want to contact the spirit world—whether to reach God or to reach demons—they build altars. The altar is the spiritual telephone booth. It's the dimensional portal. It's the connection point.

When Jacob built an altar at Bethel, he dreamed of angels ascending and descending (Genesis 28:12). The altar became a portal for heavenly traffic.

When people build altars to demons, they're opening portals for demonic traffic. They're establishing communication lines with darkness. They're saying: "Dark powers, you have access here. You can come and go. This is your entry point."

9. AN ALTAR IS A PLACE OF FELLOWSHIP

1 Corinthians 10:20 again: "The things which the Gentiles sacrifice they sacrifice to demons and not to God, and I do not want you to have fellowship with demons."

The word "fellowship" is *koinōnia*—communion, partnership, participation. When you sacrifice at an altar, you're entering into fellowship with whatever spirit receives that sacrifice.

You cannot have fellowship with demons and fellowship with God. You cannot drink the cup of the Lord and the cup of demons (1 Corinthians 10:21). It's one or the other.

IN SUMMARY, AN ALTAR:

- Is a place of slaughter for something worshipped
- Is a place of sacrifice
- Is a place where blood is shed and crying
- Is a spiritual dining table for spirits
- Is a place of exchange (life for life)
- Is a place of contact with the spirit world
- Is a place of fellowship with spirits
- Is a place of spiritual traffic (angels or demons)
- Is a place of covenant establishment
- Is a place of deliberation, decisions, and action

ALTARS, COVENANTS, EVIL DEDICATION

FAMILY ALTARS

Beloved, this is where it gets personal. Satan has a habit of copying God's institutions, perverting them, and using them for destruction. God established family altars for worship (think of Abraham commanding his household to follow the Lord). Satan has established family altars for destruction.

Take your mind back to your village or town. Is there a shrine there? A family idol? A sacred grove? A ritual space? Do you come from a royal family where they buried living people with the dead? Or from a place where humans were buried alive at major crossroads?

Who taught our forefathers these things? The devil. He's been in the deception business for millennia.

I remember a man who brought something to me and said, "This is Ayelala [a traditional deity]." I asked, "Where did you get this?" He said, "It's been in my family for six hundred years. We just inherit it." I asked what he did with it. He said, "I pour *ogogoro* [local gin] on it every morning. Some in my family kill chickens and spill the blood on it. Some pour oil on it."

Beloved, that family heirloom wasn't just a carved piece of wood. It was an **altar to the kingdom of darkness**. For six hundred years, that family had been pouring libations, spilling blood, maintaining covenant with demons. And they wondered why certain patterns kept repeating in their family line!

I know a brother who was running a business that kept failing. He couldn't understand why. One night in prayer, God showed him a vision: two pregnant women fighting until they killed each other. The elders of that land had buried those women right where his business was located. God told him: "Your business is sitting on an altar. Until you break that altar, nothing you put there will prosper."

All these local altars give dark powers authority over parcels of land, over households, over families. If there's a shrine in your family compound, your ancestors handed over that land—and everyone born there—to the spirits they worshipped. Even if you're now born again, filled with the Spirit, living in holiness—that covenant still stands until you break it by spiritual authority.

Those spirits still consider that land theirs. They still consider the family theirs. Because a covenant was made, and covenants are binding until revoked by higher authority.

CAR DEDICATIONS

I've seen people buy new cars and pour libations on them. I've seen people pour dog's blood on engines. What they're doing is dedicating that vehicle to evil spirits—often what they call "the demon of iron" or "the spirit of the road."

When you dedicate something to a demon, you covenant it to that demon. The person driving that car is now under that demon's influence. Whether they believe it or not, whether they agree with it or not, they're covenanted.

Here's a practical danger: what if you buy a second-hand car that someone previously dedicated this way? The car might look fine. The engine might run well. But spiritually, it belongs to someone else. You're a trespasser in a vehicle that has demonic ownership papers. Don't be surprised if that car develops mysterious problems, if accidents keep nearly happening, if it seems to have a mind of its own.

This is why we teach believers to pray deliverance over second-hand items, especially cars and houses. You need to break previous dedications, cleanse with the blood of Jesus, and rededicate to God.

DEMONIC BUSINESS

Let me give you insight about certain businesses. A believer once bought a *danfo* bus (Volkswagen van) for transport business. At Oyingbo bus stop in Lagos, he called "Yaba! Yaba!"

and 14 passengers entered. Out of those 14, 10 were witches and 2 were members of a secret society. He took them to Sabo. Four got down, four more entered. He took them to Yaba. There he called "Oyingbo!" and 9 new passengers entered—all with familiar spirits, plus one witchdoctor and three more secret society members.

Was he running a profitable business or a demonic transport service? Some passengers wouldn't even pay, but he'd feel like they did. He was transporting spiritual cargo he knew nothing about.

If you're in certain businesses—transport, hospitality, entertainment—you need to understand: you're interacting with people carrying spiritual baggage. Your bus, your hotel, your club becomes an altar by proxy if you're not careful.

Even selling wood—did you know some spirits live in trees? When you cut down trees and sell the wood, you're demolishing spiritual houses. Those spirits might attack you. This doesn't mean don't do the business; it means cover it in prayer, anoint it with oil, dedicate it to God before you start.

HOUSE DEDICATIONS

Perhaps when the foundation of your house was laid, it was done the traditional way: things were buried there. Live birds. Animals. Eggs. Palm fronds. Concoctions. If so, the foundation of your house is an altar to Satan. The house is covenanted.

Don't be surprised if strange things happen in that house. Don't be shocked if children born there have issues. Don't wonder why peace seems elusive there. The foundation is spiritually polluted.

Even now that you're born again, only aggressive prayer and land deliverance can nullify that foundation-laying ceremony. You need to pray through every room, anoint every doorway, plead the blood over every square inch.

And let me address something I've seen: some people plant Bibles or crosses in their foundation, thinking this Christianizes it. Beloved, that makes your house an altar to religious spirits! The Bible isn't a magic charm. The cross isn't a good luck symbol. You don't bury the Word; you live the Word. You don't hide the cross; you carry it.

DEAD CHURCHES

Why are many orthodox churches spiritually dead and full of secret society members? History gives us clues. In the early days of missionary work in Africa, when churches wanted land to build, local rulers often gave them demonic forests—places known for spiritual activity, places where sacrifices were made. The missionaries, not understanding spiritual realities, built there.

Over time, the demons that owned those forests entered the churches. They became elders, then deacons, then priests. They took over. And the churches became dead, formal, religious but not spiritual.

That's why some people say, "My great-grandfather died in this church, my grandfather died here, my father died here, and I'll die here." They're covenanted to a building, not to God. They're loyal to tradition, not to truth.

MARKETS

Many traditional markets are built on altars. In some, humans were buried alive during foundation ceremonies. This is one of Satan's strategies with our people: get them buying and selling on satanic altars.

Have you noticed when someone starts going mad, the first place they often go is the market? Why? They're looking for an altar. The market has a spiritual draw for confused minds.

Most of our traditional festivals are celebrated in markets. Masquerades entertain there. Markets are satanic stadiums. They're recruitment grounds for the enemy.

If God opened your eyes to see what's really sold in some markets, you'd go on a 40-day fast. Some people sit inside their wares (spiritually). Some sit upside down (in the spirit). Some sell blood (literally or spiritually).

"But," you say, "I'll just go to supermarkets!" Those are worse—they have educated demons! PhD demons! Demons that understand economics, psychology, and marketing!

So what do we do? Stop eating? No! We pray over our food. We cover our markets in prayer. We do business with discernment.

I remember a woman who sold *moin-moin* (bean cakes) in a market. Hers was so delicious that no one else could sell until she finished. One day she came to a crusade, the fire of God fell on her, and she confessed: "The *moin-moin* you've been eating? I cook it with human blood." One man who had just eaten some tried to vomit, but it was too late—already digested.

We have to pray, beloved. We have to cover what enters our bodies.

The moment someone offers sacrifice to a spirit, they become that spirit's messenger. That's why many forests are demonic altars. Unless God sends you there or you're powerfully anointed, some forests are spiritually dangerous.

Now, after all this, you might feel afraid. Altars in villages. Altars in families. Altars in markets. Altars in forests. Many people are prisoners and don't know it. There are towns where women never have settled homes because they're slaves to the altars there.

RECOGNISING PRISONERS OF LOCAL ALTARS

Brothers and sisters, good evening. I want to speak to you tonight from a place of burden. A burden for the many believers who are living far below their inheritance in Christ, not because of a lack of faith, not because of a lack of prayer, but because of unseen, unrecognized spiritual entanglements. The Bible says in **Hosea 4:6**, *"My people are destroyed for lack of knowledge."* It is this knowledge—this spiritual discernment—that I pray the Holy Spirit imparts to us tonight.

We've been discussing the power of covenants and altars. We understand that an altar is not just a pile of stones or a patch of earth. It is a place of spiritual transaction. A place where the physical and the spiritual intersect. Where blood is shed, words are spoken, and covenants—binding agreements—are sealed. In the Bible, godly men built altars to the Lord: Abraham, Isaac, Jacob, Moses, Elijah. These were places of worship, sacrifice, and encounter with the living God.

But listen to me carefully: The enemy is a counterfeiter. He has his own altars. He has his own priests. He has his own covenants.

And many of us, our families, our lands, have been unknowingly dedicated, sacrificed, or covenanted at these altars of darkness. You may be born again, Spirit-filled, and serving God, yet you find yourself battling the same cycles of failure, the same patterns of defeat. Why? Because you may be a *prisoner of local altars*. Your life, your blessings, your destiny may be held captive in the spiritual realm, tied to a piece of land, a family shrine, a village idol, or a demonic agreement made generations ago.

How do you know? How can you discern if this is your portion? Let's walk through these signs together, not to instill fear, but to bring revelation that leads to liberation. For **2 Timothy 2:26** tells us that we must *"recover ourselves out of the snare of the devil, who are taken captive by him at his will."* To recover yourself, you must first recognize the snare.

---

1. DREAMING OF YOUR PLACE OF BIRTH FREQUENTLY

When you close your eyes at night, where does your spirit go? Do you find yourself, again and again, walking the paths of your childhood village? Are you in your grandfather's compound? At the stream where you fetched water? These are not mere nostalgia. In the realm of the spirit, dreams are highways. If you are constantly transported back to a specific geographical location, it is a powerful indicator that a part of your spirit—your identity, your inheritance—is still anchored there.

Think of Jacob in **Genesis 28**. He left Beersheba and journeyed toward Haran. He slept and dreamed of a ladder to heaven, and God gave him a monumental promise. When he awoke, he said, *"Surely the LORD is in this place, and I did not know it."* He set up a stone, anointed it, and called the place Bethel—the house of God. That place became a spiritual marker.

Now, consider the opposite. What if the place you frequent in dreams is not a *Bethel* (House of God) but a *Beth-aven* (House of Wickedness)? What if it is a place where your ancestors made pacts with idols? That land, that village, can hold a spiritual claim over you. It's as if there is a spiritual umbilical cord tying you to that altar, pulling you back in your subconscious, reminding the powers there that you belong to them. You need to do as Jacob eventually did: return to that place in the spirit through prayer, confront it, and reconsecrate it to the God of Bethel. You must sever that cord with the sword of the Spirit.

2. BEING PURSUED BY SERPENTS IN DREAMS

This is a profound and common sign. Throughout Scripture, the serpent is a symbol of the devil, deceit, and demonic covenants (**Genesis 3:1, Revelation 12:9**). To dream of serpents chasing you, biting you, or wrapping around you is rarely just a biological fear. It often signifies that you are being pursued by the enforcement spirits of a covenant.

Perhaps a covenant was made using the symbol or power of a serpentine deity. In many traditional settings, there are shrines to serpent spirits—they are worshipped for protection, power, or vengeance. If your family ever sought protection or power from such a source, a covenant was established. That serpent spirit now sees you as its property. It pursues you in the dream to intimidate you, to drain your vitality, or to reinforce its claim.

But hear this, child of God: **Luke 10:19** declares, *"Behold, I give you the authority to trample on serpents and scorpions, and over all the power of the enemy, and nothing shall by any means hurt you."* The dream is revealing the battle, but the Word of God gives you the authority to crush the head of that serpent, just as our Lord Jesus crushed the head of Satan on the cross.

3. BLOCKAGES AT THE EDGE OF MIRACLES

This is one of the most painful and frustrating signs. You pray, you fast, you believe. The promotion letter is almost signed. The marriage proposal is about to be made. The business deal is in its final stage. The cheque is literally being printed. And then... nothing. It collapses. Silence. A mysterious withdrawal. A sudden, unexplainable problem.

You are left bewildered, asking God, "Why? Why does this always happen at the finish line?" It can feel like a spiritual law of "non-achievement" is working against you.

This, beloved, is a classic trademark of altar interference. In the spirit realm, your blessing has been released from heaven. The angels are dispatching it. But as it descends into your realm, there is a local altar—a demonic checkpoint—that intercepts it. The "priests" at that altar see your blessing coming and they say, "This one belongs to us. His father dedicated him here. Her grandmother promised her here. Stop it. Divert it. Consume it."

It's like the story in **Daniel 10**. Daniel prayed, and from the first day, the word was issued. But the prince of the kingdom of Persia withstood the angel for 21 days. There was a territorial power blocking the answer. Michael had to come help. Your persistent blockages may be the work of a "prince" or power assigned to a local altar, blocking your answers at the edge of breakthrough. This requires not just prayer, but *strategic, violent, authoritative warfare* to command that blockage to be shattered in Jesus' name.

4. RESTLESSNESS IN MARRIAGE

You entered marriage with love and hope. But instead of peace, there is constant, unexplained strife. Bitterness erupts over trivial matters. There is a spirit of discontent, a longing to be elsewhere, or a constant friction that has no logical root. You may even look at your spouse and think, "I married the wrong person," despite them being a good person.

While there can be natural causes, a pervasive, unexplained restlessness can be the fruit of an altar. How? In many traditions, marriages are sealed not just before God and man, but before local idols. The list of items—42 yams, 42 kola nuts, alligator pepper, the pouring of libations—these are not cultural ornaments. They are sacrificial items that form a covenant with the spirits of that land. If your marital union was "sealed" on such an altar, you have invited demonic third parties into your marriage. These spirits work to undermine unity, foster distrust, and create agitation.

Furthermore, if you or your spouse were spiritually "married" to a spirit husband or wife at a local altar before your physical marriage, that entity will see your human spouse as an intruder. It will fight to destroy the marriage. The restlessness is that entity's presence, creating discord. You must evict every ungodly spiritual participant from your marriage and re-consecrate your union solely on the altar of Christ.

5. BEING PURSUED BY MASQUERADES IN DREAMS

In our African context, the masquerade is a powerful spiritual symbol. It often represents the manifestation of ancestral spirits or community deities. To be chased or threatened by masquerades in dreams is a direct spiritual confrontation. These entities are often the enforcement officers of community or family covenants.

They pursue you for two main reasons: to frighten you into compliance (to make you return to traditional practices), or to punish you for "abandoning" the family gods after you gave your life to Christ. They are saying, "You are ours. You cannot just walk away." Their pursuit is an attempt to reinforce fear and bondage.

But remember the words of **Isaiah 54:17**: *"No weapon formed against you shall prosper, and every tongue which rises against you in judgment You shall condemn. This is the heritage of the servants of the LORD..."* That masquerade is a weapon formed against you. You have the heritage—the birthright—to condemn its pursuit. You are not under its jurisdiction; you are a citizen of Zion. Command every pursuing masquerade spirit to be bound and consumed by the fire of God.

6. INABILITY TO COMPLETE BUILDING PROJECTS

You save, you plan, you buy land, you lay a foundation. Then, problems swarm like bees. Funds evaporate. Contractors disappear or cheat you. Materials are stolen. Strange disputes arise over the land. You finish building, but you can't live in it peacefully, or it continually demands repairs, draining your finances.

Land has a spiritual consciousness. In **Genesis 3:17**, God cursed the *ground* because of Adam. In **Numbers 35:33**, the Bible says blood pollutes the land. The land you build on may be crying out against you because it has been dedicated to another master. If sacrifices were made on that land to appease earth spirits or to secure it from evil, a covenant exists. If someone was buried there ritualistically, or if it was a former shrine, the demons assigned to that land see your building as an invasion. They will fight you to a standstill.

Before you build, you must spiritually prosecute the land. Like Joshua confronting Jericho, you must walk around your property in prayer, not with trumpets of rams' horns, but with the powerful name of Jesus, claiming it from the powers of darkness. You must break every covenant of the land and plead the blood of Jesus over every inch of it.

7. UNPROFITABLE TENANTS

If you have rental property that consistently attracts terrible tenants—those who refuse to pay, who destroy property, who bring chaos—consider the spiritual dimension. The problem may not be your screening process. The land or the house itself may be under a curse from altar activities, making it a place of strife and poverty. Demons can influence people's behavior, making them rebellious and destructive when they live on that property.

The property itself may be an "altar of poverty," programmed to swallow money and generate loss. You must do a spiritual audit: What happened on this land before? Was it used for idolatry? Was it a crossroads where sacrifices were left? Reclaim that property from being a citadel of loss and rededicate it as a place of blessing and peace.

8. AMPUTATED FINANCES & 9. SPIRITUAL BACKWARDNESS

We will take these together. Amputated finances—money comes, but you cannot hold it. An emergency arises, a sudden loss, a bizarre expense. It's as if your pocket has a hole. Spiritual backwardness—you pray, but feel dry. You read the Bible, but it seems like letters. You struggle to grow in faith, in holiness, in spiritual gifts.

These are signs that your spiritual and financial pipelines are being tapped by parasitic spirits connected to altars. It is a spiritual form of *leaking*. **Haggai 1:6** describes it: *"You have sown much, and bring in little; You eat, but do not have enough; You drink, but you are not filled with drink; You clothe yourselves, but no one is warm; And he who earns wages, Earns wages to put into a bag with holes."*

The "bag with holes" is often an altar covenant that mandates you to fund spiritual darkness. Your increase is siphoned off to maintain demonic systems you may know nothing about. Your spiritual vitality is drained to feed the spirits your ancestors served. You must locate the hole and seal it with the blood of Jesus. You must command every spiritual siphon, every parasitic attachment connected to any altar, to be disconnected and burned.

10. IMAGINARY ENEMIES & 11. CONSISTENT ERRORS

A pervasive sense of being watched, followed, or hated without cause. Making foolish, repetitive mistakes that cost you dearly—

sending an email to the wrong person, missing a critical deadline, misplacing important documents.

These can be the fruits of a spell or curse orchestrated from an evil altar. The purpose is to keep you in fear and failure. It is a cloud of confusion and paranoia, sent from the pit of hell to disorient and disarm you. It's the spirit of **Isaiah 19:14**: *"The LORD has mingled a perverse spirit in her midst; And they have caused Egypt to err in all her work, As a drunken man staggers in his vomit."* You must rebuke the spirit of error and the spirit of fear, and command your mind to be garrisoned by the peace of God.

12. FAMILY WOMEN SENT AWAY FROM MARITAL HOMES

This is a specific, powerful pattern. If the women from your family line consistently have broken marriages, if they are always returning to their father's house, investigate the family house itself. Is it merely a home, or is it a *shrine*? Were there idols kept there? Was it a place of ritual? The family house can act as a spiritual magnet, pulling back its "property." It can be an altar that rejects the transfer of its daughters to other families, thereby sabotaging their marriages. The women are prisoners of that local altar.

13. CONSTANT FAILURES

Beloved, let's get real. How many times have you started something with great passion, only to watch it crumble for no logical reason? You open a business—it fails. You start a ministry—it stalls. You enroll in school—you drop out. You plant a farm—the harvest is blighted. The pattern is so consistent it feels like a curse. You begin to internalize it: "Maybe I'm just not good enough. Maybe it's my destiny to fail."

STOP. That is the voice of the accuser, reinforced by the ledger of an evil altar. Failure is not your portion. **Deuteronomy 28:13** says, *"And the Lord will make you the head and not the tail; you shall be above only, and not be beneath..."* If you are perpetually beneath, if you are the tail, something is pressing you down.

These constant failures are often the harvest of a seed sown at an evil altar. Perhaps a jealous relative went to a shrine and said, "Let nothing they do prosper." Maybe an ancestor, in a bid for quick power, traded the success of his lineage at the altar of a demon. Now, every time you rise, a command from that ancient altar is activated: *"Pull them down."*

You must trace the failure not just to your actions, but to its spiritual root. It's not about working harder; it's about praying smarter. You must confront that altar of failure and command its decrees over your life to be nullified by the blood of Jesus. You must decree, as it is written in **Isaiah 8:10**, *"Take counsel together, but it will come to nothing; Speak a word, but it will not stand, For God is with us."* Let every counsel of failure from the pits of hell be scattered now!

14. REPEATED PROBLEMS

This is similar but more specific. It's the same *type* of problem arising in different areas of your life. For example:

- **Financial:** You get a job, then a sudden tax bill cleans you out. You receive an inheritance, then a family crisis demands all the money.

- **Relational:** Every friendship ends in betrayal. Every business partnership ends in dispute.
- **Health:** One sickness is treated, another immediately appears. It's a carousel of infirmity.

This is the spirit of *trouble* assigned to you from an altar. It's a demonic specialist whose only job is to generate specific problems in your life. In **Job**, we see a man targeted for trouble. His problems were not random; they were orchestrated. Your repeated problems are orchestrated.

The altar serves as the command center. It's like a spiritual server that keeps running the same program—"Program Trouble: Version [Your Surname]." Every time you reboot your life, the same malware loads. You need a spiritual antivirus. You need the fire of the Holy Ghost to scan the deep files of your spirit and soul, find that recurring program written against you at the local altar, and **DELETE IT PERMANENTLY** in Jesus' name. Pray with specificity: "Every program of repeated [name the problem] written against my life at any altar, be erased by the blood of Jesus!"

15. SEEING THINGS OTHERS DON'T SEE

Now, this is critical. I'm not talking about the gift of discerning of spirits, which is holy and controlled. I'm talking about involuntary, fearful sightings. You see shadows moving at the periphery of your vision. You see dark figures in your room at night. You see fleeting images of faces, especially of dead relatives. Your children say, "Daddy, who is that man in the corner?" and you see nothing.

This is often a sign that you have what is called an "open door" or a "second sight" that was activated at a local altar. In many traditional initiations, parts of the body (like the eyes) are ritually opened to see into the spiritual realm—but it's a covenant with darkness. This "gift" becomes a curse, a channel for fear and torment. You are seeing the activities of the demons assigned to you or your household.

The Bible speaks of the "*veil*" that lies over the hearts of those who don't know Christ (**2 Corinthians 3:15**). For some prisoners of altars, there is a different kind of veil—one that is thin and transparent to darkness, but thick to the light of God. You need the veil torn! You need the prayer of **Ephesians 1:17-18**: "*That the God of our Lord Jesus Christ... may give to you the spirit of wisdom and revelation in the knowledge of Him, the eyes of your understanding being enlightened...*" Command your spiritual eyes to be closed to darkness and opened only to the revelations of God.

16. INABILITY TO FEED PROPERLY / CURSED SUSTENANCE

This is profound. It goes beyond physical hunger. It's a spiritual principle found in **Haggai 1:6**: "*You eat, but you do not have enough; you drink, but you are not filled with drink...*" You consume food, but it doesn't translate to vitality. You earn money, but it brings no satisfaction. There's a disconnect between intake and outcome.

Why? The food or the source of your sustenance may be *covenanted*. If you are farming on land that is dedicated to an idol, the food from that land carries a spiritual signature. You are not just eating cassava; you are eating "cassava from the shrine's field." You are ingesting the covenant of that land. If you run a business in a market built on a ritual burial ground, the profits from that business are tagged. You are not just receiving money; you are receiving "money from the altar of the marketplace demon."

This creates a spiritual leak. The nourishment, the blessing, is syphoned off to feed the demonic covenant. You must break the covenant on your food, your land, your income. You must pray over everything that enters your mouth and your pocket. Like Daniel who refused the king's defiled food (**Daniel 1:8**), you must, in the spirit, refuse the defilement attached to your sustenance. Command the curse on your bread and water to be broken (**Isaiah 65:13-15**).

17. BUSINESS FAILURES (EXPANDED)

We touched on failure, but business failure deserves its own spotlight because it's a major battlefield. You have a brilliant idea. You have capital. You have a good plan. You launch. For a while, things go well. Then, mysterious setbacks: key staff suddenly quit. Loyal customers vanish. Reliable suppliers fail. The bank loan falls through at the last minute. Fire, theft, or litigation strikes.

This is more than bad luck; it's a targeted spiritual siege. Often, the *premises* of the business is the problem. Was the land cleansed before you started? Was it previously a bar, a brothel, a shrine, a cemetery? The spirits that operated there see your godly enterprise as an invasion. They will marshal their forces to evict you.

Furthermore, if your source of start-up capital was "strange money"—money from a questionable source, money from someone in covenant with darkness—that money acts as a

Trojan horse. It brings the spirit of that covenant into the foundation of your business. You must spiritually audit your business foundation. You must evict every sitting tenant spirit from your business premises and reclaim the territory for the Kingdom of God. Command the wealth of the sinner, laid up for the just, to be transferred to you (**Proverbs 13:22**).

18. AMPUTATED FINANCES (EXPANDED)

This is the cousin of business failure, but it affects personal finances with surgical precision. Your finances are *amputated*—cut off right at the moment of flow.

- You receive a salary, and an unexpected school fee takes all of it.
- You get a bonus, and your car breaks down, costing the exact amount.
- Money enters your hand, but you cannot account for how it left.

It feels like you are a conduit, not a reservoir. The blessing flows *through* you, not *to* you. This is the work of the "spirit of the devourer" that God promises to rebuke for those who bring their tithes (**Malachi 3:11**). But what if the devourer has a legal right? That right often comes from an altar where a covenant of poverty was established. Perhaps an ancestor vowed perpetual poverty to a spirit in exchange for something. Perhaps a poverty curse was placed on your lineage.

You must locate the point of amputation. In the spirit, see your financial pipeline. Where is it being cut? Command the hands of the evil altar priests holding the machete to wither. Apply the blood of Jesus as a divine seal over your finances. Decree that you are no longer a canal but a reservoir of blessing. Decree that every financial artery severed by the enemy is now reconnected and supernaturally healed.

My brother, my sister, these 18 signs are a mirror. Don't look and be condemned. Look and be *liberated*. Recognition is the *first* step to recovery. God is showing you these things not to shame you, but to shame the devil. He is exposing the hidden snare so you can crush it under your feet.

You are not a prisoner. You are a prophet, a priest, and a king in Christ Jesus. That local altar, no matter how ancient, cannot withstand the authority of the name that is above every name. That covenant, written in demonic blood, cannot stand against the covenant written in the precious blood of the Lamb.

The journey to freedom begins with a prayer of renunciation, continues with violent faith, and ends in total restoration. You will dream new dreams. You will walk in new breakthroughs. You will build and live in it. You will eat and be satisfied. Your business will flourish. Your finances will overflow. For the yoke of the altar is being destroyed because of the anointing upon your life.

Let's move from recognition to reclamation. Let's pray.

THE WAY OUT: BREAKING THE POWER OF EVIL ALTARS

My brothers and sisters, we have diagnosed the problem. We've looked at the symptoms—the dreams, the blockages, the failures, the relentless cycles. We've recognized that many of us, through no conscious fault of our own, are prisoners of local altars. Our lives, our blessings, and our destinies have been entangled in covenants made in darkness, on patches of earth dedicated to gods that are not God.

But tonight, I come with a word from the throne: **There is a way out.** The prison door is not locked. It has been open since Calvary. Jesus Christ didn't just die to save your soul from hell; He died to redeem your *life* from every curse, every covenant, and every captivity. **Galatians 3:13-14** declares it: *"Christ hath redeemed us from the curse of the law, being made a curse for us... That the blessing of Abraham might come on the Gentiles through Jesus Christ..."* Your redemption is comprehensive! It covers ancestral sin, it breaks ancient covenants, and it recovers stolen territory.

So, how do we walk out of this prison? It's not a passive hope. It's a proactive, spiritual prosecution. It's a legal case you bring before the court of heaven, using the blood of Jesus as your evidence and His Word as your gavel. Let me give you the seven-fold strategy—the Way Out.

---

1. REPENTANCE FROM THE SCHOOL OF CONSTRUCTING UNGODLY ALTARS

This is the foundation. You cannot break a covenant while still secretly honoring it. Repentance is not just saying "sorry"; it's a complete *turnaround*. It's changing your mind, your allegiance, and your spiritual citizenship.

You must repent for yourself. Search your heart. Have you, in ignorance or fear, participated in anything that erected or honored an ungodly altar? That "small" traditional ceremony for your child? That visit to the native doctor when medicine failed? That libation you poured "just to respect tradition" at a family gathering? In the spirit, that was masonry work on the wall of your prison. Repent. **Acts 3:19** says, *"Repent ye therefore, and be converted, that your sins may be blotted out..."*

But you must also repent on behalf of your ancestors. This is a biblical principle. Daniel prayed, *"We have sinned... to our fathers we have sinned"* (**Daniel 9:5-8**). Nehemiah confessed the sins of his fathers (**Nehemiah 1:6**). You are the legal representative of your bloodline. You stand in the gap. You say, "Father, on behalf of my great-grandfather who consulted the oracle, I repent. On behalf of my grandmother who dedicated her children to the river goddess, I repent. On behalf of my father who laid the foundation of our house with eggs and palm wine, I repent. We have built altars to strange gods. We have entered covenants with demons. We have worshipped creation instead of the Creator. Forgive us, Lord."

This repentance severs the legal hold of generational sin. It's the first blow against the prison wall.

2. RENOUNCE THE COVENANTS

Repentance deals with the *sin*. Renunciation deals with the *contract*. A covenant is a binding agreement. You must now, with your voice—the voice of authority given to you by Christ—annul that agreement.

You stand up and you speak to the spirit realm. You address the parties of that dark covenant: the demons, the idols, the ancestral spirits. You say:

"In the name of Jesus Christ of Nazareth, I renounce, I revoke, and I declare null and void every covenant, pact, oath, or agreement made on my behalf, or by my ancestors, at any altar, shrine, river, forest, or crossroads. I renounce the covenant of protection from

the village idol. I renounce the covenant of prosperity from the marketplace spirit. I renounce the marital covenant made with any spirit husband or wife. I renounce the covenant of initiation into any secret society. By the authority in the blood of Jesus, I cancel every signature, every mark, every token of these covenants. They are worthless papers in the court of heaven. I am not a party to them. I am free."

This is not a whisper. This is a decree. **Job 22:28** says, *"Thou shalt also decree a thing, and it shall be established unto thee..."* Decree your disassociation.

3. RELEASE YOUR LIFE'S BENEFITS FROM THEIR HANDS

Demons are not just tormentors; they are thieves. **John 10:10** says the thief comes to steal. What have they stolen? Your benefits! Your peace, your health, your marriage, your children, your prosperity, your joy, your divine purpose. These blessings are rightfully yours in Christ, but they are being held in escrow by demonic forces who say, "This belongs to our altar."

Now, you must issue a release order. You command the garnishment on your blessings to be lifted. You pray:

"I speak to every demonic warehouse, every satanic bank, every spiritual prison cell where my blessings are held captive. In the name of Jesus, I command you to RELEASE THEM NOW! Release my healing. Release my financial breakthrough. Release my marital harmony. Release my children's destiny. Release my creative ideas. Release my divine opportunities. You have no right to withhold what God has bequeathed to me. Let them go, in the name of Jesus!"

Remember the parable of the **strong man** in **Matthew 12:29**. You must first *bind the strong man* (which we'll get to), then you can *spoil his goods*. Releasing your benefits is the spoiling of his goods!

4. RECOVER YOUR LOST BLESSINGS

Releasing is one thing. Recovery is another. The blessing might be released, but it's wandering in the spiritual wilderness, disoriented. Or the enemy has spent it, consumed it, or corrupted it. God's promise is not just to stop the theft, but to *restore*. **Joel 2:25**: *"And I will restore to you the years that the locust hath eaten..."*

This prayer is aggressive and specific. You move from defense to offense. You don't just ask God to give you new blessings; you demand the restoration of what was stolen.

"Father, in the name of Jesus, I claim a seven-fold restoration of all that the altars of darkness have stolen from me and my lineage. I recover the years of health consumed by sickness. I recover the wealth swallowed by poverty and strange debts. I recover the peace devoured by turmoil. I recover the joy eaten up by depression. I recover the destinies of my children that were traded at idol shrines. I recover lost territories, lost opportunities, lost virtues. Holy Spirit, track every stolen blessing, locate it in the spirit realm, and orchestrate its supernatural return to my life. Nothing shall be missing, nothing shall be broken. I receive my recovery now!"

This is the prayer of David in **1 Samuel 30**. When the Amalekites stole everything, David inquired of the Lord, pursued, *and recovered all.*

5. REFUSE TO RENEW THE CONTRACT

Your freedom is a new covenant—the New Covenant in Christ's blood. You must guard it jealously. The enemy will try to trick you into renewing the old contracts. How?

- Through **cultural pressure**: "Just come for the annual festival, it's just culture." NO. That festival is a renewal ceremony for the village altar.
- Through **family sentiment**: "Wear this family talisman, it's your grandfather's." NO. That talisman is a covenant token.
- Through **fear**: "If you don't participate in this rite, something bad will happen." NO. That is the threat of the slave-master to a freed slave.

You must be like the three Hebrew boys: **Daniel 3:16-18**. They refused to bow, even under threat of death. You say, "I will not bow. I will not eat. I will not drink. I will not participate. My covenant is with the Lamb. I am a signatory to His blood alone."

Make a conscious decision: *I will not set foot on that shrine land again. I will not contribute money to that idolatrous festival. I will not eat food sacrificed to idols. I will not wear the jewelry of slavery.* Burn the bridges back to Egypt.

6. PARALYSE THE STRONGMAN

Every altar has a ruler, a principality, a strongman. This is the demonic CEO, the arch-spirit assigned to enforce the covenants of that place. You can't just deal with the foot soldiers; you must paralyze the headquarters.

Matthew 12:29 gives us the strategy: *"How can one enter into a strong man's house, and spoil his goods, except he first bind the strong man? and then he will spoil his house."*

You must identify and bind the strongman over your life, your family, and your territory. Is it the *Spirit of Python* from the river shrine? The *Queen of Heaven* spirit from the family idol? The *Marine Spirit* from the coastal altar? The *Spirit of Death and Hell* from the burial shrine?

You address them directly:

"You strongman, ruling spirit over the altar of [name the place/practice], I bind you now in the name of Jesus Christ! I paralyze your operations. I freeze your assets. I silence your commands. I strip you of your armor. By the power in the blood of Jesus and the keys of the Kingdom, I render you powerless, impotent, and useless over my life and my family's life. Your house is being spoiled tonight!"

7. VIOLENTLY ADDRESS THE ALTAR

This is the climax. Most people pray *about* their problem. You must learn to pray *to* your problem. The altar is not an inanimate object. It is a spiritual entity, a point of contact, a throne. And it can hear.

Look at **1 Kings 13:1-5**. A man of God cried *against the altar* at Bethel. He didn't just pray to God about King Jeroboam; he prophesied directly to the altar: *"O altar, altar, thus saith the LORD..."* And the altar responded! It split apart, and the ashes poured out.

You must do the same. You locate, in the spirit, the specific altars holding you captive. The altar in your village square. The shrine in your family compound. The river altar where you were dedicated. The market altar. The crossroads altar.

And you speak to it. With holy rage and divine authority, you declare:

"Altar of [Name], hear the word of the Lord! Your covenant is broken. Your power is nullified. Your priesthood is disbanded. The blood of Jesus speaks against every sacrifice ever made on you. I command the fire of God to fall upon you now and burn you to ashes. I command the earthquake of the Spirit to split you apart. I command every voice, every cry, every claim coming from you to be silenced forever. You are dismantled, in the name of Jesus!"

Beloved, this is spiritual warfare. It's not casual. It's not polite. It's violent faith that takes the Kingdom by force (**Matthew 11:12**). It will require time. It will require tears. It will require your voice to be hoarse from decreeing. You may need to fast—to weaken your flesh and strengthen your spirit for the battle.

And what about your name? If your name is a prayer to an idol (like *Esubiyi* – "the devil has given birth to this one"), you need to renounce its power. You don't necessarily have to change it legally (though you can), but you must spiritually divorce yourself from its meaning. Declare: "I am no longer defined by this name. I am defined by the name of Jesus Christ. Every curse, every linkage, every destiny attached to that name is broken. I am a new creation."

Tonight, we move from diagnosis to deliverance. We move from prisoners to prosecutors. We are serving eviction notices to every squatter spirit, and repossession orders on every stolen blessing.

The aggression is not from a place of fear, but from a place of furious love for the freedom Christ purchased. It's the aggression of a mother bear rescuing her cubs. It's the aggression of a king reclaiming his plundered territory.

Get ready to pray. Get ready to fight. Get ready to recover *all*. For it is your Father's good pleasure to give you the Kingdom. And no local altar, no matter how ancient, can stand in the way of that promise.

THE PRAYER OF LIBERATION FROM EVIL ALTARS

Beloved family, we have come to the moment of engagement. We have studied the prison. We have identified the jailers. We have located the chains. Now, we are going to do violence to the kingdom of darkness. This is not a time for timid whispers. This is a time for authoritative decrees. This is not a request session; this is an eviction notice. This is not a quiet meditation; this is a spiritual uprising.

We are going to pray as the prophets prayed—with fire in our bones and the Word of God as our hammer. We are going to pray as the apostles prayed—with Kingdom authority that shakes foundations. We are going to pray as Jesus taught us to pray—declaring His will to be done on earth, in our lives, as it is in heaven.

Get into position. This is physical because we are spiritual beings in physical bodies. Place your right hand on your head—

the seat of your mind, your will, your identity, your authority. Place your left hand on your navel—the center of your being, the place of generational connection, the womb of your destiny. You are connecting your authority (head) to your heritage and destiny (navel). You are standing as a priest before God, intervening for your own life.

Take a deep breath. Fill your lungs with the breath of God. Now, let's begin this holy assault.

---

1. THE DECREE OF RELEASE

Pray: "I RELEASE MYSELF FROM THE BONDAGE OF EVIL ALTARS! IN THE NAME OF JESUS!"
Say it once with all the faith you can muster. Now, begin to repeat it: **"I RELEASE MYSELF! IN THE NAME OF JESUS!"**

Don't stop. Don't be concerned with how you sound. This is warfare. The chains have been on for generations; they won't fall off with a polite request. You are enforcing the legal verdict of Calvary. **Isaiah 52:2** cries out: "*Shake thyself from the dust; arise, and sit down, O Jerusalem: loose thyself from the bands of thy neck, O captive daughter of Zion.*" God is saying, **YOU** loose yourself! Use the authority I've given you!

As you repeat "I RELEASE MYSELF!", visualize it. See those spiritual chains—chains of poverty from the marketplace altar, chains of sickness from the river altar, chains of failure from the family shrine—snapping like rotten thread. Hear the metal screeching as it breaks. Feel the weight falling off your shoulders. You are not asking God to do it; you are commanding it to be so, based on what He has already done.

Now, pray this corporate prayer with me:

"O Lord Almighty, God of Abraham, Isaac, and Jacob, I stand in the gap now. I call upon the blood of the Lamb that speaks better things than the blood of Abel. Let every reader of this word, every listener to this prayer, whose parents or ancestors covenanted them to a piece of land, to a village shrine, to a family idol, or to a territorial spirit—BE RELEASED RIGHT NOW by the power in the blood of Jesus!

You spirit of the land holding them captive, RELEASE THEM! You shrine deity claiming their destiny, LET THEM GO! The blood of Jesus is your demand notice. You have no legal right. The document of covenant has been nailed to the cross. Colossians 2:14-15 is your eviction order!

All those who have been covenanted to spirit husbands or spirit wives in their dreams or through family rituals—BE RELEASED IN THE NAME OF JESUS! That demonic wedding is annulled! That phantom marriage is dissolved by the fire of the Holy Ghost! I command you to collect your wedding rings back, your spiritual tokens, your demonic jewelry, and GET OUT! You are not his wife! You are not her husband! You are the bride of Christ alone! COME OUT OF THAT COVENANT NOW!"

Keep repeating: **"I RELEASE MYSELF!"** until your spirit feels a shift, until you feel a lightness, until you know in your knower that something has broken.

---

2. THE PURGE OF POISON

Pray: "I VOMIT EVERY SATANIC POISON I HAVE SWALLOWED! IN THE NAME OF JESUS!"

We are not speaking of physical vomiting, but a spiritual expulsion. You have ingested poison. Not just through literal food sacrificed to idols, but through:

- The **poison of evil words** spoken over you at altars.
- The **poison of curses** mixed into your food or drink in the spirit.
- The **poison of demonic deposits** placed in your body through ritual incisions or sexual sin.
- The **poison of sinful entertainment** that defiled your soul.
- The **poison of ancestral iniquity** flowing in your spiritual bloodstream.

Revelation 3:16 says God will spew the lukewarm out of His mouth. Tonight, you are going to spew the demonic out of your system. The word "vomit" is violent. It is the body's emergency rejection of toxicity. Your spirit is now in emergency mode, rejecting every satanic toxin.

Pray this aggressively:

"Father, for all who have ever eaten food from the table of idols—whether at a traditional ceremony, a festival, or through dream eating—I call for Your fire! Let the fire of the Holy Ghost strike their stomachs now! Let it travel through their intestines, their bloodstream, their lymphatic system!

Let Your fire begin to torment every hidden spirit, every occult power, every demonic food deposit until they run out of their hiding places! Let the whole stomach, the whole digestive system, the whole body be packed full of the fire of God! Let the heat rise until every satanic poison is forced out—through the mouth, through the nose, through the ears, through the pores, through every possible opening!

I command every seed of idolatry, every egg of witchcraft, every larva of perversion, every viral curse planted through consumption to BURN TO ASHES and be FLUSHED OUT! Let the living water from the throne of God flow through my system as a spiritual detox! I am cleansed! I am purged! I am sanctified!"

Cough slightly if you need to. Prime the expulsion. Refuse to swallow your saliva for a moment, as a sign of rejecting the poison. Command it out!

---

3. THE CANCELLATION OF DEDICATION

Pray: "I CANCEL EVERY DEMONIC DEDICATION! IN THE NAME OF JESUS!"

Now repeat with holy anger: **"I CANCEL YOU! IN THE NAME OF JESUS!"**

A dedication is a setting apart. You were set apart for demons. Tonight, you cancel that setting apart and you are re-consecrated to God. You are using your God-given authority to revoke the dedication certificate signed in hell.

"All those reading this who have been dedicated to demons at birth, in childhood, or through any ritual—BE RELEASED IN THE NAME OF JESUS! That dedication to the river god is CANCELLED! That dedication to the god of iron is CANCELLED! That dedication to the family deity is CANCELLED!

All those who have ever carried sacrifices to the crossroads, who have poured libations, who have taken offerings to shrines—BE

RELEASED! The cross of Jesus is the only crossroads that has power! Every other crossroads altar is a fraud, a mockery of Calvary! I cancel your participation in it! The blood of Jesus washes away every guilt, every stain, every legal claim from those actions!

I am not a child of Ogun! I am not a servant of Sango! I am not a devotee of any river goddess! I AM A CHILD OF THE LIVING GOD! My dedication is to Yahweh alone! I cancel every other claim!"

---

4. THE SHATTERING OF EVIL AUTHORITY

(Keep your hands on your head. Feel the seat of your authority.)

Pray: "I BREAK EVERY EVIL AUTHORITY OVER MY LIFE! IN THE NAME OF JESUS!"

Now decree it to specific powers: **"I BREAK YOU! IN THE NAME OF JESUS!"**

Authority is the right to rule. These spirits have ruled areas of your life by the authority granted through covenants and dedications. You are now revoking that grant. You are dethroning them.

"Witchcraft authority operating over my life, my family, my destiny—BREAK IN THE NAME OF JESUS! Your spells are powerless! Your incantations are empty noise!

Spirit of infirmity and sickness, you have authority over my body no longer—BREAK! I revoke your license to make me sick!

Spirit of backwardness and stagnation, your authority to hold me down is BROKEN! I am moving forward!

Every serpentine spirit, python spirit, cobra spirit that has wrapped itself around my progress—BREAK YOUR HOLD! Loose me and let me go!

All those whose hair was cut for evil purposes, whose nail clippings were taken, whose personal items were used in rituals—BE RELEASED FROM THAT SYMBOLIC BONDAGE! Your hair has grown back in the spirit! Your identity is reclaimed! I break the power of every symbolic covenant made with your substance!"

---

5. THE TARGETED ANNIHILATION

Now, we get specific. We name the strongholds. For each of these four evil authorities, you will say the word **"BREAK!"** seven times. Seven is the number of completion, of perfection. You are completely and perfectly destroying these authorities.

A. "EVERY EVIL AUTHORITY OF FAMILY SHRINE OR IDOL—BREAK! BREAK! BREAK! BREAK! BREAK! BREAK! BREAK!"
That little god in your father's house, that idol passed down for generations—its authority over your lineage ends tonight. The shrine in your village compound—its voice is silenced.

B. "EVERY EVIL AUTHORITY OF WITCHCRAFT AND FAMILY SPIRITS—BREAK! BREAK! BREAK! BREAK! BREAK! BREAK! BREAK!"
The collective power of witchcraft in your family line. The familiar spirits that know your name. The ancestral spirits that demand worship. Their council is dissolved.

C. "EVERY EVIL AUTHORITY OF REMOTE CONTROL POWERS—BREAK! BREAK! BREAK! BREAK! BREAK! BREAK! BREAK!"
Spirits that manipulate you from afar. Spirits that use your photograph, your name, your belongings to afflict you. Their signals are jammed. Their remote is smashed.

D. "EVERY EVIL AUTHORITY OF THE STRONG MAN—BREAK! BREAK! BREAK! BREAK! BREAK! BREAK! BREAK!"
The arch-demon, the CEO of the oppression over your life. The one who coordinates the others. His backbone is snapped. His command center is in chaos.

With each "BREAK!", imagine a mighty hammer from heaven—the hammer of God's Word (**Jeremiah 23:29**)—smashing down on that authority. See it shatter into a million pieces.

---

6. THE RETURN-TO-SENDER ORDER

Finally, we send the packages back. You are not a dump site for demonic garbage.

Pray: "EVERY OWNER OF EVIL LOAD, CARRY YOUR LOAD! IN THE NAME OF JESUS!"

This is divine justice. **Galatians 6:5** says every man shall bear his own burden. The burdens placed on you by witchcraft, by curses, by altars—they are not yours to carry. They belong to the one who sent them.

"You spirit of sickness, this infirmity is your load. Carry it back to the sender! You spirit of poverty, this lack is your assignment. Take it back to the coven from whence it came! You spirit of failure, this

pattern of defeat is your merchandise. Return it to the altar that produced it!

I am not your mule! I am not your donkey! I refuse to carry what you designed for me. Every evil load of depression, anxiety, confusion, debt, barrenness, marital strife—I identify your owner. Now, owner of the load, come and pick up your property! Carry it away from my life, from my home, from my body!

Let every curse return to its roots! Let every spell revert to its caster! Let every demonic attachment be reattached to the one who sent it! I send it back now, in the name that is above every name—JESUS!"

Beloved, do you feel that? The atmosphere is shifting. The spiritual pressure is lifting. Chains are hitting the floor. Seals are breaking. Doors are swinging open. You have just engaged in a spiritual transaction of monumental proportions.

You have moved from being a *prisoner* of the altar to being a *prosecutor* of the altar. You have served legal documents written in the blood of Jesus. The case is closed in your favor.

This is just the beginning. This kind of warfare may need to be repeated. Strongholds don't always fall in one night. But tonight, a critical blow has been struck. The foundation of the prison has been cracked. The wall has been breached.

Walk out into the new air of your freedom. You are no longer defined by what was done at an altar. You are defined by what was done on the altar of Calvary. And that work is complete.

CHAPTER 05

DELIVERANCE FROM EVIL ALTARS: A CALL TO SPIRITUAL WARFARE

My beloved brothers and sisters in Christ, tonight we gather not as passive listeners but as active warriors. We come not to simply receive information but to engage in liberation. The title of this message is clear and direct: **DELIVERANCE FROM EVIL ALTARS**. This is not a theoretical discussion. This is a battle plan. This is our Exodus moment, where we confront the altars of Egypt and march toward our promised land of freedom.

Look with me at **Exodus 20:24-26**. God gives specific instructions: "*An altar of earth thou shalt make unto me... if thou wilt make me an altar of stone, thou shalt not build it of hewn stone... Neither shalt thou go up by steps unto mine altar...*" Why these details? Because God is holy, and His worship must be pure, undefiled by human manipulation or fleshly exposure. The altar to God is a place of humility, of raw materials offered as they are. But Satan, the great counterfeiter, has taken this holy concept and created perverse replicas—altars of manipulation, control, and destruction.

THE BATTLE OF MIZPEH: THE ALTAR THAT BRINGS VICTORY

Our foundation scripture is **1 Samuel 7:7-11**. Let me paint the scene for you:

The Philistines, archetypes of oppressive, demonic systems, are marching against Israel. Panic sets in. The people run to Samuel, their prophet, and they cry out with words we must remember: "*Cease not to cry unto the LORD our God for us, that he will save us out of the hand of the Philistines.*"

Notice what Samuel does. He doesn't just gather a prayer meeting. He doesn't only prophesy. **He goes straight to the altar.** "*And Samuel took a sucking lamb, and offered it for a burnt offering wholly unto the LORD: and Samuel cried unto the LORD for Israel; and the LORD heard him.*"

Here is the divine sequence:

1. **Recognition of the Enemy** (The Philistines are coming)
2. **Recourse to the Prophet/Priest** (They go to Samuel)
3. **Return to the Altar** (Samuel offers a sacrifice)
4. **Release of Heavenly Power** (The LORD thundered with a great thunder)

5. **Rout of the Enemy** (The Philistines were discomfited and smitten)

While Samuel was at the altar—while the smoke of the sacrifice was ascending—the enemy drew near. But God intervened from the place of accepted sacrifice. The altar became the artillery base from which heaven launched its attack.

Beloved, your deliverance from evil altars will not come from avoiding the spiritual realm; it will come from establishing a superior altar—the altar of your prayer life, the altar of your sacrifice of praise, the altar of your obedience—and from that position of strength, you demolish the altars of darkness.

The Holy Ghost has trained us in the expensive school of experience. We've learned that Satan will not politely hand over your stolen blessings. The kingdom of heaven suffers violence, and the violent take it by force (**Matthew 11:12**). It's time to move beyond "God, please bless me" prayers to "Devil, I command you to release what you've stolen" decrees.

THE NATURE OF THE CONFLICT: POSITIVE VS. NEGATIVE ALTARS

We must understand this dichotomy clearly.

Positive Altars are raised to the One True God:

- **The Altar of Prayer:** Where you meet with God. Is your prayer altar strong, or is it weak from neglect?
- **The Altar of Holiness:** Where the flesh is sacrificed. Is your holiness altar compromised?

- **The Altar of the Cross:** Where Jesus, the perfect Lamb, was sacrificed once for all. This is the ultimate positive altar, the source of all our authority.

Negative Altars are demonic counterfeits raised to steal, kill, and destroy (**John 10:10**). They are communication centers with hell. They are spiritual transaction points where:

- Names are submitted for monitoring.
- Curses are issued and sealed with sacrifices.
- Covenants are made to bind destinies.
- Blessings are intercepted and hijacked.

The enemy didn't invent this system; he corrupted it. He was in heaven, he saw how the altar of incense functioned before God's throne (**Revelation 8:3-4**). He understands the power of a dedicated place of spiritual exchange. Now, he has taught his agents—witchdoctors, shrine priests, family elders engaged in idolatry—to erect these perverted altars.

And for many of us, our problems are directly linked to traffic at these altars. Imagine a spiritual control room. On a screen is your name. A demon says, "Bring the file on [Your Name]." They pull it. "He's about to get a promotion. Send the spirit of sabotage." Another says, "She's about to be married. Activate the spirit of discord and the marine spouse." It's a traffic of assignments going up and down concerning your life. This is why you can be praying, yet feel blocked. The altar is working against you.

THE ENEMY'S ARSENAL: IDENTIFYING THE FORTIFICATIONS OF DARKNESS

Beloved congregation, we are at war. Not a war with flesh and blood, but a spiritual conflict of cosmic proportions. The Apostle

Paul didn't write Ephesians 6:12 as a metaphor—he wrote it as a battlefield report: "*For we wrestle not against flesh and blood, but against principalities, against powers, against the rulers of the darkness of this world, against spiritual wickedness in high places.*"

Tonight, I want to take you on a reconnaissance mission. Before Joshua could conquer Jericho, he sent spies to see the land. Before David could face Goliath, he had to identify the giant's armor. Before you can destroy the enemy's fortifications, you must recognize them. You cannot demolish what you refuse to acknowledge. You cannot liberate territory you don't know is occupied.

The enemy has established strongholds—local altars—across our lands, our families, and even in the spiritual realm connected to our lives. These are not mere superstitions; they are demonic installations with specific functions. Let us examine this arsenal, this demonic inventory, with the discerning eyes of the Spirit.

---

1. CROSSROADS ALTARS: THE BLASPHEMOUS PARODY

The crossroads—where two paths meet—has been perverted into one of Satan's most common altars. Why the crossroads? Because it's a place of decision, of intersection. But the enemy has corrupted this into a place of demonic summoning.

Spiritual Reality: At a crossroads altar, practitioners believe they can summon spirits from all four directions—north, south, east, west. That chicken you see with its throat slit, placed at a crossroads with candles? That's not just garbage. It's a demonic invitation. A summoning circle. They're calling upon territorial spirits to converge at that point to execute an assignment.

Biblical Parallel: In **Deuteronomy 27-28**, God commanded blessings from Mount Gerizim and curses from Mount Ebal. The enemy counterfeits this by calling curses from all directions at crossroads. But hear this: **The only cross with power is the cross of Calvary!** Every crossroads altar is a mockery of the place where Jesus' arms were stretched out to the north, south, east, and west to draw ALL humanity to Himself.

If you find a sacrifice at your doorstep or workplace, recognize it for what it is: a satanic subpoena. They're serving you papers from hell's court. But you have the right to refuse service! The blood of Jesus voids every demonic legal document.

---

2. TREE ALTARS: LIVING GATEWAYS OF DARKNESS

Throughout Scripture, trees have spiritual significance. The Tree of Life. The Tree of Knowledge of Good and Evil. Jesus cursed a fig tree. He said we'd know false prophets by their fruits.

But certain trees—especially ancient, massive ones like the Iroko, Baobab, or sacred groves—have become demonic gateways. Why? Because people have worshipped there for generations. That cloth tied around the tree? That's not decoration. It's an altar cloth. The tree has become a "high place" (**2 Kings 17:9-11**).

Spiritual Reality: Demonic spirits attach themselves to these trees. They become watching posts, listening devices, and snaring points. The Bible warns about worshipping under "every green tree" (**Jeremiah 3:6**). That's not just poetry—it's identifying actual centers of idolatry.

When you pass certain trees and feel sudden fear, depression, or dizziness, you may be passing a tree altar. Those spirits recognize the light of Christ in you and react. Don't just feel afraid—command that tree to be cut down in the spirit! Like Jesus said in **Luke 13:7**, "*Cut it down; why cumbereth it the ground?*"

---

3. ROCK ALTARS: DEMONIC PORTALS AND HIDDEN CITIES

The story shared earlier is not fantasy. Two prophetesses in church, one transports them into a rock where they see rooms, electronic equipment, kitchens. This reveals a terrifying reality: certain rocks, mountains, and caves are not just physical formations—they're demonic portals to hidden spiritual dimensions.

Biblical Foundation: In **Matthew 16:18**, Jesus said the gates of hell would not prevail against His church. The word "gates" implies an entry point. Rocks and caves have often been seen as entrances to the underworld in various cultures. Remember the demons begged Jesus not to send them into the "abyss" (**Luke 8:31**). These rock altars can be localized entry points to demonic dimensions.

Spiritual Reality: Just as Jacob saw a ladder between heaven and earth at Bethel (**Genesis 28**), these rock altars can function as "inverse Bethels"—connecting points between earth and dark spiritual realms. They're demonic headquarters in your region.

---

4. PHOTOGRAPH ALTARS: THE SPIRITUAL POINT OF CONTACT

This is one of the most common yet overlooked altars. Your photograph in the hands of someone with evil intent becomes more than paper—it becomes a spiritual point of contact.

Spiritual Principle: In the Bible, names carried power and identity. Your image similarly carries your spiritual signature. When an enemy takes your photograph to a shrine, places it before an idol, and begins to chant, they're establishing a direct link to your spirit. This is why you might suddenly feel oppressed when nothing has changed in your environment.

Biblical Example: Remember the teraphim—the household idols that Rachel stole from Laban (**Genesis 31**)? These weren't just statues; they were points of spiritual connection and inheritance. Your photograph used in this way becomes a modern teraphim.

If you've given someone a picture and now sense oppression, you need to break that linkage. Command every photograph of you in enemy hands to be supernaturally destroyed by fire from heaven.

---

5. IMAGE ALTARS (EFFIGIES): VOODOO IS REAL

An effigy—a doll, a carved image, a symbol made to represent you—isn't child's play. It's serious spiritual warfare.

Biblical Foundation: The Second Commandment forbids graven images for a reason beyond mere art criticism (**Exodus 20:4-5**). When you make an image for worship or manipulation, you open a door for spiritual transfer. The effigy becomes a spiritual receptacle that can be manipulated.

Spiritual Reality: What is done to the effigy in the spiritual realm affects the person it represents. Pins stuck in a doll's head translate to migraines. Binding the doll's hands translates to stagnation. This isn't magic—it's demonic manipulation through symbolic representation.

But here's your victory: **You are created in God's image (**Genesis 1:27**)**, not in the image of some doll! Your true spiritual identity cannot be captured or controlled by any effigy. Command every effigy representing you to explode in the fire of the Holy Ghost!

---

6. REPORTING ALTARS: THE SPIRITUAL TELEPHONE EXCHANGE

Imagine a dark room where demons gather around an altar, chanting your name continuously. This is a reporting altar—a spiritual telephone exchange where your name is dialed repeatedly, waiting for you to answer.

Spiritual Principle: In the spirit realm, when you answer to your name being called, you acknowledge the caller's right to communicate with you. This is why you might hear your name whispered when no one is there. It's a spiritual phishing attempt!

Biblical Example: When God called Samuel, he answered, "*Speak, for thy servant heareth*" (**1 Samuel 3:10**). That was a divine connection. But when demons call your name, they're seeking the same type of connection—a demonic one.

Your protection? **Isaiah 43:1**: "*Fear not: for I have redeemed thee, I have called thee by thy name; thou art mine.*" Only answer to the voice of your Shepherd (**John 10:27**). To every other voice, declare: "*I only answer to the name of Jesus Christ! My ears are deaf to every other call!*"

---

7. CLOTHING ALTARS: GARMENTS OF CURSING

Your clothing—especially intimate apparel—carries your spiritual signature more powerfully than almost anything else. Why? Because it touches your skin, absorbs your sweat, carries your scent and DNA.

Biblical Foundation: When the woman with the issue of blood touched Jesus' garment, virtue flowed from Him to her (**Matthew 9:20-22**). Spiritual transfer happens through garments. Conversely, when Achan took the "accursed thing"—a Babylonian garment—it brought a curse on all Israel (**Joshua 7**).

Spiritual Reality: If an enemy obtains a piece of your clothing—especially underwear—they have a powerful point of contact. They can weave spells into that fabric. They can tie knots while speaking curses. They can use it to create spiritual clones or attachments.

This is why you must be careful with laundry, with where you discard old clothes. Pray over new clothes before wearing them. And if you suspect your garments have been compromised, don't just throw them away—spiritually burn them with the fire of God in prayer before disposal.

---

8. RIVER/WATER ALTARS: THE MARINE KINGDOM

Across Africa and indeed many coastal regions, river and water altars are among the most powerful. Dedications to "Mami Wata," river goddesses, and marine spirits create profound bondage.

Biblical Perspective: Water spirits are real. In **Revelation 12:15**, the serpent spews water like a flood to destroy the woman. In **Luke 8**, the demons called "Legion" begged not to be sent into the "abyss"—often associated with watery depths.

Spiritual Reality: Many people are dedicated to water spirits as children. Others have made covenants at riversides for success, beauty, or power. These marine altars create spiritual spouses, financial drains (money flows like water away from you), and emotional turbulence.

But remember: **You have been baptized into Christ, not into river spirits!** The only water with saving power is the living water that flows from the throne of God (**Revelation 22:1**). Command every marine covenant to be dissolved in Jesus' name!

---

9. FOREST ALTARS: THE NOCTURNAL ASSEMBLY POINTS

Dark groves, deep forests—these have been places of pagan worship for millennia. The Bible repeatedly mentions "groves" in connection with idolatry (**1 Kings 14:23**).

Spiritual Reality: While you sleep, your enemies may be awake in forest altars, chanting your name, performing rituals against you. The forest provides secrecy and a connection to "nature spirits" or elemental demons.

These altars are where covens gather, where witches convene, where spells are woven under the cover of darkness. But greater is He that is in you than all the forest demons combined! Declare what Elisha declared: "*Lord, open his eyes that he may see*" (**2**

Kings 6:17). See the chariots of fire surrounding you, rendering every forest altar impotent!

---

10. ALTARS OF BODY PARTS: COVENANTS THROUGH BIOLOGICAL MATERIAL

This is perhaps the most invasive altar type. Your hair, nail clippings, placenta, blood, even bodily fluids—these contain your biological and spiritual signature.

Biblical Principle: The Nazirite vow involved not cutting hair as a sign of consecration to God (**Numbers 6**). Why? Because hair carried spiritual significance. When Absalom's hair was cut annually, it was weighed—showing its importance (**2 Samuel 14:26**).

Spiritual Reality: In many traditions, when a child's hair is first cut, the hair is carefully kept or ritually disposed of. Why? Because it can be used to covenant that child to spirits. Placenta burial under certain trees creates lifelong connections. Blood extracted during rituals creates unbreakable ties.

But hear this: **Your body is the temple of the Holy Spirit (**1 Corinthians 6:19**)**, not a collection of ritual components! Every part of you is sanctified by the blood of Jesus. Command every biological material taken from you to lose its power and connection to you!

---

11. ASTRAL ALTARS (STAR ALTARS): CURSES THROUGH THE HEAVENS

While astrology is condemned in Scripture (**Isaiah 47:13-14**), its demonic counterpart is very real. Astral altars are where your birth chart, your "star," is used to program curses against your destiny.

Spiritual Reality: Just as the wise men followed a star to Jesus (**Matthew 2**), demonic practitioners study stars to trace and influence destinies. They identify "weak points" in your astrological chart and launch spiritual attacks during certain planetary alignments.

But you are not under the stars—you are under the God who created the stars! **Psalm 147:4** says He counts and names the stars. Declare that your destiny is written in the Lamb's Book of Life, not in the stars! Command every astral curse to be nullified!

---

12. ALTARS OF EVIL TRANSFER: SPIRITUAL ROBBERY

These are specialized altars where your virtues, anointing, success, or blessings are siphoned and transferred to another person.

Biblical Example: This is what Saul tried to do to David—steal his anointing. This is what Jacob did to Esau—transferred the birthright. This is what the witch of Endor did—brought up Samuel to give Saul direction he'd lost access to.

Spiritual Reality: Through rituals, your spiritual "assets" can be hijacked. That's why someone might suddenly rise as you fall, succeed where you fail, prosper while you struggle—without any logical explanation. It's spiritual transfer.

But declare with Job: "*The LORD gave, and the LORD hath taken away; blessed be the name of the LORD*" (**Job 1:21**). Only God has the right to give and take what is yours! Command every transfer altar to reverse its flow! Demand a sevenfold return of everything stolen!

---

13. THE FAMILY SHRINE: THE GENERATIONAL STRONGHOLD

This is arguably the most potent altar for many believers. That idol in the family house, that shrine passed down for generations, is not just an artifact—it's an active monitoring station.

Spiritual Reality: Through the family shrine, ancestral spirits monitor the entire lineage. They enforce covenants made by forefathers. They punish those who abandon family "traditions." They claim ownership of every child born into that family.

This is why you can be born again, Spirit-filled, yet still struggle with certain patterns. The family shrine is the headquarters of the "strong man" over your bloodline (**Matthew 12:29**).

But you have been translated from the kingdom of darkness into the kingdom of God's dear Son (**Colossians 1:13**)! You are no longer under the jurisdiction of the family shrine. You are under the bloodline of Jesus! Command the family shrine to lose all authority over your life!

---

14. PHYSICAL ALTARS: THE LITERAL DEMONIC ALTAR

We must not spiritualize this away: there are literal, physical altars of stone, mud, or wood where demonic priests minister. These might be in hidden groves, secret rooms, or even disguised as innocent-looking objects.

Biblical Mandate: God commanded Israel to destroy the altars of the Canaanites (**Exodus 34:13**). Not ignore them, not pray about them—destroy them!

Spiritual Reality: These physical altars are power points where demonic energy is concentrated. They're recharge stations for evil spirits. They're where curses are concocted and launched.

You may never see these physical altars, but in the spirit, you can target them. Like Elijah on Carmel, you can call fire down on every physical altar raised against you.

---

15. ALTARS OF CURSES: THE RITUAL SEALING OF SPOKEN WORDS

The story of the bus driver with the viper's tooth illustrates this perfectly. Spoken words alone have power, but when ritualistically sealed at an altar, they become exponentially more potent.

Biblical Truth: Death and life are in the power of the tongue (**Proverbs 18:21**). Curses spoken by someone in authority or with spiritual knowledge can indeed affect reality.

Spiritual Reality: At altars of curses, spoken words are mixed with sacrifices, sealed with blood or ritual actions, and launched like spiritual missiles. They travel until they find their target.

But you have a better covenant! **Galatians 3:13**: "*Christ hath redeemed us from the curse of the law...*" Every curse launched against you must pass through the filter of Calvary. At the cross, every curse was transformed. Declare that every curse is returning to its sender with sevenfold force!

Beloved, this is not meant to frighten you, but to enlighten you. The enemy's arsenal is extensive, but our Lord's armory is infinite. You now know the enemy's fortifications. You've seen his playbook. You've identified his strongholds.

Armed with this knowledge, you are no longer fighting an invisible, unknown foe. You see his fortifications. You recognize his tactics. And with the name of Jesus, the blood of the Lamb, and the Word of your testimony, you are more than equipped to demolish every altar, plunder every stronghold, and reclaim every inch of territory Satan has stolen.

The reconnaissance is complete. Now comes the assault. Now comes the victory.

THE WAY OF VICTORY: THE SEVEN-STRATEGY BATTLE PLAN

Beloved family, soldiers of the Most High God, we have completed our reconnaissance. We have surveyed the enemy's territory. We have identified his fortifications—the crossroads altars, the tree altars, the river altars, the family shrines, the entire demonic arsenal arrayed against our lives and destinies. Knowledge without application is torment. Revelation without implementation is frustration.

But tonight, we transition from intelligence gathering to active engagement. We move from knowing *what* we're fighting to knowing *how* to fight. The Apostle Paul didn't just tell us about our enemies in Ephesians 6; he gave us a complete battle plan: the whole armor of God.

I present to you now not just principles, but a proven, biblical, seven-strategy approach to total victory over every evil altar. This is not theory. This is battlefield-tested spiritual warfare. This is how the giants of faith brought down strongholds. This is how you will walk in complete deliverance.

STRATEGY 1: RECOGNIZE THEIR OPERATIONS – THE EYES OF THE SPIRIT

The first casualty in any war is often truth. The enemy's primary weapon is deception. He wants you to call a demonic attack "bad luck." He wants you to label a generational curse "family tendency." He wants you to spiritualize a satanic blockade as "God's will" or "divine timing."

Biblical Mandate: *"Lest Satan should get an advantage of us: for we are not ignorant of his devices"* **(2 Corinthians 2:11)**. Ignorance is not innocence; it is vulnerability. God expects us to know the enemy's strategies.

How to Implement This:

- **Become a Spiritual Detective:** Examine the patterns in your life. Does failure consistently happen at the edge of breakthrough? Do relationships collapse at the same point? Does financial increase always evaporate? These aren't coincidences—they are signatures. They reveal the *modus operandi* of the spirit working against you.
- **Trace the Source:** Like a physician diagnosing an illness, trace the symptom to its root. That persistent sickness—

could it be linked to a river altar dedication from childhood? That marital strife—could it be connected to a traditional wedding ceremony that invoked idols? That business failure—could the land be a former shrine?

- **Document the Evidence:** Keep a spiritual journal. Record your dreams, your struggles, the timing of attacks. Patterns will emerge. The Holy Spirit will connect dots for you. As **John 16:13** says, the Spirit of truth will guide you into *all* truth—including truths about what's operating against you.

Recognition is the first act of war. When you stop saying "Why does this keep happening to me?" and start declaring "I recognize the spirit behind this pattern, and I command it to cease!"—you have taken your first victorious step.

STRATEGY 2: REPENT FOR ANY INVOLVEMENT – THE CLEANSING OF THE SOLDIER

You cannot effectively fight an enemy you're secretly in covenant with. You cannot break an agreement you're still honoring, even if unconsciously. Repentance is not weakness; it is the strategic severing of enemy supply lines.

Biblical Foundation: "*If I regard iniquity in my heart, the Lord will not hear me*" **(Psalm 66:18)**. Unconfessed sin, especially involvement with idolatry, gives the enemy legal ground. It's like leaving a spare key under your mat for a thief.

How to Implement This:

- **Personal Repentance:** Search your heart ruthlessly. Have you ever, in fear or ignorance:

  - Participated in a traditional ceremony "just to keep peace"?
  - Worn charms or talismans for "protection"?
  - Consulted diviners or fortune-tellers?
  - Eaten food you knew was sacrificed to idols?
  - Used traditional medicine involving incantations or rituals?

  Repent specifically. Name the act. Feel the grief of having dishonored God.
- **Generational Repentance:** Stand in the gap for your bloodline. As Daniel prayed in **Daniel 9:4-19**, confess the sins of your fathers. "Father, I repent on behalf of my grandfather who consulted the oracle. I repent for my grandmother who dedicated her children at the river. I repent for every altar built, every sacrifice made, every covenant established by my ancestors that has opened doors to darkness in my lineage."
- **Renounce the Benefits:** Some covenants brought temporary benefits—protection, success, favor. You must renounce these demonic benefits. "Lord, I reject every blessing that came from an evil altar. I would rather have Your delayed blessing than the devil's premature provision."

Repentance cleanses your spiritual uniform. It ensures you approach the battle in righteousness, not in mixture. A clean soldier is a confident soldier.

STRATEGY 3: RENOUNCE THEM PUBLICLY – THE DECLARATION OF INDEPENDENCE

In the spirit realm, silence is agreement. What you do not renounce, you endorse. Renunciation is the legal revocation of demonic contracts. It is you standing before the court of heaven and hell and announcing: "This covenant is null and void!"

Biblical Precedent: In **Acts 19:18-19**, new believers "came, and confessed, and shewed their deeds. Many of them also which used curious arts brought their books together, and burned them before all men." Public renunciation! They didn't quietly stop practicing magic; they made a spectacle of their break with darkness.

How to Implement This:

- **Verbalize Your Renunciation:** Open your mouth and speak to the spirit realm. "I renounce, revoke, and declare null and void every covenant, oath, pact, or agreement made on my behalf or by my ancestors at any altar, shrine, river, forest, or crossroads. I renounce my dedication to [name the spirit]. I renounce the covenant of protection from the family idol. I renounce every spiritual marriage. By the authority in the blood of Jesus, I cancel every signature, every mark, every token."
- **Be Specific:** The more specific your renunciation, the more effective. Don't just say "all altars." Name the types you recognize: "I renounce the crossroads altar operating in my village. I renounce the river altar where I was dedicated. I renounce the family shrine in my compound."
- **Do It Audibly:** The spiritual realm responds to spoken words. **Proverbs 18:21**: "*Death and life are in the power of the tongue.*" Your renunciation is a death sentence to demonic claims over your life.

This is your spiritual Declaration of Independence. You are serving the enemy with eviction papers written in the blood of Jesus.

STRATEGY 4: RESIST THEM WITH THE WORD – THE SWORD OF THE SPIRIT

You cannot fight spiritual battles with natural weapons. Your opinions, your feelings, your arguments are useless against principalities. You need a divine weapon: the living Word of God.

Biblical Arsenal: "*And take the helmet of salvation, and the sword of the Spirit, which is the word of God*" **(Ephesians 6:17)**. This is not just carrying a Bible; it is wielding specific Scriptures like a skilled swordsman.

How to Implement This:

- **Scriptural Bullets Against Altars:**
    - Against generational altars: "*Christ hath redeemed us from the curse of the law...*" **(Galatians 3:13)**.
    - Against idolatrous altars: "*Thou shalt have no other gods before me...*" **(Exodus 20:3)**.
    - Against curses from altars: "*No weapon formed against thee shall prosper...*" **(Isaiah 54:17)**.
    - Against demonic priests: "*Let God arise, let his enemies be scattered...*" **(Psalm 68:1)**.
    - Against territorial altars: "*He hath delivered us from the power of darkness, and hath translated us into the kingdom of his dear Son*" **(Colossians 1:13)**.
- **The "It Is Written" Protocol:** When Jesus was tempted, He didn't argue with Satan; He said, "*It is written...*" **(Matthew 4:4, 7, 10)**. This is the model. When

you feel the oppression of an altar, don't just complain—declare Scripture. "It is written: I am seated with Christ in heavenly places, far above all principality and power! Therefore, every altar under the earth is under my feet!"

- **Personalize the Promises:** Turn Scripture into first-person decrees. Don't just say "God is a refuge"; declare "You, O Lord, are *my* refuge and fortress! Therefore, no altar-formed storm can overwhelm me!" **(Psalm 91:2)**.

The Word in your mouth becomes a hammer that shatters rocks **(Jeremiah 23:29)**. Those rocks include stone altars!

STRATEGY 5: KILL THE PRIESTS AT THE ALTAR – THE ELIJAH ANOINTING

This is where many believers falter. We're comfortable binding spirits, but hesitant to confront their human agents. Yet, Scripture is clear: for complete deliverance, you must deal with the priesthood maintaining the altar.

Biblical Precedent: When Elijah confronted the prophets of Baal on Mount Carmel, he didn't just pray for God to ignore them. After God answered by fire, Elijah commanded: "*Take the prophets of Baal; let not one of them escape. And they took them: and Elijah brought them down to the brook Kishon, and slew them there*" **(1 Kings 18:40)**. Radical? Yes. Necessary? Absolutely.

How to Implement This (In Prayer):

- **Identify the Priesthood:** In the spirit, discern who is ministering against you. Is it a living witchdoctor? A family elder maintaining the shrine? A marine priest? A coven of witches? You may not know their natural names, but you can address their spiritual office.

- **Pray for Divine Judgment:** This is not about personal vengeance; it's about enforcing God's justice. Pray as the martyrs did in **Revelation 6:10**: *"How long, O Lord, holy and true, dost thou not judge and avenge our blood on them that dwell on the earth?"*
- **Decree Specific Judgments:**
    - "Let every priest ministering at altars against me be struck with the blindness of the men of Sodom **(Genesis 19:11)**!"
    - "Let the sword they've drawn against me fall upon their own heads **(Psalm 7:16)**!"
    - "Let their own snares capture them, let them fall into the pits they've dug for me **(Psalm 57:6)**!"
    - "Let their tongues cleave to the roof of their mouths, let their incantations turn to silence **(Psalm 137:6)**!"
- **Call for Their Conversion or Removal:** Pray: "Father, either save them by Your mighty power, or remove them from the earth. Let their altars be left without priests, their shrines without attendants!"

This is serious warfare prayer. It requires holy boldness. But remember: these priests are actively working to destroy lives, families, and destinies. Your prayer is an intervention for the innocent.

STRATEGY 6: WITHDRAW YOUR SPIRITUAL ASSETS – THE GREAT RECLAMATION

Your name, your blessings, your health, your prosperity, your anointing—these are spiritual assets. At evil altars, demons often act as custodians of what rightfully belongs to you. They hold them in demonic escrow, releasing just enough to keep you alive but never thriving.

Biblical Principle: "*I will restore to you the years that the locust hath eaten...*" **(Joel 2:25)**. Restoration implies something was taken. Withdrawal is the act of taking it back.

How to Implement This:

- **The Withdrawal Prayer (Hand on head):** "I withdraw my name from every evil altar, in the name of Jesus! Remove my name from every demonic register, every satanic ledger, every scroll of affliction!"
- **Withdraw Specific Blessings:**
    - Hand on chest: "I withdraw my health from every infirmity altar!"
    - Hand on head: "I withdraw my mental clarity from every altar of confusion!"
    - Hands outstretched: "I withdraw my financial prosperity from every poverty altar!"
    - Hands on womb/stomach: "I withdraw my fertility and children's destinies from every altar of barrenness and destruction!"
- **Visualize the Withdrawal:** See in the spirit your blessings being released from dark storehouses. See your name being erased from demonic lists. See angels of God carrying your possessions back to you.
- **Issue Receipts:** "I acknowledge receipt in the spirit of all my withdrawn assets! I now possess what the enemy has withheld!"

This is not begging God to give you something new; it's commanding the release of what is already yours in Christ but has been held captive.

STRATEGY 7: DESTROY THE ALTAR ITSELF – THE FINAL DEMOLITION

Binding spirits is good, but if you leave the altar standing, new spirits will come to occupy it **(Matthew 12:43-45)**. You must demolish the structure itself.

Biblical Blueprint: The prophet in **1 Kings 13:1-5** didn't pray about the altar; he spoke directly to it: "*O altar, altar, thus saith the LORD... the altar shall be rent, and the ashes poured out.*" He addressed the inanimate object because in the spirit, it was animate—a living point of demonic contact.

How to Implement This:

- **Address the Altar Directly:** "You altar of [name location/purpose], hear the word of the Lord! Your foundation is cursed. Your stones are scattered. Your fire is quenched. Your covenant is broken. Be dismantled now!"
- **Call for Elemental Destruction:**
    - **Fire:** "Let the fire of God fall and consume you to ashes!" (As on Carmel)
    - **Earthquake:** "Let the earthquake of the Spirit split you apart and swallow you!" (As when God's presence shook Sinai)
    - **Water:** "Let the flood of God's judgment wash you away!" (As in Noah's day)
    - **Wind:** "Let the whirlwind of God scatter your pieces to desolate places!" (As with Job's trial)
- **Salt the Ground:** As Elisha salted the waters of Jericho **(2 Kings 2:21)**, declare: "I salt the ground of this altar with the covenant of God's eternal Word. Nothing shall ever

grow here again—no demonic plant, no recurrent problem, no resurrected curse!"

- **Plant the Cross:** "Upon the ruins of this altar, I plant the cross of Jesus Christ! This ground is now redeemed by the blood! It is now a place of prayer and testimony to the living God!"

The Question Stands: Are you ready to deal with evil altars? This is not a one-time prayer. This is a campaign. Some altars, especially ancient family or territorial ones, may require sustained, violent prayer over days or weeks. You may need to fast. You may experience intensified warfare as the enemy fights to keep his ground.

But I ask you again: **DO YOU WANT TO BE FREE?** Then you must want it more than you want comfort. More than you want the approval of family who may not understand. More than you want to avoid spiritual conflict.

The weapons of our warfare are not carnal, but mighty through God to the pulling down of strongholds **(2 Corinthians 10:4)**. You have just been handed the divine blueprint for that demolition.

The recognition, the repentance, the renunciation, the resistance, the removal of priests, the withdrawal of assets, the final demolition—this is the complete victory cycle.

Now, soldier, to your post. The battle is yours to fight. The victory is yours to claim. The altar is yours to destroy. And the freedom is yours to walk in forever.

THE PRAYER ASSAULT: THE BATTLE CRY OF DELIVERANCE

Church, family, warriors of the Most High God—we are at the moment of engagement. All the teaching, all the revelation, all the understanding of the enemy's arsenal means nothing if we do not now take up the weapons of our warfare and storm the gates of hell. This is not a time for quiet meditation. This is not a moment for polite requests. This is the hour of violent faith, of holy aggression, of taking back by force what the enemy has stolen.

Listen to me carefully: **If you are not willing to pray with everything in you—with your voice, with your spirit, with your whole being—then you might as well remain seated in silence.** This is not a game. This is not a religious exercise. This is life-and-death spiritual combat for your destiny, for your family, for your future. The devil has played for keeps; now you must pray for keeps.

Get ready. Stand up on your feet if you are able. If you cannot stand, sit up straight. Square your shoulders as a soldier would. Lift your head—you are not a slave begging for mercy; you are a son or daughter enforcing your inheritance. You are about to address the powers of hell not as a victim, but as a victor. Not with your own authority, but with the all-powerful name that is above every name—the name of JESUS.

Take a deep breath. Fill your lungs with the breath of the Holy Spirit. Now, we pray. And we pray not *about* the problem, but *to* the problem. Not *around* the altar, but *against* the altar itself.

PRAYER 1: THE NEUTRALIZATION DECREE

"I RENDER EVERY AGGRESSIVE ALTAR IMPOTENT, IN THE NAME OF JESUS!"

Say it! Mean it! **"I RENDER EVERY AGGRESSIVE ALTAR IMPOTENT, IN THE NAME OF JESUS!"**

What does it mean to render something impotent? It means to strip it of power, to make it ineffective, to neutralize its potency. You are declaring that every altar that has been aggressively working against you—the altar that never sleeps, the altar where your name is mentioned daily, the altar that fires arrows at your progress—is now POWERLESS.

Biblical Foundation: In **Colossians 2:15**, it says that Jesus "*having spoiled principalities and powers, he made a shew of them openly, triumphing over them in it.*" The word "spoiled" means He stripped them, disarmed them, rendered them impotent. You are enforcing that finished work.

Visualize in the spirit: Every demonic altar that has been a power station against your life—its circuits are frying, its generators are failing, its connections are shorting out. It is now a dead monument, a useless pile of stones. Its fire is cold. Its voice is silent. Its influence is null.

PRAYER 2: THE DISGRACE DECLARATION

"EVERY EVIL ALTAR ERECTED AGAINST ME AND MY FAMILY, BE DISGRACED, IN JESUS' NAME!"

Shout it! **"BE DISGRACED!"**

You are calling for public, spiritual humiliation. In the ancient world, to be disgraced meant your enemies would mock you, your allies would abandon you, your power would be visibly broken.

Biblical Precedent: Remember Dagon, the Philistine idol? When the Ark of God was placed before it, **1 Samuel 5:3-4** records: "*And when they of Ashdod arose early on the morrow, behold, Dagon was fallen upon his face to the earth before the ark of the LORD... and the head of Dagon and both the palms of his hands were cut off upon the threshold; only the stump of Dagon was left to him.*" That is disgrace! The idol was face down, headless, handless—publicly shamed before the presence of God.

Decree that every altar working against you experiences its "Dagon moment." Let its fire be extinguished in the sight of the demons who tend it. Let its sacrifices be rejected and rot before they can be consumed. Let the spirits who minister there laugh at its impotence and abandon it. A disgraced altar is an abandoned altar.

PRAYER 3: THE NULLIFICATION COMMAND

"ANYTHING DONE AGAINST MY LIFE UNDER DEMONIC ANOINTING, BE NULLIFIED, IN THE NAME OF JESUS!"

Declare it with authority! **"BE NULLIFIED!"**

"Demonic anointing" is a real and terrible thing. It's the counterfeit power that energizes curses, spells, and rituals. It's the unholy unction upon the words of a witch doctor, upon the herbs of a native doctor, upon the incantations of a shrine priest. That anointing gives their words and actions supernatural potency.

But you are canceling the very power source of their operations. To nullify is to make legally void, to invalidate, to cancel out.

Biblical Authority: Isaiah 8:10 declares: "*Take counsel together, and it shall come to nought; speak the word, and it shall not stand: for God is with us.*" The plans made at demonic altars are "counsel together." The curses spoken are "the word." You are decreeing that they come to NOUGHT. They shall NOT STAND.

Every ritual performed with your name, every symbolic action done with your photograph or belongings, every curse sealed with blood at an altar—I command the demonic anointing upon those actions to be VACATED. Let their power be drained away like water into sand. Let their words become empty noise, their actions meaningless gestures.

PRAYER 4: THE RIGHTEOUS CURSE

"I CURSE EVERY LOCAL ALTAR FASHIONED AGAINST ME, IN THE NAME OF JESUS!"

This is bold, biblical, and necessary. Understand this: you are not cursing people; you are cursing demonic structures, systems, and installations. You are pronouncing God's judgment on the works of darkness.

Biblical Model: The prophet in **1 Kings 13:2** cried against the altar at Bethel: "*O altar, altar, thus saith the LORD...*" He spoke directly to the inanimate object because in the spirit, it was an active entity, a point of satanic contact. He pronounced its destruction.

You are doing the same. You are addressing:

- The crossroads altar: "I curse you!"

- The river altar: "I curse you!"
- The family shrine: "I curse you!"
- The marketplace altar: "I curse you!"
- The forest altar: "I curse you!"
- The astral altar: "I curse you!"

Foundation: Proverbs 26:2 says, *"As the bird by wandering, as the swallow by flying, so the curse causeless shall not come."* Your curse is NOT causeless. These altars have CAUSED affliction, bondage, and theft in your life. You are issuing a righteous, judicial curse upon them. You are calling for divine justice to dismantle them.

PRAYER 5: THE DIVINE HAMMER

"LET THE HAMMER OF THE ALMIGHTY GOD SMASH EVERY EVIL ALTAR ERECTED AGAINST ME, IN JESUS NAME!"

Visualize this! See in the spirit the mighty hammer of God—not a carpenter's hammer, but the sledgehammer of divine judgment.

Biblical Imagery: Jeremiah 23:29: *"Is not my word like as a fire? saith the LORD; and like a hammer that breaketh the rock in pieces?"* The Word is God's hammer. And **Daniel 2:34-35** shows the stone cut without hands that smashes the great image to pieces, becoming a great mountain that fills the whole earth.

That stone is Christ. You are that stone in Christ's hand, His hammer of judgment. See God's hammer rising and falling upon:

- The altar of sickness—SMASHED!
- The altar of poverty—SHATTERED!
- The altar of marital strife—PULVERIZED!
- The altar of stagnation—CRUSHED TO DUST!

Feel the impact in the spirit. Hear the sound of breaking stone, splintering wood, crumbling earth. Every altar is being reduced to irreparable fragments.

PRAYER 6: THE HEAVENLY FIRE

"O LORD, SEND YOUR FIRE TO DESTROY EVERY EVIL ALTAR FASHIONED AGAINST ME, IN THE NAME OF JESUS!"

Now you are calling for the element of divine purity and judgment—FIRE.

Biblical Precedent: On Mount Carmel, Elijah prayed and "*the fire of the LORD fell, and consumed the burnt sacrifice, and the wood, and the stones, and the dust, and licked up the water that was in the trench*" (**1 Kings 18:38**). God's fire consumed even the stones of the altar!

Call for that same fire—not natural fire, but the fire of God's holy presence that consumes everything unlike Him. Let it fall on:

- The hidden altar in the forest—let it be a raging inferno!
- The underwater river altar—let the water boil and the altar melt!
- The family shrine in the compound—let it be ash by morning!
- The altar in the market—let traders see supernatural flames and run!

This fire does not just burn; it SANCTIFIES the ground. Where the altar stood, it now becomes holy ground, purified by God's fire.

PRAYER 7: TARGETING THE PRIESTHOOD (PART 1)

"EVERY EVIL PRIEST MINISTERING AGAINST ME AT THE EVIL ALTAR, RECEIVE THE SWORD OF GOD, IN THE NAME OF JESUS!"

Shift your focus from the altar to the ministers. Every altar has attendants—human or demonic priests who maintain it, offer sacrifices, and chant incantations.

Biblical Justice: Psalm 35:5-6: "*Let the angel of the LORD chase them... let their way be dark and slippery: and let the angel of the LORD persecute them.*"

You are calling for divine law enforcement. Let the angel of the Lord, with the sword of God, pursue every priest who has taken your case to an altar. Let the sword of the Spirit—the Word of God—pierce their operations, their minds, their very spirits.

Whether it's the native doctor in your village, the witch in your family, or the marine priest at the coast—let the sword of God find its mark. Let their ritual knives turn against them. Let their incantations become their own indictment.

PRAYER 8: TARGETING THE PRIESTHOOD (PART 2)

"LET THE THUNDER OF GOD SMITE EVERY EVIL PRIEST WORKING AGAINST ME ON THE EVIL ALTAR AND BURN THEM TO ASHES, IN THE NAME OF JESUS!"

Increase the intensity! Thunder represents God's terrifying, irresistible power. It is His voice of judgment (**Psalm 29:3-9**).

Biblical Example: When the Philistines captured the Ark, they placed it in the house of Dagon. God didn't just tip the idol; He smote the people of Ashdod with tumors (**1 Samuel 5:6**). Divine retribution came upon the priests and people serving the idol.

Decree that the thunder of God—His powerful, judicial voice—strikes every evil priest. Not just a setback, but complete consumption: "BURN THEM TO ASHES." Let their physical bodies, their influence, their occult knowledge be reduced to nothing. Let them become a warning to others.

PRAYER 9: THE FINAL JUDGMENT ON THE PRIESTHOOD

"LET EVERY SATANIC PRIEST MINISTERING AGAINST ME AT EVIL ALTARS FALL DOWN AND DIE, IN THE NAME OF JESUS!"

This is the ultimate spiritual judgment. This is warfare prayer at its most intense.

Biblical Precedent: In **Acts 5:1-10**, Ananias and Sapphira fell down and died for lying to the Holy Spirit. Peter didn't pray for them to get sick; he pronounced judgment, and it happened. In **Acts 13:11**, Paul told Elymas the sorcerer, "*Behold, the hand of the Lord is upon thee, and thou shalt be blind,*" and immediately he was blinded.

You are operating in that apostolic, judicial anointing. You are declaring the consequence of opposing God's anointed. These priests have declared war on a child of the King. Let the sentence be executed.

This is not hatred; this is divine justice. It is the removal of cancerous cells to save the body. Pray with a clean heart, free from personal vengeance, but full of holy zeal for God's kingdom to advance.

PRAYER 10: THE PREEMPTIVE DEFENSE

"ANY HAND THAT WANTS TO RETALIATE OR ARREST ME BECAUSE OF ALL THESE PRAYERS I AM PRAYING, DRY UP AND WITHER IN THE NAME OF JESUS!"

When you attack the kingdom of darkness, it will counter-attack. They will try to "arrest" you—spiritually detain you, bring new accusations, launch fresh assaults. They will "retaliate"—seek vengeance.

But you are nullifying their counter-offensive before it begins.

Biblical Example: 1 Kings 13:4 – When King Jeroboam stretched out his hand from the altar, saying, "Lay hold on him!" (the prophet), his hand dried up and he could not pull it back. God defended His prophet.

Decree the same defense over yourself. Every hand raised to curse you in response to your prayers—let it wither. Every spiritual warrant for your arrest—let it be torn up. Every retaliation planned in secret meetings—let it backfire on the planners.
You are building a wall of fire around yourself (**Zechariah 2:5**). No retaliatory strike can penetrate it.

NOW PAUSE!

Don't rush on. The enemy is in disarray. The altars are smoking ruins. The priests are fleeing or falling.

SING A SONG OF VIOLENT PRAISE! Shout "HALLELUJAH!" with all your might. Clap your hands. Stamp your feet. Do a victory dance!

Why? **Psalm 149:6-9** says: "*Let the high praises of God be in their mouth, and a twoedged sword in their hand; To execute vengeance upon the heathen, and punishments upon the people; To bind their kings with chains, and their nobles with fetters of iron; To execute upon them the judgment written: this honour have all his saints. Praise ye the LORD.*"

Your praise is a weapon! It confuses the enemy's camp. It establishes God's presence on the battlefield. It's the sound of victory before the war is fully over. SING LOUDER THAN YOU PRAYED!

PRAYER 11: THE BOOMERANG DECREE

"EVERY STUBBORN EVIL ALTAR PRIEST, DRINK YOUR OWN BLOOD, IN THE NAME OF JESUS!"

After praise, return to the fray with this powerful decree. You are turning their own weapons against them.

Biblical Principle: Psalm 7:15-16: "*He made a pit, and digged it, and is fallen into the ditch which he made. His mischief shall return upon his own head, and his violent dealing shall come down upon his own pate.*"

The blood they have shed in sacrifices—let them be forced to drink it. The poisons they have prepared for others—let them ingest them. The curses they have spoken—let those words lodge in their own organs.

This is poetic justice. This is the law of spiritual reciprocity in operation. Let every stubborn priest who refuses to cease their operations experience the full taste of their own medicine.

PRAYER 12: THE POSSESSION PROCLAMATION
"I POSSESS MY POSSESSION STOLEN BY THE EVIL ALTAR, IN JESUS' NAME!"

Finally, you shift from pure defense and destruction to OFFENSE and RECOVERY. This is the triumphant declaration of repossession.

Biblical Foundation: Obadiah 1:17: *"But upon mount Zion shall be deliverance, and there shall be holiness; and the house of Jacob shall possess their possessions."*

What are your possessions that altars have stolen?

- Your health
- Your prosperity
- Your marital joy
- Your children's destinies
- Your mental peace
- Your spiritual vitality
- Your divine opportunities
- Your time, your years, your seasons

You are not asking for them; you are possessing them. You are laying claim to what is rightfully yours in Christ. See in the spirit angels carrying back to you what was taken. See doors of opportunity swinging open. See health flooding your body. See financial channels unclogging.

Declare with confidence: **"I POSSESS MY HEALTH NOW! I POSSESS MY WEALTH NOW! I POSSESS MY FAMILY NOW! I POSSESS MY DESTINY NOW! EVERYTHING THE ALTAR STOLE, I RECOVER IT NOW IN JESUS' NAME!"**

Beloved, you have just completed a spiritual assault of monumental proportions. You have not merely prayed; you have prophesied. You have not just requested; you have commanded. You have addressed altars, priests, and powers directly. Heaven has recorded your decrees. Hell has felt the impact.

Now, walk in the victory you have proclaimed. Guard your freedom. Maintain your deliverance with consistent prayer, the Word, and holy living. You are no longer a prisoner of altars. You are a destroyer of altars. The same power that raised Christ from the dead has worked in you tonight.

Go, and live as the free person you truly are.

THE GREAT WITHDRAWAL: THE DIVINE REPOSSESSION

Church, family, heirs of the Kingdom—we have arrived at the moment of reclamation. We have waged war, we have demolished strongholds, we have scattered the enemy's camp. But victory is not complete until what was stolen is recovered. Deliverance is not finished until the plunder is possessed.

Listen to me: The children of Israel didn't just walk out of Egypt; they **spoiled the Egyptians** (**Exodus 12:36**). They went out with the wealth of their oppressors. David didn't just defeat the Amalekites; he **recovered all** (**1 Samuel 30:19**). Every person, every possession, every piece of livestock.

This is where we are now. This is the Great Withdrawal. You are about to spiritually repossess everything the enemy has held in demonic escrow, everything that has been intercepted at evil altars, everything that has been locked in satanic storehouses.

Get into position. This is physical because we are spiritual beings. Your body is participating in this spiritual transaction.

Place your right hand firmly on your head. Your head is the seat of your identity, your authority, your mind, your will. This is where your name is spiritually inscribed. This is where your thoughts are processed. This is where your decisions are made. Your hand on your head symbolizes you taking authority over your own identity and destiny.

WITHDRAWAL 1: THE NAME WITHDRAWAL

"I WITHDRAW MY NAME FROM EVERY EVIL ALTAR, IN THE NAME OF JESUS!"

Say it with conviction! **"I WITHDRAW MY NAME!"**

Your name is not just a label; it is your spiritual signature. In ancient cultures, to know someone's name was to have power over them. Throughout Scripture, names carry destiny and identity. Abram became Abraham. Jacob became Israel. Saul became Paul.

Biblical Foundation: Revelation 3:5 promises: "*He that overcometh... I will not blot out his name out of the book of life, but I will confess his name before my Father, and before his angels.*" Your name is written in the Lamb's Book of Life. But the enemy has counterfeit books—demonic ledgers where they record names for destruction, for monitoring, for assignment.

At evil altars, your name has been:

- Written on pieces of paper and buried
- Chanted in incantations
- Inscribed on eggs and thrown into rivers
- Carved on candles and burned
- Whispered to idols and spirits

You are now erasing your name from every demonic register. See in the spirit: Your name, written in blood on a scroll at a crossroads altar—the ink is fading, the parchment is crumbling. Your name, chiseled on a stone at a family shrine—the letters are being supernaturally chipped away. Your name, echoing in a dark cavern where witches gather—the sound is being swallowed by holy silence.

"I WITHDRAW MY NAME FROM THE ALTAR OF SICKNESS! I WITHDRAW MY NAME FROM THE ALTAR OF POVERTY! I WITHDRAW MY NAME FROM THE ALTAR OF BARREMNESS! I WITHDRAW MY NAME FROM THE ALTAR OF FAILURE! I WITHDRAW MY NAME FROM EVERY ALTAR IN MY VILLAGE, IN MY FAMILY COMPOUND, AT EVERY CROSSROADS, IN EVERY FOREST, IN EVERY RIVER!"

Your name is coming home to where it belongs—under the covering of the name that is above every name: JESUS.

WITHDRAWAL 2: THE BLESSING WITHDRAWAL

(Now move your hand from your head to your chest, over your heart.)

"I WITHDRAW MY BLESSINGS FROM EVERY EVIL ALTAR, IN THE NAME OF JESUS!"

Your chest is the center of your being, the place of life, emotion, and spirit. Your blessings are not just material; they are spiritual, emotional, relational.

What are your blessings? The **Psalm 103** blessings: forgiveness, healing, redemption, love, compassion, satisfaction, renewal. The **Ephesians 1** blessings: every spiritual blessing in heavenly places. The **Deuteronomy 28** blessings: blessed in the city and field, blessed fruit, blessed basket, blessed coming in and going out.

These blessings have been:

- Intercepted at the point of release
- Held hostage in demonic warehouses
- Converted to curses through altar manipulations
- Transferred to others through evil altars of transfer

Biblical Promise: Malachi 3:10-11 speaks of God opening the windows of heaven and pouring out blessing, and rebuking the devourer. The devourer has been consuming your blessings at the altar. You are now rebuking him and commanding the release of what he's devoured.

Visualize the heavenly storehouses. See angels carrying packages with your name on them—packages of peace, joy, health, favor, divine connections. These packages were diverted to dark altars. Now, command them to be rerouted to your spiritual address.

"I WITHDRAW THE BLESSING OF HEALTH THAT WAS SACRIFICED AT THE SHRINE OF SICKNESS! I WITHDRAW THE BLESSING OF PEACE THAT WAS STOLEN AT THE ALTAR OF STRIFE! I WITHDRAW THE BLESSING OF WISDOM THAT

WAS TRADED AT THE ALTAR OF CONFUSION! I WITHDRAW THE BLESSING OF FAVOR THAT WAS BURIED AT THE CROSSROADS!"

Every blessing has a divine GPS. Reset its coordinates to your life in Christ.

WITHDRAWAL 3: THE BREAKTHROUGH WITHDRAWAL

(Move your hand back to your head.)

"I WITHDRAW MY BREAKTHROUGHS FROM EVERY EVIL ALTAR, IN THE NAME OF JESUS!"

Your head is again the place of authority, but now specifically for breakthroughs—mental breakthroughs, strategic breakthroughs, directional breakthroughs.

What is a breakthrough? It's a sudden, dramatic advance past an obstacle. It's that promotion that was blocked. That contract that was intercepted. That admission letter that never arrived. That business idea that was stolen. That ministry opportunity that was hijacked.

Biblical Example: Remember the story in **Daniel 10**. Daniel prayed, and from the first day, the answer was released. But it was hindered for 21 days by the "prince of Persia." That prince was a territorial spirit operating through altars in Persia. Your breakthroughs have been similarly hindered by "princes" guarding evil altars.

These altars have been:

- **Altars of Delay:** Where your breakthroughs are put on permanent hold
- **Altars of Substitution:** Where your breakthroughs are given to someone else
- **Altars of Destruction:** Where your breakthroughs are ritually destroyed before they reach you

You are now commanding the princes to stand down. You are withdrawing your breakthroughs from their control.

"I WITHDRAW MY PROMOTION FROM THE ALTAR OF DEMOTION! I WITHDRAW MY CONTRACT FROM THE ALTAR OF REJECTION! I WITHDRAW MY ADMISSION FROM THE ALTAR OF FAILURE! I WITHDRAW MY BUSINESS SUCCESS FROM THE ALTAR OF POVERTY! I WITHDRAW MY MINISTRY DOORS FROM THE ALTAR OF CLOSED DOORS!"

See in the spirit: That job position with your name on it—it's being released from a demonic filing cabinet. That signed document—it's being pulled from a satanic briefcase. That opportunity—it's escaping a dark stronghold. It's now in transit to you.

WITHDRAWAL 4: THE GLORY WITHDRAWAL

(Keep your hand on your head, but lift your face upward.)

"I WITHDRAW MY GLORY FROM EVERY EVIL ALTAR, IN THE NAME OF JESUS!"

Your glory is the radiant manifestation of God's presence upon your life. It's your divine distinction, your God-given excellence, the weight of His presence that makes you stand out for His purposes.

Biblical Identity: Isaiah 60:1 says, "*Arise, shine; for thy light is come, and the glory of the LORD is risen upon thee.*" **Haggai 2:9** declares, "*The glory of this latter house shall be greater than of the former.*"

But your glory has been:

- Dimmed at altars of obscurity
- Tarnished at altars of shame
- Stolen at altars of envy
- Buried at altars of humiliation

Evil altars specialize in glory theft. They take the glory God gave you and attempt to transfer it to idols or to people serving darkness. That's why you might feel constantly overshadowed, unnoticed despite your gifts, or robbed of the honor due to your work.

You are now reclaiming your glory. The glory that makes you the head and not the tail. The glory that causes kings to come to your rising (**Isaiah 60:3**).

"I WITHDRAW THE GLORY UPON MY LIFE FROM THE IDOL THAT HAS BEEN FEEDING ON IT! I WITHDRAW THE GLORY UPON MY MINISTRY FROM THE SHRINE THAT HAS BEEN SUCKING IT! I WITHDRAW THE GLORY UPON MY FAMILY FROM THE ALTAR THAT HAS BEEN BURYING IT! I WITHDRAW THE GLORY UPON MY DESTINY FROM EVERY PLACE WHERE IT HAS BEEN HELD CAPTIVE!"

Feel the weight of glory returning to your spirit. Feel the divine radiance being restored. The enemy's camp is becoming darker as your light increases.

WITHDRAWAL 5: THE PROSPERITY WITHDRAWAL

(Now place your hand firmly on your chest again.)

"I WITHDRAW MY PROSPERITY FROM EVERY EVIL ALTAR, IN THE NAME OF JESUS!"

Prosperity is not just money; it's shalom—complete well-being: spiritual, physical, financial, relational. But financial prosperity has been specifically targeted because money is a spiritual gatekeeper. With resources, you fund the Gospel, care for the poor, and establish God's kingdom.

Biblical Promise: 3 John 1:2: "*Beloved, I wish above all things that thou mayest prosper and be in health, even as thy soul prospereth.*" **Psalm 35:27**: "*Let them shout for joy, and be glad, that favour my righteous cause: yea, let them say continually, Let the LORD be magnified, which hath pleasure in the prosperity of his servant.*"

Your prosperity has been:

- Swallowed by "money-eating" altars
- Blocked by altars of debt and lack
- Converted to spiritual money in demonic banks
- Cursed at altars of poverty so it never satisfies

There are altars specifically designed to create financial leaks, mysterious debts, bad investments, and business failures. Every time money comes to you, these altars activate to siphon it off.

You are now plundering the enemy's storehouse. You are executing **Isaiah 45:3**: "*And I will give thee the treasures of darkness, and hidden riches of secret places, that thou mayest* *know that I, the LORD, which call thee by thy name, am the God of Israel."*

"I WITHDRAW MY FINANCES FROM THE DEMONIC BANK WHERE THEY'VE BEEN DEPOSITED! I WITHDRAW MY WEALTH FROM THE MONEY-EATING ALTAR! I WITHDRAW MY INHERITANCE FROM THE SHRINE OF POVERTY! I WITHDRAW MY BUSINESS INCREASE FROM THE MARKETPLACE ALTAR! I WITHDRAW MY FINANCIAL BREAKTHROUGHS FROM EVERY CROSSROADS WHERE THEY'VE BEEN BURIED!"

See in the spirit: Gold, silver, resources flowing BACK to you from dark places. Bank accounts being supernaturally restored. Debt records being erased. Wealth transfers happening in the heavenlies.

WITHDRAWAL 6: THE COMPLETE REPRESENTATION WITHDRAWAL

(Now place one hand on your head and the other on your chest simultaneously.)

"I WITHDRAW ANYTHING REPRESENTING ME FROM EVERY EVIL ALTAR, IN JESUS' NAME!"

This is the comprehensive withdrawal. Beyond your name, beyond specific blessings—anything that carries your spiritual signature, anything that represents you in the spirit realm.

What represents you?

- Photographs

- Personal belongings (clothing, jewelry, hair, nail clippings)
- Spiritual symbols connected to you
- Covenantal tokens
- Dream representations of you
- Spiritual clones or doubles created by witchcraft

Biblical Warning: In **Ezekiel 13**, God condemns those who sew pillows to armholes and make kerchiefs to hunt souls. These were symbolic objects used in magical practices to capture and control people's lives.

At evil altars, these representations of you are:

- Pinned with needles
- Buried in coffins
- Tied with cords
- Burned with curses
- Placed before idols for monitoring

You are now severing every symbolic connection. You are declaring that no object, no symbol, no representation has power over the real you—the you who is hidden with Christ in God (**Colossians 3:3**).

"I WITHDRAW MY PHOTOGRAPH FROM THE SHRINE WHERE IT'S BEEN DISPLAYED! I WITHDRAW MY CLOTHING FROM THE ALTAR WHERE IT'S BEEN USED IN RITUALS! I WITHDRAW MY HAIR AND NAILS FROM THE POT WHERE THEY'VE BEEN BURIED! I WITHDRAW MY DREAM BODY FROM THE DREAM ALTAR WHERE IT'S BEEN MANIPULATED! I WITHDRAW EVERY SPIRITUAL REPRESENTATION OF ME FROM EVERY DARK REALM!"

Visualize these objects losing their connection to you. The photograph—the image fades to blank paper. The clothing—the spiritual fibers disintegrate. The hair—it becomes mere dead matter with no link to your life.

WITHDRAWAL 7: THE BODILY RESTORATION WITHDRAWAL

Now, this is personal and specific. Lay both hands on any part of your body that has been under attack. If it's internal, place your hands over the area. If it's systemic, place hands on your chest or stomach.

Begin to decree:

"I WITHDRAW YOU [NAME THE ORGAN OR SYSTEM] FROM EVERY EVIL ALTAR, IN THE NAME OF JESUS!"

Say it SEVEN TIMES with holy fury. Seven is the number of completion, perfection. You are completely severing the connection between that body part and every altar that has claimed jurisdiction over it.

For a woman struggling with reproductive issues, lay hands on the womb:

"I WITHDRAW MY WOMB FROM THE ALTAR OF BARREMNESS! I WITHDRAW MY WOMB FROM THE RIVER ALTAR WHERE I WAS DEDICATED! I WITHDRAW MY WOMB FROM THE FAMILY SHRINE THAT CLAIMS MY CHILDREN! I WITHDRAW MY WOMB! I WITHDRAW MY WOMB! I WITHDRAW MY WOMB! I WITHDRAW MY WOMB! I WITHDRAW MY WOMB! I WITHDRAW MY WOMB!"

For someone with chronic headaches or mental issues, lay hands on the head:

"I WITHDRAW MY BRAIN FROM THE ALTAR OF CONFUSION! I WITHDRAW MY MIND FROM THE SHRINE OF MADNESS! I WITHDRAW MY MEMORY FROM THE CROSSROADS WHERE IT WAS SCATTERED! I WITHDRAW MY MIND! I WITHDRAW MY MIND! I WITHDRAW MY MIND! (seven times)"

For financial struggle, lay hands on the hands (instruments of work):

"I WITHDRAW MY HANDS FROM THE ALTAR OF FAILURE! I WITHDRAW MY LABOR FROM THE MARKETPLACE ALTAR OF POVERTY! I WITHDRAW MY SKILL FROM THE SHRINE OF FRUSTRATION!"

For someone with blood disorders or genetic issues:

"I WITHDRAW MY BLOOD FROM EVERY ALTAR WHERE IT WAS POLLUTED! I WITHDRAW MY DNA FROM EVERY GENERATIONAL ALTAR THAT HAS CURSED IT! I WITHDRAW MY BLOODLINE FROM EVERY FAMILY SHRINE THAT CLAIMS IT!"

For eye problems or sinful patterns:

"I WITHDRAW MY EYES FROM THE ALTAR OF LUST! I WITHDRAW MY VISION FROM THE SHRINE OF BLINDNESS! I WITHDRAW MY SPIRITUAL SIGHT FROM EVERY DARK ALTAR THAT HAS CLOUDED IT!"

As you say "I WITHDRAW YOU!" seven times, feel the release. Feel the spiritual cords being severed. Feel the dark attachments being peeled away. Feel the life of God flowing into that area, healing what was damaged, restoring what was stolen.

Beloved congregation, what have we just done? We have executed the most comprehensive spiritual withdrawal in modern spiritual warfare. We have not merely prayed a prayer; we have conducted a divine transaction.

We have moved from the courtroom of heaven (where we won our case through the blood of Jesus) to the warehouse of hell (where our possessions were held) with a repossession order signed by the Judge of all the earth.

The thunder of God has been invoked—His voice of power that shakes the foundations of hell.

The fire of God has been released—purifying what was polluted, consuming what was demonic.

The altars are crumbling—their stones scattered, their fires quenched, their priests scattered.

Your name is being erased from their ledgers—you are no longer on their list of targets.

Your blessings are now in transit—angels are dispatching what belongs to you, with compound interest for the years of delay (**Joel 2:25**).

Walk out of this place differently than you came in. Your shoulders should feel lighter—the burdens have been lifted. Your head should be held higher—your identity has been reclaimed. Your chest should feel fuller—your blessings are returning.

You are no longer a VICTIM of altars. You are a DESTROYER of altars. You are no longer a PRISONER of covenants. You are an HEIR of the New Covenant in Christ's blood.

The withdrawal is complete. The repossession is underway. Now, live in the freedom you have proclaimed. Guard it with prayer. Maintain it with the Word. And never again allow the enemy to establish an altar in your life.

Go, and possess your possessions. The Lord has given you the land.

CHAPTER 06

THE BLOOD COVENANT TRAP

The Prison Without Walls

My brothers and sisters, there is perhaps no prison more terrible than the one you don't know you're in. Let me explain something to you. If a man who is mad begins to notice that his clothes are dirty, that's the beginning of his healing. But if he's sitting there ironing filthy clothes and tearing them apart, then his madness is actually increasing. Now think about this: a man locked in a police cell cannot release himself if the key is in the pocket of the policeman. Someone from the outside must bring the key.

Tonight, I'm talking about perhaps the most binding, most powerful, and most deceptive prison of all: **The Blood Covenant Trap**. And the key to this prison isn't in any man's pocket—it's in the wounded hands of our Lord Jesus Christ.

The Sacred and the Profane: Understanding Blood

Let me take you straight to **Ezekiel 16:6**:
"And when I passed by thee, and saw thee polluted in thine own blood. I said unto thee when thou wast in thy blood, Live; yea, I said unto thee when thou wast in thy blood, Live."

Did you hear that? **Polluted in thine own blood.** This is one of the most profound statements in Scripture. Blood—the very substance of life—can become polluted. Not chemically, but spiritually.

Now listen to **Leviticus 17:11**:

"For the life of the flesh is in the blood: and I have given it to you upon the altar to make an atonement for your souls: for it is the blood that maketh an atonement for the soul."

Do you understand what God is telling us? Blood isn't just a biological fluid. It's spiritual. It carries life. It makes atonement. Without blood, there is no remission of sins. That's why when Adam and Eve sinned, God Himself killed an animal and clothed them with its skin. The first blood shed in human history wasn't by Cain—it was by God Himself, to cover man's shame.

Leviticus 17:14 goes further:

"For it is the life of all flesh; the blood of it is for the life thereof... whosoever eateth it shall be cut off."

Why such a severe warning? Because blood contains LIFE. Not just biological life, but spiritual identity, destiny, and covenant potential.

The Mystery of Blood, Water, and Spirit

Now, let's go to **1 John 5:8**, one of the most mysterious verses in Scripture:

"And there are three that bear witness in earth, the spirit, and the water, and the blood: and these three agree in one."

Why these three? Blood, water, and spirit? Because these are the three mysterious elements that carry spiritual signatures:

- **Water** covers about 70% of our bodies and 70% of the earth
- **Blood** circulates life to every cell
- **Spirit** gives us consciousness and connection to God

From the beginning, the Spirit of God moved upon the waters. Fire changes everything it touches. Electricity powers our world. But blood... blood is unique. Medical science tells us amazing things:

- Blood carries oxygen from our lungs to every cell
- Blood carries nutrients from our food
- Blood regulates our body temperature
- Blood contains white blood cells—"security agents" that attack sickness
- Every cell in your body gets new blood every 50 seconds!

But with all our science, we still don't fully understand blood. Why? Because it's not just physical—it's spiritual. And here's the terrifying truth: **Once your blood is spiritually polluted, your entire life is polluted.**

Blood Speaks and Remembers

In **Genesis 4:10**, God says to Cain:

"What hast thou done? the voice of thy brother's blood crieth unto me from the ground."

Abel's blood was crying out for justice! Blood has a voice. It remembers. It testifies.

In **Revelation 6:10**, the martyrs cry out:

"How long, O Lord, holy and true, dost thou not judge and avenge our blood on them that dwell on the earth?"

Their blood is speaking! That's why Jesus told the Pharisees: *"That upon you may come all the righteous blood shed upon the earth, from the blood of righteous Abel unto the blood of Zacharias... Verily I say unto you, All these things shall come upon this generation"* (Matthew 23:35-36).

Blood covenants don't expire. They echo through generations. That's the power—and the danger—of blood.

THE COVENANT: GOD'S MASTERPIECE AND SATAN'S COUNTERFEIT

My brothers and sisters, I want you to understand something tonight that will change how you see your entire spiritual journey. Everything God creates, Satan counterfeits. Everything God establishes, Satan perverts. Everything God ordains for life, Satan twists for death. And there is no clearer example of this than the concept of **covenant**.

Let me take you to **Zechariah 9:11** once more, but let's read it in its full context:

"As for thee also, by the blood of thy covenant I have sent forth thy prisoners out of the pit wherein is no water."

Do you hear the beauty in that? "By the blood of thy covenant." Whose blood? The blood of Jesus. Whose covenant? God's eternal covenant with humanity. What does it do? It sends forth prisoners out of the pit where there is **no water**—no refreshment, no life, no hope, just dry, desperate bondage.

That's God's covenant. That's the real thing. But let me show you how the enemy has taken this holy concept and created a demonic distortion.

Understanding Covenant: It's in God's DNA

First, you need to understand: **Covenant is God's idea.** It's how He relates to us. From Genesis to Revelation, God is a covenant-making, covenant-keeping God.

Look at the covenants in Scripture:

1. **The Adamic Covenant** (Genesis 3:15) - The promise of redemption
2. **The Noahic Covenant** (Genesis 9:9-17) - The promise to never flood the earth again
3. **The Abrahamic Covenant** (Genesis 15, 17) - The promise of land, descendants, and blessing
4. **The Mosaic Covenant** (Exodus 19-24) - The Law given at Sinai
5. **The Davidic Covenant** (2 Samuel 7) - The promise of an eternal kingdom
6. **The New Covenant** (Jeremiah 31:31-34, Luke 22:20) - The covenant in Christ's blood

Every one of these covenants involved **blood**. Every one of them was **cut** (that's what the Hebrew word "karat berit" means—to cut a covenant). Every one of them established a relationship with terms, conditions, and promises.

The Ancient Ritual: Walking Between the Pieces

Now, to truly understand blood covenants—both divine and demonic—you must understand the ancient ritual. In **Jeremiah 34:18-19**, God reminds Judah:

"And I will give the men that have transgressed my covenant, which have not performed the words of the covenant which they had made before me, when they cut the calf in twain, and passed between the parts thereof, The princes of Judah, and the princes of Jerusalem, the eunuchs, and the priests, and all the people of the land, which passed between the parts of the calf."

What's happening here? Let me paint the picture:

1. **The Selection of the Animal** - Usually the best of the flock, without blemish
2. **The Cutting in Two** - The animal is sliced down the middle, lengthwise
3. **The Arrangement** - The two halves are laid opposite each other, creating a bloody pathway
4. **The Walk of Death** - The covenant partners walk together between the pieces
5. **The Unspoken Vow** - "May what happened to this animal happen to me if I break this covenant"

This is what God did with Abraham in **Genesis 15:9-17**. God had Abraham prepare a heifer, a goat, a ram, a turtledove, and a pigeon. Abraham cut them in two (except the birds). Then a deep sleep fell on Abraham, and God Himself—represented by a smoking furnace and burning lamp—passed between the pieces. God was saying: "Abraham, if I break My promise to you, may I be torn apart like these animals."

But here's the mind-blowing part: In that covenant walk, only God passed through. Abraham was asleep. Why? Because God was making a **unilateral covenant**—a promise that depended entirely on God's faithfulness, not Abraham's performance. That's grace! That's the Gospel in Genesis!

Satan's Counterfeit: The Demonic Blood Covenant

Now, Satan saw this. He understood the power of covenant. He understood that covenant establishes legal rights in the spiritual realm. So he created his own version. The same steps, but with demonic intent.

Let me walk you through the anatomy of a demonic blood covenant—the kind that has trapped millions:

1. The Discussion of Terms (The Negotiation with Hell)

This isn't a casual conversation. It's a spiritual negotiation. The human party (sometimes willingly, sometimes coerced) sits with demonic representatives or human agents (witchdoctors, shrine priests) and discusses:

- What the human wants (wealth, power, protection, revenge)
- What the demons want in return (worship, sacrifices, the person's firstborn, their destiny, their lineage)

- The duration (sometimes a lifetime, sometimes for generations)

This is exactly what happened with Faust in literature—trading his soul for knowledge and power. It's what happens in secret society initiations. It's what happens when a desperate person visits a native doctor.

2. The Exchange of Gifts (The Down Payment)

In ancient covenant-making, parties exchanged gifts. In demonic covenants, the gifts are sinister:

- The human might give a lock of hair, nail clippings, a piece of clothing (something carrying their DNA or spiritual signature)
- The demonic party might give a talisman, a ring, a staff (something that becomes a point of contact)
- Often, the most precious possession is demanded. For many, that's their **virginity** or their **firstborn child**

This is why Exodus 22:29 commands: "*Thou shalt not delay to offer the first of thy ripe fruits, and of thy liquors: the firstborn of thy sons shalt thou give unto me.*" God wants our first and best to prevent us from giving them to demons.

3. The Blood Mingling (The Spiritual DNA Fusion)

This is the most critical—and most dangerous—step. The parties cut themselves (usually on the wrist or forearm) and let their blood drip into a common cup, often containing wine or some other liquid. They mix it. Then they both drink from it.

Do you understand what's happening spiritually? **They are exchanging spiritual DNA.** They are becoming one at the blood level. This is why sexual immorality creates such powerful covenants—because in sex, there's a mingling of fluids, a mingling of lives.

In **1 Corinthians 6:16**, Paul asks: "*What? know ye not that he which is joined to an harlot is one body? for two, saith he, shall be one flesh.*" He's talking about spiritual union, not just physical.

When you drink someone's blood in a covenant ritual, you're not just drinking a biological fluid. You're ingesting their spiritual identity, their destiny, their curses, their blessings. You're creating a bond that death itself struggles to break.

4. The Scar (The Permanent Reminder)

After the bloodletting, gunpowder or ash is often rubbed into the wound. This creates a keloid—a permanent raised scar. Every time the person looks at that scar, they remember the covenant. Every time they touch it, they renew it unconsciously.

This is the demonic perversion of **circumcision**. God gave Abraham circumcision as a sign of the covenant (Genesis 17:11). It was a physical reminder of a spiritual reality. Satan creates his own "circumcision"—these ritual scars that bind people to darkness.

5. The Curses (The Spiritual Fine Print)

After the blood mingling, the administering priest (whether human or demonic) pronounces curses. These aren't empty words. They're spiritual contracts. They might sound like:

- "If you break this covenant, may you die a sudden death"
- "If you reveal our secrets, may your tongue rot in your mouth"
- "If you turn to another god, may your children perish before your eyes"

These curses are **legally binding** in the spirit realm. They give demons the right to enforce the covenant through affliction, tragedy, or oppression.

6. The Unity (The Blood Brotherhood)

Finally, the two parties are declared "blood brothers" or "covenant partners." They are no longer two separate entities but one in purpose, one in destiny, one in spiritual connection.

This is the demonic perversion of what happens when we take communion. In **1 Corinthians 10:16-17**, Paul says: *"The cup of blessing which we bless, is it not the communion of the blood of Christ? The bread which we break, is it not the communion of the body of Christ? For we being many are one bread, and one body: for we are all partakers of that one bread."*

When we take communion, we're declaring our unity with Christ and with each other in Him. In demonic blood covenants, people declare unity with demons and with other covenant partners in darkness.

The Generational Reach: You Can't Outrun a Covenant

Now here's what most people—even many believers—don't understand: **Covenants have generational reach.**

When two parties make a blood covenant, they're not just representing themselves. They're representing their entire lineage—past and future. They're saying: "Not just me, but my children, my grandchildren, and all who come from me are bound to this covenant."

This is biblical! In **Exodus 20:5**, God says He visits "*the iniquity of the fathers upon the children unto the third and fourth generation of them that hate me.*" Why? Because covenants—even sinful ones—have generational consequences.

When your great-grandfather made a covenant with a river goddess for protection...
When your grandmother dedicated your mother to a shrine at birth...
When your father consulted an oracle before your birth...
They weren't just making decisions for themselves. They were making decisions for you.

That's why you can be born again, Spirit-filled, serving God, and yet still struggle with certain patterns of failure, sickness, or oppression. There's a generational covenant that hasn't been broken.

The Ilorin Testimony: When the Spiritual Becomes Visible

Let me tell you more about that testimony from Ilorin. This wasn't just two birds randomly fighting. This was spiritual warfare manifesting in the natural realm.

The brother shared that during an intense deliverance session for someone bound by blood covenants, suddenly these two large birds—birds that weren't common to that area—flew into the open-air meeting. They didn't just fly in; they attacked each other with such violence that feathers were flying everywhere. They were pecking at each other's eyes, clawing at each other's bodies.

The ushers tried to shoo them away, but the birds were so consumed with fighting each other that they wouldn't leave. Finally, the ushers had to physically catch them and remove them.

What was happening in the spirit? The person being prayed for was coming out of a powerful blood covenant. The demons assigned to enforce that covenant saw their "property" slipping away. They began to fight among themselves. One faction was saying, "We must stop this deliverance!" Another faction was saying, "It's too late—the blood of Jesus is too powerful!" Their internal conflict manifested as the fighting birds.

This is why **Mark 3:24-26** says:

"And if a kingdom be divided against itself, that kingdom cannot stand. And if a house be divided against itself, that house cannot stand. And if Satan rise up against himself, and be divided, he cannot stand, but hath an end."

When you pray aggressively against blood covenants, you don't just attack the demons—you cause confusion in their ranks. You turn them against each other.

The Geography of Bondage: You Can't Outrun It

Some people think geographical distance breaks spiritual ties. "If I move to America, I'll leave these African spiritual problems behind." My friend, that's like thinking if you move to another city, your shadow will stop following you.

Blood covenants don't respect geography. They're not bound by continents or oceans. They're spiritual contracts that follow the bloodline.

Let me give you a modern example: A Nigerian man makes a covenant with a marine spirit for success in business. The spirit gives him wealth but demands his firstborn son. The man has a son but doesn't surrender him. He thinks, "I'll just move my family to London. The marine spirit is in Nigeria—it can't follow us to England."

So he moves. His son grows up in London, becomes a professional, gives his life to Christ. But at age 35, he begins to experience strange things: dreams of drowning, fear of water, recurring failures in relationships and business. He prays, fasts, goes to church—but the problems persist.

Why? Because the covenant his father made with the marine spirit is still binding on him. The demonic rights established through that covenant give marine spirits legal access to his life, regardless of where he lives physically.

This is why **deliverance must address covenants specifically**. You can't just pray general prayers. You must identify and break the specific covenants giving demons legal rights over your life.

The Blood of Jesus: The Superior Covenant

But here's the glorious news: **Every demonic blood covenant meets its match in the blood of Jesus.**

The writer of Hebrews says it perfectly in **Hebrews 12:24**: *"And to Jesus the mediator of the new covenant, and to the blood of sprinkling, that speaketh better things than that of Abel."*

Abel's blood cried out for vengeance (Genesis 4:10). Jesus' blood cries out for mercy, for forgiveness, for redemption, for deliverance!

When you apply the blood of Jesus to a demonic blood covenant, here's what happens:

1. **Superior Blood Meets Inferior Blood** - The sinless, divine blood of Jesus confronts polluted, human/demonic blood. Jesus' blood doesn't just neutralize the demonic covenant—it obliterates it.
2. **The Legal Transfer** - Your sins and the sins of your ancestors were placed on Jesus at the cross. The curses from broken covenants were placed on Him. **Galatians 3:13** says: *"Christ hath redeemed us from the curse of the law, being made a curse for us: for it is written, Cursed is every one that hangeth on a tree."*
3. **The New Covenant Established** - When you break an old covenant, you don't leave a vacuum. You establish a new one. Jesus said in **Luke 22:20**: *"This cup is the new testament in my blood, which is shed for you."* You're transferring from the kingdom of darkness to the kingdom of light. From Satan's covenant to God's covenant.
4. **The Generational Reset** - Not only are you freed, but your children are freed. Your lineage is reset. As for you and your house, you will serve the Lord (Joshua 24:15).

The Urgent Question: What Covenants Are Binding You?

Tonight, I need you to ask yourself some hard questions:

1. **What covenants did my ancestors make that might still be affecting me?**
    - Were there shrine priests in your family line?
    - Were children dedicated to idols?
    - Was there involvement in secret societies?
2. **What covenants have I made knowingly or unknowingly?**
    - Through sexual relationships?
    - Through rituals or traditional practices?
    - Through vows or promises made in moments of desperation?
3. **What patterns in my life suggest covenant bondage?**
    - Repeated failure at the edge of breakthrough?
    - Unexplainable sicknesses?
    - Financial patterns where money comes but doesn't stay?
    - Relationship patterns that always end the same way?

You see, ignorance is not bliss when it comes to covenants. **Hosea 4:6** says: "*My people are destroyed for lack of knowledge.*" You can be destroyed by covenants you don't even know exist.

But tonight, knowledge is coming. Light is shining. Understanding is dawning. And with understanding comes responsibility. With knowledge comes the mandate to act.

You now know about blood covenants—both God's and Satan's. You now understand their power, their reach, their consequences. You cannot claim ignorance anymore.

The question is: **What will you do with this knowledge?**

Will you continue living as if these covenants don't exist? Will you continue struggling with patterns you can't explain? Will you pass these bondages on to your children?

Or will you rise up tonight—in this very moment—and begin the process of covenant breaking? Will you take the blood of Jesus and apply it to every ungodly covenant over your life? Will you become the generation that says, "The buck stops here. The covenants end with me. My children will inherit freedom, not bondage"?

The power is in your hands. The authority is in the name of Jesus. The legal precedent has been set at Calvary. All that's missing is your decision to enforce what Jesus already accomplished.

Will you enforce it tonight?

RECOGNIZING THE PRISONERS: THE TELL-TALE SIGNS OF BLOOD COVENANT ENTANGLEMENT

Beloved congregation, tonight I want to serve as a spiritual physician. I want to help you diagnose a condition that many are suffering from but few can name. You see, in the natural, a good doctor doesn't just treat symptoms—he looks for patterns. He connects dots. He recognizes syndromes.

In the spirit, it's the same. The enemy doesn't want you to recognize that your struggles are connected. He wants you to think you just have "bad luck" or that you're "unlucky" or that "this is just how life is." But I'm here to tell you tonight: Your patterns are speaking. Your struggles are testifying. Your repeated failures are crying out, revealing a deeper spiritual reality.

Let me walk you through these seventeen signs—not to condemn you, but to liberate you. Not to frighten you, but to enlighten you. For as Jesus said in **John 8:32**: *"And ye shall know the truth, and the truth shall make you free."* The first step to freedom is recognizing the prison.

---

1. ANTI-HARVEST FORCES: THE CROP THAT NEVER RIPENS

The Pattern: You sow diligently, you water faithfully, you tend carefully—but just as the harvest should come, something happens. The crop fails. The business deal collapses. The promotion vanishes. The contract is canceled. It's as if an invisible hand reaches down at the last moment and snatches away your fruit.

The Spiritual Reality: This is the spirit of the devourer at work. In **Malachi 3:11**, God promises: *"And I will rebuke the devourer for your sakes, and he shall not destroy the fruits of your ground; neither shall your vine cast her fruit before the time in the field, saith the LORD of hosts."* But what if the devourer has legal rights? What if a blood covenant gave him permission to devour your harvest?

In ancient agrarian covenants, people would sometimes sacrifice the first fruits of their harvest to idols to ensure the rest would be protected. They were essentially saying, "I give you the first so you'll protect the rest." But the enemy is a thief—he takes the first, then comes back for the rest. If your ancestors made such covenants, you're reaping the consequences.

The Biblical Parallel: Remember **Haggai 1:6**? "*Ye have sown much, and bring in little; ye eat, but ye have not enough; ye drink, but ye are not filled with drink; ye clothe you, but there is none warm; and he that earneth wages earneth wages to put it into a bag with holes.*" That's not just poor economics—that's covenant-induced leakage.

---

2. CONSTANT MARITAL FAILURE: THE RELATIONSHIP CYCLE

The Pattern: Relationship after relationship follows the same tragic script. You meet someone, there's attraction, things progress, but just as commitment deepens, something unravels. Sometimes it's infidelity. Sometimes it's inexplicable conflict. Sometimes one party just walks away. For others, marriage happens but becomes a battlefield rather than a sanctuary.

The Spiritual Reality: This often indicates a **spiritual marriage** or **soul tie** created through blood covenants. When two people have sex outside marriage, they become "one flesh" (**1 Corinthians 6:16**), creating a spiritual bond. But when that sexual encounter was with someone in covenant with darkness, you didn't just bond with the person—you bonded with their demons.

Even more serious: Some people were "spiritually married" as children through family rituals. A girl might be promised to a river spirit or a shrine deity. That spiritual husband then fights every human suitor, sabotaging relationships until the covenant is broken.

The Biblical Example: Samson and Delilah (**Judges 16**). Samson's strength wasn't just in his hair—it was in his Nazirite covenant with God. When he gave his secret to Delilah (a woman with Philistine loyalties), he wasn't just breaking a vow—he was violating covenant. The result? Capture, blindness, bondage.

---

3. FINANCIAL LEAKS: THE BAG WITH HOLES

The Pattern: Money comes in, but it never stays. You get a salary, but bills swallow it. You receive a bonus, but an emergency consumes it. You start saving, but unexpected expenses drain it. It's not that you're irresponsible—it's that your finances seem to have invisible drainage pipes.

The Spiritual Reality: This is often linked to what I call **poverty covenants**. In many traditional settings, people would make covenants with spirits of poverty, essentially saying: "Keep me poor, and I'll serve you." Or ancestors might have cursed their descendants with perpetual poverty out of jealousy or resentment.

But there's another dimension: **Money with spiritual tags**. If you receive money from someone in covenant with darkness, or if you engage in dishonest gain, that money carries a curse. It becomes a Trojan horse in your finances.

The Biblical Warning: Proverbs 13:22 says: "*The wealth of the sinner is laid up for the just.*" But the reverse can also be true: The wealth of the just can be hijacked by the sinner through covenants.

---

4. INABILITY TO SUSTAIN SUCCESS: THE TEMPORARY BREAKTHROUGH

The Pattern: You get the promotion—then get demoted six months later. You start the business—it booms then busts. You buy the house—then lose it to foreclosure. Success comes, but it's fleeting. It's like trying to hold water in a sieve.

The Spiritual Reality: This is the **spirit of temporary breakthrough**. In some blood covenants, the terms are: "I'll give you success, but you can't keep it. I'll give you fame, but it will fade. I'll give you wealth, but it will vanish." The enemy is fine with you tasting success—as long as you never feast on it.

This spirit often works with the **spirit of sabotage**. Just as things are going well, something internally or externally sabotages the success. You make an uncharacteristic mistake. A trusted associate betrays you. Market conditions suddenly shift.

The Biblical Example: King Saul. Anointed, chosen, victorious initially. But disobedience opened doors, and his success became temporary. His throne was given to another. His legacy was cut short.

---

5. UNEXPLAINABLE BUSINESS FAILURE: THE ENTERPRISE THAT CRUMBLES

The Pattern: You have a brilliant idea. You develop a solid plan. You secure funding. You assemble a good team. The launch is successful. Then, inexplicably, things unravel. Key employees quit. Major clients leave. Suppliers fail. The market turns. Every business venture follows this same discouraging trajectory.

The Spiritual Reality: This often indicates a **territorial spirit** assigned to keep you from economic dominion. In many traditional business openings, libations are poured, sacrifices are made to "the god of the market." If you start a business without breaking these territorial claims, you're essentially setting up shop on another spirit's property.

Additionally, if the capital used to start the business came from questionable sources—money from occult practices, inheritance from idol worshipers, loans from corrupt institutions—that money carries spiritual contamination that sabotages the business.

The Biblical Principle: Deuteronomy 28:8 promises: "*The LORD shall command the blessing upon thee in thy storehouses, and in all that thou settest thine hand unto...*" But the opposite is also true: Demonic forces can command curses upon your storehouses and enterprises through covenants.

---

6. RECURRING SICKNESS: THE MALARIA THAT WON'T LEAVE

The Pattern: Especially in tropical regions: recurring malaria-like symptoms—fever, chills, body aches—that don't respond fully to treatment. Or mysterious ailments that doctors can't diagnose. Or chronic conditions that improve temporarily but always return.

The Spiritual Reality: This is often **covenant-induced infirmity**. In many traditional healing practices, people would go to native doctors who would "transfer" sickness to an animal or another person through blood rituals. If that ritual was done on your behalf, you might carry the covenant of that sickness.

Also, some blood covenants include clauses like: "If you break this covenant, may sickness waste your body." When you begin to move toward freedom, these curse clauses activate.

The Biblical Example: The woman with the issue of blood for twelve years (**Mark 5:25-34**). Twelve years of doctors, treatments, expenses—no cure. Why? Possibly generational or covenant-related infirmity. But when she touched Jesus—the covenant-breaker—she was healed instantly.

---

7. FINANCIAL ABORTIONS: THE OPPORTUNITY THAT DIES IN BIRTH

The Pattern: A job opportunity emerges—the interview goes perfectly—the offer is coming—then silence. A business deal is almost sealed—the handshake has happened—the papers are being prepared—then it falls through. It's not just rejection; it's death at the point of birth.

The Spiritual Reality: This is **financial miscarriage**. Just as natural miscarriage can have spiritual causes, financial miscarriage often does too. It's often related to **blood covenants involving abortion**. The blood of aborted babies cries out (**Genesis 4:10**), and one of the areas affected is the womb of financial productivity.

Additionally, if there are curses on your "seed" (both biological and metaphorical—your ideas, your projects, your opportunities), they will be aborted before coming to fruition.

---

8. FAILURE AT THE EDGE OF MIRACLES: THE PROMOTION THAT VANISHES

The Pattern: The promotion letter is being typed—then the position is frozen. The visa is being stamped—then there's a "technical problem." The wedding date is set—then the fiancé disappears. It's not just delay; it's disappearance at the finish line.

The Spiritual Reality: This is the **spirit of the edge**. It specializes in last-minute sabotage. In the spirit realm, there are demons assigned as "gatekeepers" or "border patrol" to ensure certain people never cross into their promised land.

This often connects to what I call **generational ceilings**. Your grandfather never finished secondary school. Your father never finished university. You can't finish your degree. Your son can't complete his apprenticeship. It's a ceiling passed down through covenants.

The Biblical Example: The Israelites at the border of Canaan (**Numbers 13-14**). Twelve spies saw the promise. Ten saw the giants and said, "We can't." Their failure at the edge wasn't just fear—it was a spiritual stronghold that needed breaking.

---

9. DEMONIC DREAMS: THE NIGHTLY TERROR

The Pattern: Recurring dreams of eating with dead relatives, swimming in dirty water, being chased by animals (especially snakes), having sex with strangers, giving birth to strange creatures, or attending meetings where you don't want to be.

The Spiritual Reality: Dreams are one of the primary ways blood covenants are maintained and enforced. When you dream of eating, especially with the dead, you're often participating in covenant renewal rituals in the spirit realm. The food represents covenants being strengthened.

Swimming in water often indicates marine covenants. Snakes represent serpentine spirits or ancestral covenants. Sexual dreams can indicate spiritual marriages. Dreams of meetings often mean you're attending coven gatherings in your sleep.

The Biblical Warning: Ecclesiastes 5:3 says: "*For a dream cometh through the multitude of business...*" The "business" here can be spiritual business—covenant activities happening while you sleep.

---

10. CHRONIC LUST AND CONFUSION: THE MIND IN TURMOIL

The Pattern: A constant struggle with sexual thoughts, pornographic images flooding your mind, inappropriate attractions, coupled with mental confusion—inability to think clearly, make decisions, or concentrate.

The Spiritual Reality: This is often **spiritual defilement through blood covenants**. When you engage in sexual immorality, especially with multiple partners, you're not just breaking moral codes—you're creating spiritual links. Each partner adds their "software" to your spiritual "hard drive."

If any of those partners were in covenant with spirits of lust, perversion, or confusion, those spirits gained access to you. They'll bombard your mind with images and urges, then cloud your thinking so you can't resist effectively.

The Biblical Insight: 2 Timothy 2:26 speaks of those who are "*taken captive by him [Satan] at his will.*" Captivity often begins in the mind. Blood covenants give the enemy legal rights to influence your thoughts.

---

11. SPIRITUAL SERPENTS: THE CRAWLING SENSATION

The Pattern: A physical sensation of something crawling on or under your skin, especially when praying or sleeping. Sometimes visible marks appear inexplicably. A feeling of constriction around limbs or torso.

The Spiritual Reality: This is often literal **serpentine spirits** attached through blood covenants. In many traditional settings, people covenant with serpent deities for protection, power, or healing. These spirits then attach to their beneficiaries.

The crawling sensation is the spiritual manifestation becoming physically perceptible. These spirits often target the nervous system, creating strange sensations, involuntary movements, or even mimicking medical conditions.

The Biblical Parallel: When Paul was bitten by a viper on Malta (**Acts 28:3-5**), the natives expected him to die. But he shook it off into the fire. Some "bites" are physical; some are spiritual. Covenant with serpentine spirits is a spiritual viper bite.

---

12. STRANGE VOICES: THE UNSEEN CALLER

The Pattern: Hearing your name called when no one is there. Hearing whispers you can't decipher. Hearing negative thoughts spoken in first person ("You're a failure," "No one loves you," "You should end it all").

The Spiritual Reality: This is often **familiar spirits** operating through covenant rights. When someone makes a blood covenant, they often give the covenanted spirits permission to "call" them. This creates a spiritual frequency through which they can communicate.

Additionally, in some covenant rituals, the participant's name is called repeatedly by the officiating priest. Every time they answer, "Yes" or "I'm here," they're strengthening the covenant. Later, the spirits continue calling through that established channel.

The Biblical Example: Young Samuel hearing his name called (**1 Samuel 3**). At first, he thought it was Eli. But it was God. The enemy mimics this divine pattern. Not every voice calling your name is God. Some are familiar spirits using covenant access.

---

13. DIFFICULTY RECEIVING THE HOLY SPIRIT: THE BLOCKED INFILLING

The Pattern: You want the baptism of the Holy Spirit. You seek it earnestly. You pray, fast, attend meetings—but something blocks it. You might speak a few syllables in tongues, then it stops. Or you feel a presence but can't release the prayer language.

The Spiritual Reality: The Holy Spirit is a gentleman. He won't force Himself where He's not welcome. But blood covenants create **spiritual occupants** that resist His indwelling. It's like trying to move into a house still occupied by squatters with legal-looking documents.

Particularly resistant are covenants with **religious spirits**—demons that mimic spiritual experiences but are counterfeits. They'll give you a false tongues, a false prophecy, a false vision—anything to keep you from the genuine article.

The Biblical Principle: 1 Corinthians 12:3 says: "*No man can say that Jesus is the Lord, but by the Holy Ghost.*" The reverse is also true: Demons in covenant with you will resist your confession of Jesus' lordship through the Holy Spirit.

---

14. UNFRUITFUL CHRISTIAN LIFE: THE SPIRITUAL DESERT

The Pattern: You're born again. You go to church. You read your Bible. You pray. But there's no growth, no fruit, no power. Your Christian life feels like a desert—dry, barren, fruitless. You watch others bear fruit while you remain stagnant.

The Spiritual Reality: This is often **covenant-induced barrenness**. In the spiritual realm, covenants create "zones" or "environments." A covenant with darkness creates a spiritual environment hostile to spiritual growth.

It's like trying to grow a tropical plant in arctic conditions. The seed (the Word) is good. The sower (you) is faithful. But the soil (your spirit) has been conditioned by covenants to reject spiritual growth.

The Biblical Metaphor: The parable of the sower (**Matthew 13:3-23**). The seed that fell among thorns represents those whose spiritual growth is choked by "the cares of this world, and the deceitfulness of riches." But sometimes the "thorns" are covenant-induced spiritual oppressions.

---

15. UNEXPLAINABLE HATRED: THE UNPROVOKED OPPOSITION

The Pattern: People who should help you inexplicably oppose you. Employers who should promote you instead sabotage you. Family members who should support you instead undermine you. It's not just normal human conflict—it's irrational, persistent opposition.

The Spiritual Reality: This is often **covenant-induced rejection**. In some blood covenants, especially those made for protection or advancement, there are clauses that say: "Anyone who tries to help you will turn against you." Or: "You will be rejected by those you need most."

Additionally, if you have covenants with **spirits of jealousy** or **competition**, they'll stir up jealousy in others toward you. You become a lightning rod for irrational hatred.

The Biblical Example: Joseph and his brothers (**Genesis 37**). Their hatred wasn't just about the coat of many colors. There was a spiritual dimension—a destiny on Joseph's life that demonic forces wanted to thwart through familial opposition.

---

16. UNRULY CHILDREN: THE REBELLION BEYOND NORMAL

The Pattern: Children who are rebellious beyond normal teenage testing of boundaries. Children with inexplicable behavioral issues. Children who seem "possessed" at times. Children who reject godly upbringing despite consistent training.

The Spiritual Reality: This is often **generational covenant transfer**. The covenants made by ancestors don't just affect the immediate participants—they're inherited. The Bible speaks of "visiting the iniquity of the fathers upon the children unto the third and fourth generation" (**Exodus 20:5**).

Additionally, some covenants specifically target the **fruit of the womb**. Spirits are assigned to ensure that children from certain lineages never serve God or fulfill destiny. They specialize in creating rebellion, waywardness, and destruction in children.

The Biblical Example: Eli's sons (**1 Samuel 2:12-17, 22-25**). They were "sons of Belial" who didn't know the Lord. Their rebellion wasn't just poor parenting—there was a spiritual dimension that even Eli's prayers couldn't initially overcome.

---

17. SPIRIT OF FAILURE: THE CLOUD OVER EVERYTHING

The Pattern: A pervasive sense that nothing you do will succeed. A cloud of failure that follows you from project to project, relationship to relationship, endeavor to endeavor. Even when things start well, there's an underlying expectation that they'll eventually fail.

The Spiritual Reality: This is the **spirit of failure** itself—a demonic entity assigned through covenant to ensure you never fulfill destiny. It's not just individual failures; it's a comprehensive atmosphere of failure that saturates every area of life.

Often, this spirit entered through curses spoken during covenant rituals: "You will never succeed." "Everything you touch will fail." "You will be a laughingstock." These words, sealed with blood, become self-fulfilling prophecies enforced by demons.

The Biblical Contrast: Joshua 1:8 promises: "*This book of the law shall not depart out of thy mouth; but thou shalt meditate therein day and night, that thou mayest observe to do according to all that is written therein: for then thou shalt make thy way* *prosperous, and then thou shalt have good success.*" God's plan is success. The enemy's plan through covenants is failure.

THE DIAGNOSIS IS NOT THE DESTINY

Beloved, if you recognize yourself in these patterns, I want you to understand something crucial: **The diagnosis is not the destiny.** Recognizing the prison is the first step to leaving it. These patterns aren't your identity. They're symptoms of a deeper spiritual condition. And like any good physician, I haven't shown you these symptoms to condemn you, but to liberate you. You can't treat what you don't recognize.

But here's what you must understand: Symptoms treated in isolation will always return. You can pray about financial leaks, and they might improve temporarily. You can fast about marital problems, and they might ease for a season. You can rebuke sickness, and it might leave for a while.

But if you don't address the **root covenant** giving demons legal rights to maintain these patterns, the symptoms will always return. Sometimes worse than before (**Matthew 12:43-45**).

The blood of Jesus is the only solvent powerful enough to dissolve blood covenants. The name of Jesus is the only authority high enough to cancel demonic contracts. The Word of God is the only truth solid enough to replace covenant lies.

You're not just fighting individual problems. You're prosecuting a legal case in the court of heaven. You're presenting the blood of Jesus as evidence that every other covenant is null and void. You're serving eviction notices on squatters who've been living in your life through forged documents.

The recognition phase is complete. Now comes the liberation phase. Now comes the breaking phase. Now comes the season where patterns are not just identified—they're obliterated. Where symptoms are not just treated—they're eliminated at their root.

You're about to move from being a prisoner who recognizes the prison to being a free person who destroys the prison so no one else can be held there. The recognition was necessary. But it was only the beginning. The real work—the glorious work of deliverance—starts now.

THE BLOOD COVENANT TRAP

"And when I passed by thee, and saw thee polluted in thine own blood, I said unto thee when thou wast in thy blood, Live; yea, I said unto thee when thou wast in thy blood, Live."

— Ezekiel 16:6

INTRODUCTION: THE CAGE YOU DON'T SEE

Beloved, one of the most tragic conditions a human being can experience is to be locked in a cage—and not even know it. A madman who begins to notice his clothes are dirty is on the road to healing. But if he is ironing his filthy garments, tearing them apart, then his madness is deepening. And listen: if you are in a police cell and the key is in the pocket of the officer, you cannot free yourself. Someone from outside must come with authority and unlock the door.

That is exactly what we are dealing with in this chapter—the **Blood Covenant Trap**. Many of you are living in spiritual captivity, bound by covenants you never consciously made, enslaved by blood ties that happened without your consent. But today, the Key-holder—Jesus Christ—has come to set you free.

Let's begin with the Scripture. Ezekiel 16:6 shows us a powerful truth: **blood can be polluted**. God saw Israel polluted in her own blood, yet He spoke life. That means even when your blood has been contaminated spiritually, God can still speak life into you. But first, you must understand what has been done, and how it happened.

THE MYSTERY AND POWER OF BLOOD

Before we talk about the trap, we must understand what blood truly is—spiritually and physically. The Bible says in Leviticus 17:11:

"For the life of the flesh is in the blood: and I have given it to you upon the altar to make an atonement for your souls: for it is the blood that maketh an atonement for the soul."

Life is in the blood. When God created Adam, He formed him from the dust, but it was the breath of God—the *neshamah*—that made him a living soul. That life resides in the blood. Blood is not just a physical substance; it is a **spiritual carrier**. It carries identity, destiny, covenant, and curse.

Medical science tells us blood is a living liquid. It carries oxygen, nutrients, hormones, and immune cells. It regulates temperature, removes waste, and heals wounds. But spiritually, blood carries **memory**. It carries **covenant**. It carries **generational patterns**. It carries **blessings and curses**.

In 1 John 5:8, we read:

"And there are three that bear witness in earth, the Spirit, and the water, and the blood: and these three agree in one."

The Spirit, the water, and the blood. These are divine mysteries. Water cleanses, the Spirit quickens, and the blood atones. But the enemy has corrupted each one. He perverts water into rituals of bondage, he mimics the Spirit with familiar spirits, and he corrupts blood into covenants of slavery.

THE BLOOD COVENANT: GOD'S DESIGN PERVERTED

God invented covenant. When He wanted to commit irrevocably to Abraham, He made a blood covenant (Genesis 15). Animals were cut in two, and God passed between the pieces. That covenant still stands today. When God wanted to redeem humanity, He sent His Son to shed His blood—the blood of the new covenant (Matthew 26:28).

But Satan, the great counterfeiter, has created his own blood covenants. He uses the same principle—blood exchange—to bind people to himself, to demons, to idols, and to one another in destructive ways.

A blood covenant in the demonic realm is a **legal contract in the spirit world**. It gives demons legal grounds to harass, afflict, limit, and torment. It can be done consciously—through rituals, secret society initiations, or occult practices—or **unconsciously**, through things you never thought were spiritual.

Many of you are struggling with patterns of failure, chronic sickness, marital disasters, financial leaks, and spiritual dryness. You pray, fast, confess Scriptures—yet nothing changes. Why? Because there may be a **blood covenant** still in force, giving the enemy legal access to your life.

---

20 DOORS INTO BLOOD COVENANT SLAVERY

Let me show you how people enter this trap. I will walk you through twenty common doors—some you may recognize, others may shock you. But the Holy Spirit is here to expose and destroy every one of them.

1. THE VIRGIN COVENANT

Sisters, I must ask you: **Who took your virginity?** Brothers, **whose virginity have you taken?** This is not to condemn you, but to expose a spiritual reality. When a man deflowers a woman, there is blood. That blood mingles spiritually, and a covenant is formed. You become "one flesh" not just in principle, but in spiritual identity.

If that relationship did not lead to marriage, you have a **broken blood covenant**. And if the person was involved in witchcraft, idolatry, or sexual perversion, you have now been covenanted to their demons. That is why some people cannot find a godly spouse—they are still spiritually tied to the first person they slept with.

The Bible says in 1 Corinthians 6:16:

"What? know ye not that he which is joined to an harlot is one body? for two, saith he, shall be one flesh."

This is not a metaphor. It is a spiritual reality. Your blood has been mingled. Your destiny has been tied. And until that covenant is broken by the blood of Jesus, it will affect every subsequent relationship.

2. INCISIONS AND TRIBAL MARKS

In many African cultures, children are given tribal marks—incisions on the face, chest, or back—for identity or protection. But behind many of these rituals are incantations, invocations of spirits, and blood covenants.

Each cut draws blood. Each drop is offered to a spirit. The marks become **spiritual barcodes**—identifying you as belonging to a certain clan, but also to certain demons. These marks can attract sickness, poverty, and misfortune because they are covenant points.

The Bible warns in Leviticus 19:28:

"Ye shall not make any cuttings in your flesh for the dead, nor print any marks upon you: I am the LORD."

God forbade it because He knew the spiritual implications. Those marks are not just cultural; they are contractual.

3. SEX OUTSIDE MARRIAGE

Every act of fornication or adultery is a blood covenant. Why? Because in the sexual act, there is an exchange of bodily fluids, but also an exchange of **spiritual DNA**. You give a part of yourself and receive a part of the other person.

If you sleep with a witch, you may unknowingly find your spirit attending witchcraft meetings. If you sleep with someone involved in secret societies, you may find demons from their lineage now attached to you. This is why some people struggle with perverse dreams, unnatural desires, or spiritual oppression after immoral relationships.

You must repent, renounce, and break every ungodly sexual covenant.

4. ANIMAL SACRIFICES

Perhaps your parents or grandparents sacrificed a goat, a chicken, or a cow on your behalf when you were born, when you were sick, or during a festival. They may have thought they were protecting you, but in reality, they were making a **blood covenant with demons**.

That animal's blood was offered to a spirit—maybe the "god of thunder," the "river goddess," or the "family deity." In exchange, the spirit promised protection, but it was really claiming ownership over your life.

Hebrews 10:4 says:

"For it is not possible that the blood of bulls and of goats should take away sins."

But demonic powers accept such blood as payment for access to a human life. You may be serving God today, but if that covenant is not broken, you are still sharing your life with demonic landlords.

5. ABORTION

This is a painful but necessary truth. Abortion sheds innocent blood. That blood cries out to God, just like Abel's blood cried from the ground (Genesis 4:10). It creates a covenant of guilt, shame, and curse.

Many women who have had abortions struggle with depression, reproductive issues, and broken relationships. Men who paid for or encouraged abortions carry the same covenant. There is a spirit of death attached to that bloodshed, and it will affect subsequent children unless it is cleansed by the blood of Jesus.

6. TATTOOS

Before you get defensive, hear me out. I am not saying every tattoo is demonic. But the **process** of tattooing involves repeatedly piercing the skin, drawing blood. In many cultures, tattoos are part of ritual initiations—into gangs, cults, or occult groups.

Even if you got a tattoo innocently, if the artist was involved in the occult, or if the symbol is pagan (dragons, skulls, pentagrams, etc.), you may have received a **demonic stamp**. Your skin has been marked, and your blood has been drawn. That can become a point of demonic contact.

Leviticus 19:28 applies here as well. God wanted His people set apart, not marked like the pagans.

7. BLOOD TRANSFERS THROUGH BITE MARKS

This may sound extreme, but in the realm of the occult, vampires and blood drinkers are real. They bite their victims, drink blood, and transfer covenants. Even in some secret societies, members drink one another's blood to become "blood brothers."

If you have ever been bitten in a strange way—maybe in a dream, or during a physical attack—your blood may have been taken and used in a covenant.

8. CIRCUMCISION RITUALS

Circumcision itself is not evil—God commanded it for Israel. But when circumcision is performed with **ritual incantations**, invoking spirits, or dedicating the child to idols, it becomes a blood covenant. The blood from that cut is often collected and used in sacrifices.

Many men suffer from sexual brokenness, perversion, or marital strife because their reproductive organ was covenanted to demons during circumcision.

9. HOSPITAL BLOOD TRANSFUSIONS

I am **not** telling you to refuse medical treatment. But you must cover any medical procedure with the blood of Jesus. Some hospitals—especially in certain regions—have satanic agents who work as nurses or doctors. They deliberately contaminate blood supplies or use blood for ritual purposes.

Before you receive a transfusion, pray! Plead the blood of Jesus over that blood. Ask God to sanctify it and break any covenant attached to it.

10. SATANIC COMMUNION

If you take communion from a pastor or priest who is living in sin, involved in Freemasonry, or engaged in occult practices, you are entering into **covenant with his demons**. Communion is not just bread and wine—it is a covenant meal. When an unholy person administers it, it becomes a demonic initiation.

This is why some church members suffer from strange illnesses, financial loss, or family breakdown after taking communion in certain churches. They have unknowingly covenanted with the spirits operating through their leader.

11. BLOOD BATHS

In some traditions, people bathe in animal blood to cleanse themselves of curses or to gain power. This is an abomination. You are literally bathing in covenant blood, dedicating your body to the spirit to whom that blood was offered.

12. ANOINTING WITH BLOOD

Some witchdoctors and false prophets anoint people with blood—on the forehead, on the hands, on the feet—to "seal" a prayer or a prophecy. That blood is often from sacrificed animals, and it seals you to the demon behind the ritual.

13. BLOOD LIBATIONS

Pouring blood on the ground, on a building foundation, on a car, or on business premises is a common practice to "invite blessings." But it is actually a blood covenant dedicating that property to demons. If you buy or inherit such property, you inherit the covenant.

14. UNCONSCIOUS COVENANT THROUGH WOUNDS

If you are bleeding—from an accident, a fight, or surgery—and someone touches your blood and then licks their finger or uses it in a ritual, they have made a covenant with you. This is why in some cultures, enemies collect blood from wounds to perform witchcraft.

15. INHERITED COVENANTS

Your ancestors may have made blood covenants with idols, spirits, or secret societies. Those covenants are legally binding on the family line until someone breaks them. You may be born again, Spirit-filled, and serving God, but if those ancestral covenants are still intact, you will keep hitting invisible walls.

Exodus 20:5 says:

"I the LORD thy God am a jealous God, visiting the iniquity of the fathers upon the children unto the third and fourth generation of them that hate me."

But praise God, Galatians 3:13 says:

"Christ hath redeemed us from the curse of the law, being made a curse for us."

You can break those inherited covenants in Jesus' name.

16. LOVERS' BLOOD COVENANTS

Young people in love sometimes cut themselves, mix blood, and swear eternal fidelity. They think it is romantic, but it is a demonic blood covenant. When the relationship ends, the covenant remains, blocking future marriages and attracting tormenting spirits.

17. EATING BLOOD

Some cultures eat blood pudding, drink blood mixed with milk, or consume blood-based foods. Leviticus 17:10-14 strictly forbids eating blood because "the life of the flesh is in the blood." When you eat blood, you are consuming life—and possibly covenant—that is not yours.

18. MULTIPLE EAR OR NOSE PIERCINGS

Piercing itself may not be sinful, but in many cultures, multiple piercings are part of idol worship or ritual slavery. Each hole can become a covenant point. In Exodus 21:6, a slave who wanted to stay with his master had his ear pierced as a sign of permanent bondage.

Some people have multiple ear piercings and wonder why they feel spiritually deaf to God's voice. It could be because those holes are giving demons access.

19. SEX DURING MENSTRUATION

Leviticus 20:18 calls this "uncovering the fountain of her blood." It is a serious defilement that creates a powerful blood covenant. The blood of menstruation is life-potential blood, and when mingled during intercourse, it can create severe spiritual entanglements.

20. BLOOD HUNTERS

Demons need blood to sustain their power. They orchestrate accidents, wars, violence, and conflicts to get blood. When husband and wife fight and draw blood, demons collect it and form covenants with them. This is why some homes are perpetually filled with strife—they are under a blood covenant of violence.

RECOGNIZING THE TRAP: SIGNS OF BLOOD COVENANT SLAVERY

How do you know if you are in this trap? Look for these signs:
Chronic, unexplained sickness

Repeated marital failure

Financial dryness despite hard work

Dreams of bleeding, being cut, or drinking blood

Attraction to blood or violent imagery

Family patterns of tragedy or early death

Inability to break free from sinful habits

Feeling spiritually heavy or oppressed after medical procedures

Strange reactions during communion

recurring nightmares involving rituals or sacrifices

If these resonate, you may be under a blood covenant.

THE WAY OUT: BREAKING THE BLOOD COVENANT TRAP

Jesus Christ shed His blood to break every evil covenant. His blood is superior to any other blood. Hebrews 9:14 says:
"How much more shall the blood of Christ, who through the eternal Spirit offered himself without spot to God, purge your conscience from dead works to serve the living God?"

Here is how to break free:

Repent thoroughly. Confess every sin related to blood covenants—fornication, adultery, abortions, idolatry, etc.

Renounce every covenant. Verbally break each one in Jesus' name.

Plead the blood of Jesus. Apply it over your life, your body, your bloodline.

Burn or destroy covenant objects. Tattoos may need to be lasered off; ritual items must be burned.

Fast and pray aggressively. Some covenants are stubborn and require spiritual violence.

PRAYER SECTION

Let us pray now. Pray with holy anger, with faith, with determination. You are not begging God; you are enforcing the victory of Calvary.

Lord Jesus, I thank You for Your precious blood that cleanses from all sin and breaks every covenant.

I repent for every involvement in blood covenants, known or unknown. Forgive me, Lord.

I renounce and break every blood covenant made through:

My virginity being taken or taken wrongly

Tribal marks or incisions

Fornication or adultery

Animal sacrifices on my behalf

Abortion

Tattoos or ritual cuttings

Occult blood transfers

Defiled circumcision

Unholy communion

Blood baths or anointing

Inherited covenants

Lovers' blood pacts

Eating blood

Piercings for bondage

Menstrual defilement

Violence and bloodshed in my home
I break them all now by the power in the blood of Jesus!

I plead the blood of Jesus over my own blood. Let every contamination be purified, every curse be reversed, every demonic mark be erased.

I withdraw my blood from every satanic altar, every demonic blood bank, every ritual vessel.

I command every spirit attached to blood covenants to leave me now—spirit of sickness, poverty, failure, marital destruction, ancestral bondage—go in Jesus' name!

I declare that I am redeemed by the blood of the Lamb. I am free. I am clean. I am restored.

FINAL WORD

Beloved, this is a deep and serious teaching, but it is a deliverance truth. Many have been set free from lifelong bondages after breaking blood covenants. Do not treat this lightly. Pray through. Be thorough. Allow the Holy Spirit to bring to your remembrance any hidden covenant.

You are not a slave. You are a child of God. The blood of Jesus speaks better things than the blood of Abel (Hebrews 12:24). It speaks freedom, mercy, redemption, and breakthrough.

Now, go and pray violently. Your deliverance is here.

THE WAY OF ESCAPE: FIVE STEPS TO FREEDOM FROM BLOOD COVENANTS

Listen to me, church. This is not a theory. This is not religious speculation. This is a **spiritual emergency protocol**. When you discover you've been trapped in a blood covenant—whether by your actions, your ancestors, or your ignorance—you don't have the luxury of polite, quiet prayers. You are in a **spiritual war zone**, and you need a battle plan that works.

The blood of Jesus is your legal right to freedom. But you must enforce that right. You must execute the judgment written (Psalm 149:9). God has given you the authority—now you must exercise it with precision, with violence in the Spirit, and with unshakable faith.

Let me walk you through the **five non-negotiable steps** to break free from any blood covenant.

STEP 1: COMPLETE REPENTANCE – THE FOUNDATION OF FREEDOM

You cannot bypass this. Repentance is not saying, "Lord, forgive all my sins." That's lazy repentance. That's generic repentance. When you're dealing with blood covenants, you need **surgical repentance**.

Why?

Because sin gives legal ground to the enemy (Ephesians 4:27). Blood covenants are **legal contracts in the spirit realm**. If you don't repent specifically, you leave legal loopholes.

How to do it:

Get before God in raw honesty. No masks. No excuses.

Name the sins specifically.

"Lord, forgive me for having sex with [name] outside marriage."

"Forgive me for that abortion in 1998."

"Forgive me for getting that dragon tattoo after I was saved."

"Forgive me for participating in that ritual sacrifice when I was a child."

"Forgive my grandfather for dedicating our family to the river goddess."

Repent for the ignorance. "Lord, forgive me for unknowingly entering into covenants through [action]. I renounce them now."

Repent for the bloodshed. Any time blood was shed in sin—abortion, violence, ritual cutting—it must be repented for. Blood cries out (Genesis 4:10).

Biblical Foundation:

"If we confess our sins, he is faithful and just to forgive us our sins, and to cleanse us from all unrighteousness." – 1 John 1:9

God is faithful to forgive, but He responds to **specific confession**. This isn't for His sake—He already knows—it's for **your legal standing**. You are revoking the enemy's license to operate.

STEP 2: VIOLENT RENUNCIATION – THE LEGAL DECREE

After repentance, you must **renounce**. To renounce means to formally declare that you reject, disown, and break every covenant.

Why violently?

Because some of these covenants are **ancient**. They've been enforced for generations. The demons guarding them are not junior spirits—they are **principalities, rulers of darkness** (Ephesians 6:12). Polite prayer won't break a 500-year-old covenant. You need **violent faith**.

How to do it:

Speak aloud. Your voice is a spiritual instrument (Proverbs 18:21). Demons hear words.

Address the covenant directly. "I renounce the blood covenant made through my premature sexual experience with [name]. I break it now in Jesus' name!"

Renounce by category. Go through the 20 doors we discussed earlier. Renounce each one you identify with.

Renounce on behalf of ancestors. "I renounce every blood covenant my ancestors made with idols, secret societies, or familiar spirits. I break their effect over my life now!"

Biblical Foundation:

"And they overcame him by the blood of the Lamb, and by the word of their testimony..." – Revelation 12:11

Your renunciation is **your testimony against the enemy in the court of heaven**. You are presenting the blood of Jesus as evidence and decreeing your freedom.

STEP 3: BIND THE SPIRIT IN CHARGE – DISARMING THE STRONGMAN

Every covenant has a **ruling spirit**. A strongman (Matthew 12:29). You must identify and bind it.

How to identify it:

What pattern has this covenant produced? Poverty? Bind the spirit of poverty.

Sickness? Bind the spirit of infirmity.

Marital failure? Bind the spirit of divorce, spirit of lust, spirit of rejection.

Recurring nightmares? Bind the spirit of fear, spirit of witchcraft.

How to bind it:

Use your authority. Jesus said, "Whatever you bind on earth will be bound in heaven" (Matthew 18:18).

Address it directly. "You spirit of [name], assigned to enforce the blood covenant of [specific covenant], I bind you now in the name of Jesus! Your power is broken! Your assignment is cancelled!"

Loose yourself from it. "I loose myself from your grip! I loose my finances, my health, my marriage, my destiny from your operations!"

Biblical Foundation:

"No man can enter into a strong man's house, and spoil his goods, except he will first bind the strong man..." – Mark 3:27

You are entering the strongman's house (the covenant) to spoil his goods (your stolen blessings). Binding comes first.

STEP 4: SPEAK DESTRUCTION TO THEIR PRODUCTS – RECLAIMING WHAT WAS LOST

Covenants produce **evil fruits**. Sickness, debt, barrenness, confusion, failure. You must not only break the covenant but also destroy its products.

How to do it:

Identify the products. What has this covenant produced in your life? Be specific.

Command destruction. "Every sickness planted in my body through blood covenants, be uprooted now! Every curse of poverty, be broken! Every spirit of failure, die now!"

Nullify their effects. "I nullify every effect of [specific covenant] in my life, my family, my ministry."

Biblical Foundation:

"Every plant, which my heavenly Father hath not planted, shall be rooted up." – Matthew 15:13

These evil products are **unplanted by God**. Therefore, you have the authority to uproot them.

STEP 5: DECREE YOUR DESIRES AGGRESSIVELY – ESTABLISHING GOD'S KINGDOM

You cannot leave a vacuum. When you cast out an evil spirit, it returns with seven worse if the house is empty (Matthew 12:43-45). You must **fill the space with God's word, God's promises, God's blessings.**

How to do it:

Decree the opposite. If the covenant produced sickness, decree healing. If poverty, decree abundance. If barrenness, decree fruitfulness.

Use Scripture. "By the stripes of Jesus, I am healed!" (Isaiah 53:5). "The Lord is my shepherd, I shall not want!" (Psalm 23:1).

Decree generational reversal. "Instead of shame, I have double honor! Instead of confusion, I have divine order! Instead of curse, I have blessing!" (Isaiah 61:7).

Biblical Foundation:

"Thou shalt also decree a thing, and it shall be established unto thee..." – Job 22:28

Your decree establishes God's reality in your life. You are not wishing—you are **legislating in the spirit realm**.

THE PRAYER OF BLOOD COVENANT BREAKING: A SPIRITUAL BATTLEFIELD MANUAL

Now, we pray. This is not a gentle devotional. This is **spiritual warfare**. If you are not willing to pray violently, with faith, with aggression, then stop now. You are about to engage ancient powers, and they will resist you. But greater is He that is in you than he that is in the world (1 John 4:4).

PREPARATION:

Find a place where you can pray aloud without restraint.

Have your Bible open to Psalm 91, Isaiah 53, Ephesians 6.

Anoint yourself with oil if led (James 5:14).

Fast if possible. Some covenants only break by prayer and fasting (Matthew 17:21).

STEP 1: REPENTANCE – THE CLEANSING FLOOD

Kneel if you can. Bow your head. Let the Holy Spirit search you.

"Heavenly Father, I come before You in the name of Jesus. I thank You for the blood of Jesus that cleanses me from all sin. Your Word says if I confess my sins, You are faithful and just to forgive me. So I confess now, specifically:

I confess the sin of fornication with [names]. Forgive me, Lord.

I confess the sin of adultery with [names]. Forgive me, Lord.

I confess the sin of abortion [number] times. Forgive me for shedding innocent blood.

I confess the sin of idolatry—participating in [ritual, festival, offering].

I confess the sin of getting tattoos with demonic symbols [describe].

I confess the sin of drinking blood/eating blood-based foods.

I confess the sin of allowing blood covenants through ignorance.

I also repent on behalf of my ancestors:

For my father/mother who [action].

For my grandparents who served [idol].

For my lineage that made pacts with secret societies.

Lord, forgive us. Cleanse us. Let the blood of Jesus wash away every stain, every guilt, every legal claim against me. I receive Your forgiveness now. In Jesus' name, amen."

STEP 2: THE BLOOD CLEANSING – FIRE IN YOUR VEINS

Stand up. Place your right hand on your head, your left hand on your stomach—the seat of your life. Pray with holy aggression.

"Holy Ghost Fire! You are the consuming fire! You are the purifier! I command You now: boil every spiritual contamination out of my blood! Burn out every demonic deposit! Incinerate every covenant signature in my bloodstream!

Begin to visualize it: See the fire of God entering your head, flowing down through your neck, into your chest, through your arms, into your stomach, through your legs. See it boiling your blood—not harming you, but purifying. Every pollutant rising as steam, leaving your body. Every demonic marker dissolving.

Keep praying: "Holy Ghost Fire, boil it out! Boil out the covenants of sin! Boil out the covenants of sickness! Boil out the covenants of poverty! Boil out the covenants of failure! Purify my blood with the fire of God! I am washed! I am clean! I am sanctified!"

Pray this for at least 5 minutes. Don't rush. Let the Spirit do deep work.

STEP 3: THE COMPREHENSIVE BREAKING – THE LEGAL DECREES

Now, with boldness, declare these prayers. Mean every word. Shout if you must. Cry if you must. But pray with authority.

"I release myself from every satanic blood covenant, in the name of Jesus!"

Feel the chains breaking.

Grip your head with both hands. "I release my head from every evil blood covenant, in the name of Jesus! My mind is free! My thoughts are free! My memory is cleansed!"

"I dismantle every stronghold of evil covenants, in the name of Jesus!"

Strongholds are mindsets, belief systems built by covenants. Command them to crumble.

"I release myself from every covenanted curse, in the name of Jesus!"

Curses attached to covenants: poverty, sickness, barrenness, accident, early death—break now!

"Let the blood of Jesus speak against every unconscious evil covenant!"
You may not know all covenants, but the blood of Jesus knows. Let it speak mercy, forgiveness, cancellation.

"I speak destruction unto the fruits of unclean spirits in my life, in the name of Jesus!"

Fruits: sickness, debt, confusion, strife. Command them to wither.

"I break every evil covenant linkage, in the name of Jesus!"
Linkages between you and other people, you and demons, you and idols. Snap them!

"I dismantle every stronghold of evil blood covenants, in the name of Jesus!"

Second decree for emphasis.

"I nullify the effects of evil access to my blood, in Jesus' name!"
Access points: injections, transfusions, rituals, sexual sin. Nullify them!

"I release myself from every covenanted-curse, in Jesus' name!"
Double confirmation.

"I release every organ in my body from the grip of evil blood covenant, in the name of Jesus!"

Name them: liver, kidneys, heart, lungs, reproductive organs, brain. "Be free!"

"I dissociate myself and my family from every territorial blood covenant, in the name of Jesus!"

Covenants tied to your land, your city, your nation. Dissolve them!

"I dissociate myself from every tribal blood covenant, in the name of Jesus!"

Covenants made by your tribe, your ethnic group. Break away!

"I dissociate myself from every inherited blood covenant, in the name of Jesus!"

Generational covenants. End them now!

"I withdraw my blood from every evil altar, in the name of Jesus!"
Where your blood was placed—withdraw it!

"I withdraw my blood from every satanic blood bank, in the name of Jesus!"

Demonic reservoirs storing blood for power—withdraw yours!

"I break every unconscious evil blood covenant, in Jesus' name!"
Unknown covenants—broken!

"Let the blood of any animal shed on my behalf loose its covenant power, in the name of Jesus!"

Chickens, goats, cows—their blood loses all power over you!

"Let every drop of blood speaking evil against me be silenced by the blood of Jesus!"

Aborted babies, menstrual blood, violence blood—silenced!

"I release myself from every collective blood covenant captivity, in the name of Jesus!"

Family, group, community covenants—released!

"I release myself from every conscious or unconscious evil blood covenant, in the name of Jesus!"

Total coverage.

"Let the blood of every evil covenant loose its power over me, in the name of Jesus!"

Their blood vs. Jesus' blood—Jesus wins!

"I defy and destroy every evil covenant agreement, in Jesus name!"

Defy: refuse to honor. Destroy: render null and void.

"Let the blood of the new-covenant speak against the blood of any evil covenant militating against me, in the name of Jesus!"

Hebrews 12:24—Jesus' blood speaks better things!

"I receive the mandate to disqualify the right of all evil blood covenants, in the name of Jesus!"

You are a judge in the spirit (1 Corinthians 6:3). Disqualify them!

"Every evil blood covenant formed with any organ of my body, be nullified by the blood of Jesus!"

Specific organs—nullified!

"I recover all the good things stolen through evil covenants by the enemies, in the name of Jesus!"

Health, money, years, opportunities, blessings—recover them!

"Let every evil blood covenant along my blood-line be neutralised, in the name of Jesus!"

Past, present, future—neutralized!

"I release myself from every curse attached to evil covenants, in the name of Jesus!"

Curses of Deuteronomy 28—broken!

"I release myself from the grip of curse-covenant breakers, in the name of Jesus!"

Spirits that enforce curses—be loosed from them!

"Let every repercussion of breaking unconscious covenants be washed away by the blood of Jesus!"

Sometimes when you break covenants, there's backlash. Let the blood protect you!

AFTER THE PRAYER: SEALING YOUR FREEDOM

Thank God aloud. "Thank You, Father, for my freedom! Thank You, Jesus, for Your blood! Thank You, Holy Spirit, for Your fire!" **Drink water in the natural.** This helps flush your physical system.

Take communion. If possible, take bread and juice/wine. "This is my body, broken for me. This is my blood, shed for me. I appropriate Your covenant of life."

Decree blessings over yourself. "I am blessed! I am healed! I am prosperous! I am free!"

Guard your freedom. Don't return to sin. Don't entertain evil thoughts. Put on the whole armor of God daily (Ephesians 6:11).

WHEN YOU FACE RESISTANCE

Some covenants don't break easily. You may pray and feel nothing. Or you may feel worse—headaches, nausea, oppression. That means the covenant is **fighting back**.

What to do:

Persist. Jesus said, "Men ought always to pray and not to faint" (Luke 18:1).

Fast. Add fasting to your prayer. It increases spiritual sensitivity and power.

Get help. Ask mature believers to pray with you.

Stand your ground. You are free. Don't negotiate with demons. Don't doubt. Stand on God's Word.

THE BIBLICAL ARMORY FOR THIS BATTLE

Meditate on these scriptures daily:

Revelation 12:11 – Overcoming by the blood and the word of testimony.

Colossians 2:14-15 – Jesus nailed the handwriting of ordinances to His cross.

Galatians 3:13 – Christ redeemed us from the curse.

Hebrews 9:14 – The blood of Christ purges conscience.

1 John 1:7 – The blood cleanses from all sin.

Ephesians 1:7 – Redemption through His blood.

1 Peter 1:18-19 – Redeemed with precious blood.

Hebrews 10:19 – Boldness to enter by the blood.

Exodus 12:13 – The blood as a token of protection.

Zechariah 9:11 – By the blood of covenant, prisoners are freed.

This is your hour of deliverance. You are not a victim. You are a victor. The blood of Jesus is your weapon, your defense, your legal argument. Use it. Pray violently. Believe fiercely. And walk into the freedom that is your inheritance.

The Testimony of Deliverance

A sister was failing her school certificate exams repeatedly. Her mother consulted an oracle who said: "Make a covenant with the river, and she'll pass." They cut the girl, used her blood to write her name on an egg, and threw it into the river. She passed—not just that exam, but went on to become a medical doctor, got married, had children.

Twenty-two years later, the demons came collecting: "We gave you success, now you must serve us." They began attacking her marriage. Her husband brought strange women home, claiming they were "business partners." One moved into their bedroom. The sister prayed for six violent hours, breaking that river covenant. The strange women fled, and her marriage was restored.

Some covenants take time to break because they're ancient and deeply rooted. Don't give up after one prayer session. You may need to pray aggressively for days or weeks. But freedom is worth the fight.

If you haven't given your life to Christ, you cannot break these covenants. The blood of Jesus is your only legal authority. If you need to surrender to Him now, pray this:

"Father, in the name of Jesus, I come before You. I claim the power of the blood of Jesus. Forgive my sins. Lord Jesus, come into my life. I make You my Lord and Savior. Thank You, Jesus. Amen."

You were created to soar like an eagle, but blood covenants have caged you. Today, that cage is breaking. The blood of Jesus—the only pure, sinless, powerful blood—is speaking a better word than all the polluted blood covenants against you.

You are coming out of the blood covenant trap. You are walking into the glorious liberty of the children of God. The blood of Jesus has set you free. Now walk in that freedom, and never return to the cage.

CHAPTER 07
PRAYER WARFARE SECTION

"Howbeit this kind goeth not out but by prayer and fasting."
— Matthew 17:21

INTRODUCTION: THE BATTLEGROUND OF PRAYER

Beloved, listen carefully. We have spent six chapters exposing the enemy's strategies—covenants, altars, curses, blood pacts. But knowledge alone does not bring freedom. **Revelation without confrontation leads to frustration.**

Jesus Himself said, **"This kind does not go out except by prayer and fasting."** What "kind"? The kind we've been discussing: ancient covenants, entrenched strongholds, generational curses, stubborn altars. These are not junior demons. These are **principalities, powers, rulers of darkness, spiritual wickedness in high places** (Ephesians 6:12).

You cannot defeat a Goliath with a slingshot of casual prayer. You need **strategic, violent, focused, sustained prayer warfare.** This chapter is not a suggestion—it is a **spiritual prescription** for your deliverance.

HOW TO PRAY RESULT-ORIENTED PRAYERS

The Five Prayer Protocols

God is a God of order. Even in warfare, there is strategy. The Holy Spirit has shown us five prayer protocols for serious spiritual battles:

A. 7 Days' Night Vigil (12 midnight – 3:00 am)

Why midnight? Psalm 119:62 says, *"At midnight I will rise to give thanks unto thee."*

Why three hours? Jesus prayed in Gethsemane for about three hours (Matthew 26:36-46).

The midnight hour is when many demonic covenants are renewed, when witches hold meetings, when curses are activated. You must **invade their time slot** with prayer. Your midnight prayer is a declaration: "This territory belongs to Jesus!"

B. 7 Days' Fast Breaking Daily (Breaking at 7:00 pm)

Fasting is not starvation; it is **focusing**. It is saying, "This matter is so important, I will set aside physical food to feast on spiritual food."

Daniel fasted 21 days and broke through demonic resistance over Persia (Daniel 10:12-13).

Breaking at 7:00 pm (evening) follows the biblical pattern—Daniel broke his fast at evening time (Daniel 10:3).

C. 21 Days' Night Vigil (12 midnight – 3:00 am)

For battles that are **ancient, entrenched, or heavily fortified**. Twenty-one days matches Daniel's breakthrough period. Some covenants have been reinforced for centuries; they require sustained assault.

D. 21 Days' Fast Breaking Daily (Breaking at 7:00 pm)

The ultimate spiritual marathon. This is for **lifelong patterns, generational strongholds, or national curses**. You are declaring war not just on a demon, but on a **dynasty of darkness**.

E. 3 or More Days of Dry Fast

A dry fast—no food, no water—is **extreme warfare**. Esther called a three-day dry fast before confronting Haman (Esther 4:16).
Warning: Do not undertake a dry fast without medical clearance if you have health issues. And always be led by the Holy Spirit.

The Non-Negotiables:

Aggressive Prayer: This is not mumbling. This is **shouting, commanding, decreeing**. Jesus said, "*The kingdom of heaven suffereth violence, and the violent take it by force*" (Matthew 11:12).

Pray in the Spirit: Praying in tongues (1 Corinthians 14:15) builds you up (Jude 1:20) and allows the Holy Spirit to pray through you with groanings too deep for words (Romans 8:26).

Use the Name of Jesus: Philippians 2:10 says "*at the name of Jesus every knee should bow.*" Demons must bow to that name. But you must use it with **authority**, not as a religious mantra.

---

1. POWER AGAINST DESERT SPIRITS

Desert spirits are spirits of **barrenness, dryness, stagnation, and isolation**. They turn your life into a wilderness—no fruit, no water, no growth. They are the opposite of the River of God.

Biblical Confessions to Personalize:

Psalm 31:2: "*Bow down thine ear to me; deliver me speedily: be thou my strong rock, for an house of defence to save me.*"

Isaiah 58:8: "*Then shall thy light break forth as the morning, and thine health shall spring forth speedily.*"

Jeremiah 1:12: "*I will hasten my word to perform it.*"

Malachi 4:2: "*But unto you that fear my name shall the Sun of righteousness arise with healing in his wings.*"

Galatians 3:13-14: "*Christ hath redeemed us from the curse of the law... that the blessing of Abraham might come on the Gentiles.*"

Colossians 2:14-15: "*Blotting out the handwriting of ordinances that was against us... nailing it to his cross.*"

Personal Declaration:

"Jesus is Lord over my spirit, soul, and body. At the name of Jesus every knee bows. I can do all things through Christ who strengthens me. The Lord is my shepherd, I shall not want. Jesus has delivered me from the powers of darkness and translated me into the kingdom of His dear Son. I have redemption through His blood, forgiveness of sins. He blotted out the handwriting against me. I am the body of Christ. I am redeemed from the curse. I have the mind of Christ."

Prayer Points:

Thank the Lord for His power to deliver from any form of bondage. Gratitude is faith in advance.

I confess the sins of my ancestors (list them). Be specific: idolatry, witchcraft, bloodshed, adultery, etc.

Ask the Lord for forgiveness. For yourself and for them.

Ask the Lord to forgive those you do not know about. Cover ignorance with the blood.

Let the power in the blood of Jesus separate me from the sins of my ancestors. Exodus 12:13—the blood causes the destroyer to pass over.

I renounce any evil dedication placed upon my life, in the name of Jesus. Dedications at shrines, to idols, to rivers, to stars.

I break every evil edict and ordination, in the name of Jesus. Demonic pronouncements over your destiny.

I renounce and loose myself from every negative dedication placed upon my life, in the name of Jesus. Double confirmation.

I command all demons associated with the dedication to leave now, in the name of Jesus Christ. Evict them.

I take authority over all the associated curses in Jesus' name. Curses of poverty, failure, sickness, early death.

Lord, cancel the evil consequences of any broken demonic promise or dedication. Nullify the fallout.

I take authority over all the curses emanating from broken dedication, in the name of Jesus. Some curses activate when you break a demonic pact.

I command all demons associated with any broken evil parental vow and dedication to depart from me now, in the name of Jesus. Parents might have vowed you to a spirit.

Ask the Lord to separate you completely from all the sins of your forefathers by the precious blood of Jesus. Ezekiel 18:20—the soul that sins shall die, but you are covered by the blood.

Ask the Lord to remove the curse if it was from Him. Sometimes God curses disobedience (Deuteronomy 28). Repent and ask for removal.

Command the curse of [name it] to be broken in the name of Jesus. Poverty curse, sickness curse, barrenness curse.

Apply the oil and command all demons associated with the curse to leave at once, in the name of Jesus. Oil is a symbol of the Holy Spirit (James 5:14).

Command any demon afflicting the [body part] or causing [problem] to leave at once, in the name of Jesus. Be specific.

Ask the Lord to heal all the damages done. Physical, emotional, spiritual damages.

I dismiss and disband from my heart every thought, image or picture of failure in these matters, in the name of Jesus. 2 Corinthians 10:5—casting down imaginations.

I reject every spirit of doubt, fear and discouragement, in the name of Jesus. 2 Timothy 1:7—God gave us power, love, and a sound mind.

I cancel all ungodly delays to the manifestation of my miracles, in the name of Jesus. Habakkuk 2:3—the vision is for an appointed time.

Let the angels of the living God roll away every stone of hindrance to the manifestation of my breakthroughs, in the name of Jesus. Like the angel rolled the stone from Jesus' tomb (Matthew 28:2).

O Lord, hasten Your word to perform it in every department of my life. Jeremiah 1:12.

O Lord, avenge me of my adversaries speedily. Luke 18:7-8.

I refuse to agree with the enemies of my progress, in Jesus' name. Do not speak their words.

(Pray the next four prayer points according to the level of your faith)

O Lord, I desire breakthroughs concerning [specify] today, in the name of Jesus. For the faith that believes for same-day miracles.

O Lord, I desire breakthroughs concerning [specify] this week, in the name of Jesus. For the faith that believes within seven days.

O Lord, I desire breakthroughs concerning [specify] this month, in the name of Jesus. For the faith that believes within thirty days.

O Lord, I desire breakthroughs concerning [specify] this year, in the name of Jesus. For the faith that sets annual goals with God.

Let there be turbulence, re-arrangement, revision, re-organisation and re-routing of situations and circumstances in order to give path to my desired miracles. In the name of Jesus. Stir up the spiritual atmosphere.

Let every hole present in the container of my life be mended, in the name of Jesus. Plug financial leaks, health leaks, relationship leaks.

I bind, plunder and render to nothing every anti-testimony, anti-miracle and anti-prosperity forces, in the name of Jesus. Bind the strongman (Matthew 12:29).

The God who answered by fire and the God of Elijah, answer me by fire, in the name of Jesus. 1 Kings 18:24.

The God who answered Moses speedily at the Red Sea, answer me by fire, in the name of Jesus. Exodus 14:21-22.

The God who changed the lot of Jabez, answer me by fire, in the name of Jesus. 1 Chronicles 4:9-10.

The God which quickeneth and calleth those things that be not as if they are, answer me by fire, in the name of Jesus. Romans 4:17.

I apply the blood of Jesus on my spirit, soul, body and my womb. Cover every area.

Let the fire of God saturate my womb, in the name of Jesus. For fertility, for healing of reproductive issues.

Let every design against my life be completely nullified, in the name of Jesus. Demonic blueprints, evil plans.

Let all evil labels fashioned by the camp of the enemy against my life be rubbed off by the blood of Jesus. Labels: "barren," "failure," "poor," "sickly."

Sing the song "HOLY GHOST FIRE, FIRE FALL ON ME" with full concentration and in faith. Music is spiritual warfare (1 Samuel 16:23).

I vomit every satanic deposit in my life, in the mighty name of Jesus. (Prime the expulsion of these things by coughing slightly. Refuse to swallow any saliva coming out from the mouth.) Physical action demonstrating spiritual expulsion.

I break myself loose from the bondage of stagnancy, in the mighty name of Jesus. Stagnancy in career, ministry, finances, spiritual growth.

Lord, destroy with Your fire anything that makes Your promise to fall upon my life no matter the origin. Anything that hinders God's word in your life.

As you pray No. 45, take 3-4 deep breaths determinedly expelling and flushing out spiritual contamination. Do so aggressively in the mighty name of Jesus. "Let the blood, the fire and the living water of the Most High God wash my system clean from:"

a) **Unprofitable growth in my womb** – fibroids, cysts, tumors.

b) **Evil plantation** – demonically planted sickness, poverty, failure.

c) **Evil deposits from spirit husband/wife** – spiritual marital pollution.

d) **Impurities acquired from parental contamination** – generational sins.

e) **Evil spiritual consumptions** – food sacrificed to idols, polluted communion.

f) **Hidden sicknesses** – ailments doctors cannot diagnose.

g) **Remote control mechanisms** – demonic devices manipulating you from afar.

h) **Physical and spiritual incisions** – tribal marks, ritual cuts.

I) **Satanic poisons** – slow-acting spiritual toxins.

j) **Evil stamps, labels and links** – demonic branding and connections.

Let every area of my life become too hot for any evil to inhabit. In the name of Jesus. Your life becomes a furnace of God's presence.

Evil growth in my life, be uprooted, in the name of Jesus. Matthew 15:13.

Let my body reject every evil habitation, in the name of Jesus. Your body is the temple of the Holy Spirit (1 Corinthians 6:19).

O Lord, reverse all evil arrangements attracted consciously or unconsciously to my life. Turn the enemy's plans upside down.

I reject all evil manipulations and manipulators, in Jesus' name. People used by demons to control you.

I break the power of the occult, witchcraft and familiar spirits over my life, in the name of Jesus. Cut ties with all occult practices.

Prime the expulsion of the following things by heaving deeply and applying little force upon the lower part of the abdomen:

I deliver and pass out any satanic deposit in my intestine, in the name of Jesus. Gut issues, digestive problems with spiritual roots.

I deliver and pass out any satanic deposit in my reproductive organs, in the name of Jesus. Uterus, ovaries, prostate, testes.

I deliver and pass out any satanic deposit in my womb, in the name of Jesus. Specifically for women.

In the Name of Jesus, I Declare Before All the Forces of Darkness, "Jesus Christ is Lord over Every Department of My Life." A proclamation of ownership.

You foreign hand laid on my womb, release me, in Jesus' name. Hands of witches, evil midwives, jealous relatives.

In the name of Jesus, I renounce, break and loose myself from all:

(I) demonic holds

(II) psychic powers

(III) bonds of physical illness

(IV) bondage

In the name of Jesus, I break and loose myself from all evil curses, chains, spells, Jinxes, bewitchments, witchcraft or sorcery which may have been put upon me. Comprehensive breaking.

Let a creative miracle take place in my womb and reproductive system, in the name of Jesus. For those believing for children or healing.

Father, I ask You in the name of Jesus Christ to send out Your angels and have them unearth and break all evil storage vessels fashioned against me. Vessels containing your hair, pictures, personal items used in witchcraft.

I loose myself from every evil influence, dark spirit and satanic bondage, in the name of Jesus. John 8:36—whom the Son sets free is free indeed.

I confess and declare that my body is the temple of the Holy Spirit, redeemed, cleansed, and sanctified by the Blood of Jesus Christ. 1 Corinthians 6:19-20.

I bind, plunder and render to naught every strong man assigned to my womb, reproductive system and marital life, in the name of Jesus. Matthew 12:29.

God who quickens the dead, quicken my womb and reproductive system, in the name of Jesus. Romans 4:17.

I release myself from the hold of spirits of sterility, infertility and fear, in the name of Jesus. 2 Timothy 1:7.

All spirits rooted in fornication, come out of my womb with all your root, in the mighty name of our Lord Jesus. Sexual sin opens doors to reproductive spirits.

All spirits rooted in sexual perversion, come out of my womb with all your root, in the name of Jesus. Perversion includes homosexuality, bestiality, incest.

All spirits rooted in spirit husband, come out of my womb with all your root, in the mighty name of our Lord Jesus. Demonic spiritual spouses.

All spirits rooted in masturbation, come out of my womb with all your root, in the mighty name of our Lord Jesus. Self-pollution invites demons.

All spirits rooted in guilt, come out of my womb with all your root, in the mighty name of our Lord Jesus. Guilt from abortion, fornication, etc.

All spirits rooted in pornography, come out of my womb with all your root, in the mighty name of our Lord Jesus. Pornography is spiritual adultery.

Sing this song: "There is power mighty in the blood..." Faith in the blood of Jesus.

I reverse every evil manipulation done against my womb using my menstrual pads or dates, in the name of Jesus. Witchcraft often uses menstrual blood.

I divorce every satanic marriage to my father, Jesus' name. Breaking Oedipal curses, unhealthy soul ties with parents.

I release myself from every inherited womb malformation, in the name of Jesus. Generational reproductive issues.

Lord, grant unto my womb the power to retain, maintain and safely deliver my babies, in the name of Jesus. For healthy pregnancy and delivery.

Let the blood of Jesus sanitise my womb and anoint it, in the name of Jesus. Spiritual cleansing and consecration.

I command all satanic network against my having issues to be completely broken, in the name of Jesus. Collective witchcraft against your fruitfulness.

I break every anti-marriage and anti-pregnancy curse, in the name of Jesus. Curses preventing marriage or children.

I bind every spirit of abortion and miscarriage, in Jesus' name. Spirits that kill babies in the womb.

DAILY EXERCISE (For those believing for children):

A. Speaking to your womb to retain and maintain the pregnancy till birth. Proverbs 18:21—death and life are in the tongue.

B. Barricading your spirit with the hedge of fire and blood of Jesus. Job 1:10—God's hedge of protection.

C. Binding household strongman from both sides of the family. Matthew 12:29.

D. Command the spirit of abortion and miscarriage to depart from the womb.

E. Command the spirit of death to depart from the womb.

F. Thanksgiving. 1 Thessalonians 5:18—in everything give thanks.

---

2. PRAYERS FOR PROFITABLE SALES

Confessions: Psalm 46:1; Hebrews 1:14; Philippians 4:19; Numbers 6:25; Deuteronomy 28:13; Daniel 1:17; Psalm 5:12; Psalm 119:165.

Praise Worship First – Enter His gates with thanksgiving (Psalm 100:4).

Prayer Points:

Father, I dedicate and consecrate these products to You, in the name of Jesus. Sanctify your business.

Lord, bless the efforts of all who are involved in selling my products. Team blessing.

Lord, give my people favour with the customers. Like Joseph with Potiphar (Genesis 39:3-4).

Father, help my salesmen to understand the needs of my customers. Wisdom.

Lord, help my sale representative never to oversell, but always to efficiently present my products and services. Integrity.

Father, let the Holy Spirit teach me sales promotion and increasing sales techniques. Divine marketing ideas.

Lord, help me to always remain ahead and not behind. Competitive edge.

Lord, help me to offer my products in the proper way. Excellence.

Lord, give my salesmen favour when making sales representatives. Favour with distributors.

Almighty Father, cause a hunger or request for my goods and services, in the name of Jesus. Create demand.

Lord, open new doors and provide new markets for my goods and services. Expansion.

Lord, help me to increase sales and add new markets daily. Growth.

I retrieve my products from every evil attack, in Jesus' name. Reclaim what the enemy has blocked.

I break every curse of failure upon the sales of my products, in the name of Jesus. Deuteronomy 28:12—the Lord shall open unto you His good treasure.

I command the devil to take off his legs from my goods and services, in the name of Jesus. Remove demonic sat.

Let the rod of Iron fall on any strange money passed to me, in the name of Jesus. Money with curses attached.

I use the Blood of Jesus Christ to wash my hands and my products and make them clean today, in the name of Jesus. Sanctify physically and spiritually.

Let there be a breakthrough for me in my transaction, in the name of Jesus. Sudden sales, big contracts.

Lord, let me have the spirit of favour in all my business transaction. Like Esther (Esther 5:2).

I ask for the release of prosperity on the sales of my products, in the name of Jesus. 3 John 1:2—prosper and be in health.

Let all demonic hindrances to the sales of my products be totally paralysed, in the name of Jesus. Hindering spirits (1 Thessalonians 2:18).

I break every circle of sales failure upon my products, in the name of Jesus. Repetitive patterns of loss.

Let my products be shielded away from all evil observers, in the name of Jesus. Hide from the evil eye.

Father, let Your angels lift up my products on their hands so that it does not strike its foot against a stone, in Jesus' name. Psalm 91:11-12.

I remove my products from the dominion of the powers of darkness, in the name of Jesus. Transfer from Satan's kingdom to God's (Colossians 1:13).

Let my products become a channel of blessings and a foundation of life for other business, in the name of Jesus. Your business blesses others.

I command my money being caged by the enemy to be completely released, in the name of Jesus. Let money held in demonic banks be released.

Lord, give me supernatural breakthroughs in all my present business proposals. Favour with decision-makers.

I bind and put to flight all the spirits of fear, anxiety and discouragement in the name of Jesus. 2 Timothy 1:7.

Lord, let divine wisdom fall upon all who are supporting me in selling my products. Wisdom for your team.

I break the backbone of any further spirits of conspiracy and treachery, in the name of Jesus. Betrayal in business.

Lord, hammer my matter into the mind of those who will assist me in selling my products so that they do not suffer from demonic loss of memory. Help them remember your proposals.

I paralyse the handiwork of household enemies and envious agents on selling my products, in the name of Jesus. Jealous relatives or colleagues.

You devil, take your legs away from the top of my finances, in the mighty name of Jesus. Remove demonic blockage.

Let the fire of the Holy Spirit purge my finances from any evil mark put upon me, in the name of Jesus. Money marked by witchcraft.

Father, guide and direct me to rectify any problem I have with my business. Divine troubleshooting.

Lord, forgive me for any wrong decision or wrong action or thought I engaged in. Repentance for business sins.

Father, help me to see my mistakes and faults and to do all in my power to overcome and correct them in the name of Jesus. Learn from errors.

Lord, give unto me the Eagle eye and eyes of Elisha to foresee market situations. Discernment (2 Kings 6:17).

Lord, give me wisdom to walk out of any unfavorable business situations. Discerning when to exit.

Lord, always help me to identify evil business traps. Avoid scams, bad partnerships.

Lord, help me to erect safeguards to prevent business failure. Proverbs 22:3—the prudent sees danger and hides.

Lord, help me to be on the lookout for ways to provide better products and services. Innovation.

In the mighty name of Jesus, I claim the following:

(a) **good reputation** – Proverbs 22:1.

(b) **favour with clients and customers** – like Daniel (Daniel 1:9).

(c) **abundant prosperity** – 2 Corinthians 9:8.

(d) **divine Wisdom for those who occupy important decision-making positions** – James 1:5.

(e) **Increased sales and services and expanded markets** – Deuteronomy 28:12.

(f) **new product ideas and new servicing concepts** – Exodus 31:3-4.

---

3. POWER AGAINST SEXUAL PERVERSION

Thank God for His power to deliver from every bondage. Gratitude first.

I break myself from every spirit of sexual perversion, in the name of Jesus. 1 Corinthians 6:18—flee fornication.

I release myself from every spiritual pollution emanating from my past sins of fornication and sexual immorality, in the name of Jesus. 1 Corinthians 6:11—such were some of you, but you are washed.

I release myself from every ancestral pollution, Jesus name. Generational sexual sin patterns.

I release myself from every dream pollution, in Jesus' name. Sexual dreams, wet dreams.

I command every evil plantation of sexual perversion in my life to come out with all its roots, in the name of Jesus. Matthew 15:13.

Every spirit of sexual perversion, working against my life, be paralyzed, and get out of my life, in the name of Jesus. Mark 1:25—Jesus rebuked unclean spirits.

Every demon of sexual perversion assigned to my life, be bound, in the name of Jesus. Binding the strongman.

Father Lord, let the power of sexual perversion oppressing my life receive the fire of God and be roasted, in the name of Jesus. Hebrews 12:29—God is a consuming fire.

Every inherited demons of sexual perversion in my life, receive the arrows of fire and remain permanently bound, in the name of Jesus. Generational lust spirits.

I command every force of power of sexual perversion to come against themselves, in the name of Jesus. Confusion in the enemy's camp (2 Chronicles 20:23).

Father Lord, let every demonic stronghold built in my life by the spirit of sexual perversion be pulled down, in Jesus' name. 2 Corinthians 10:4.

Let every power of sexual perversion that have summoned my life be shattered to pieces, in the name of Jesus. Demonic meetings targeting you.

Let my soul be delivered from the forces of sexual perversion, in the name of Jesus. Psalm 34:22.

Let the Lord God of Elijah arise with a strong hand against every spirit wife/husband and power of sexual perversion, in the name of Jesus. 1 Kings 18:46.

I break the hold of any evil power over my life, in Jesus' name. Romans 8:37—more than conquerors.

I nullify every effect of the bite of sexual perversion upon my life, in the name of Jesus. Like the viper's bite (Acts 28:3-5).

Every evil stranger and satanic deposit in my life, I command you to be paralyzed and get out of my life, in the name of Jesus. Eviction notice.

Holy Ghost Fire, purge my life completely, in the name of Jesus. Refiner's fire (Malachi 3:3).

I claim my complete deliverance in the name of Jesus from the spirit of fornication and sexual immorality, in the name of Jesus. John 8:36.

Let my eyes be delivered from lustfulness, in the name of Jesus. Job 31:1—I made a covenant with my eyes.

As from today, let my eyes be controlled by the Holy Spirit, in the name of Jesus. Galatians 5:16—walk in the Spirit.

Holy Ghost Fire, fall upon my eyes and burn to ashes every evil force and satanic powers controlling my eyes, in Jesus' name. Blind the lustful eye.

I move from bondage to liberty in every area of my life, in the name of Jesus. 2 Corinthians 3:17—where the Spirit is, there is liberty.

Thank God for answers to your prayers. Thanksgiving seals it.

4. ATTACKING THE ENEMY OF YOUR CALLING

I destroy the power of every satanic arrest in my life, in the name of Jesus. Arrests of destiny, ministry, progress.

All satanic-arresting agents, release me, in the name of Jesus. Angels of delay, hindering spirits.

I command every spiritual contamination in my life to receive cleansing by the blood of Jesus, in the name of Jesus. 1 John 1:7.

Let the brush of the Lord scrub out every dirtiness in my spiritual pipe. Cleansing your spiritual flow.

I destroy everything that is representing me in the demonic world with the fire of God, in the name of Jesus. Effigies, images, symbols.

Lord, teach me to die to self. Luke 9:23—deny yourself.

Every rusted spiritual pipe in my life, receive wholeness, in the name of Jesus. Restore spiritual sensitivity.

I command every power, eating up my spiritual pipe to be roasted, in the name of Jesus. Parasitic spirits draining your anointing.

Spirit of the living God, quicken the whole of my being, in the name of Jesus. Psalm 119:25—quicken me.

I command the hole in my spiritual pipe to be closed, in the name of Jesus. Plug spiritual leaks.

God, smash me and renew my strength, in the name of Jesus. Break the old man, renew the spirit.

Holy Spirit, open my eyes to see beyond the visible, to the invisible, in the name of Jesus. 2 Kings 6:17.

Lord, ignite my calling with Your fire. Jeremiah 20:9—fire in my bones.

Let my spiritual pipe receive the strength of God against any contamination, in the name of Jesus. Fortify against future attacks.

Holy Spirit, open my eyes and let me have a revelation vision of Christ, in the name of Jesus. Ephesians 1:17-18.

O Lord, liberate my spirit to follow the leading of the Holy Spirit. Romans 8:14.

I receive heavenly flushing in my spiritual pipe, in Jesus' name. Cleansing flow.

I confess that my spiritual pipe shall be effective throughout my life, in the name of Jesus. Continual flow of anointing.

Holy Spirit, teach me to pray through the problems instead of praying about it, in the name of Jesus. Pray until breakthrough.

O Lord, deliver me from the lies I tell myself. Self-deception.

Every evil spiritual padlock and evil chain hindering my spiritual growth, be roasted, in the name of Jesus. Break spiritual limitations.

I rebuke every spirit of spiritual deafness and blindness in my life, in the name of Jesus. Mark 8:18—having eyes, see not.

O Lord, deliver me from the lies the enemy tells me. John 8:44—the devil is a liar.

O Lord, empower me to resist satan that he would flee. James 4:7.

I bind the strongman behind my spiritual blindness and deafness and paralyze his operations in my life, in Jesus' name. Matthew 12:29.

I anoint my eyes and my ears with the blood of Jesus. Apply the blood spiritually.

I choose to believe the report of the Lord and no other, in the name of Jesus. Isaiah 53:1.

Let the fire of the Holy Spirit melt my resistance, in Jesus' name. Melt pride, stubbornness.

O Lord, restore my spiritual eyes and ears, in the name of Jesus. Revelation 3:18—anoint your eyes.

Lord, anoint my eyes and my ears that they may see and hear wondrous things from heaven. Psalm 119:18.

Let the fire of the Holy Spirit smash my pride, in Jesus' name. Proverbs 16:18.

O Lord, anoint me to pray without ceasing. 1 Thessalonians 5:17.

I send the fire of God to my eyes and ears to melt away satanic deposit, in the name of Jesus. Remove demonic scales.

Let my spiritual eyes and ears be wide opened, in Jesus' name. Like Elisha's servant (2 Kings 6:17).

In the name of Jesus, I capture every power behind my spiritual blindness and deafness. Take them prisoner.

Let my spiritual sight and eardrum receive healing, in the name of Jesus. Physical and spiritual healing.

Holy Spirit, rain on me now, in the name of Jesus. Outpouring.

Holy Spirit, uncover my darkest secrets, in the name of Jesus. Bring hidden things to light.

You spirit of confusion, loose your hold over my life, in the name of Jesus. 1 Corinthians 14:33—God is not the author of confusion.

In the power of the Holy Spirit, I defy satan's power, in the name of Jesus. Luke 10:19.

Holy Spirit, pour Your healing power on me, in Jesus' name. Healing for wounds from spiritual battles.

Let water of life flush out every unwanted stranger in my life, in the name of Jesus. John 7:38—rivers of living water.

You the enemies of the gospel in my life, be paralysed, in the name of Jesus. Opposition to your calling.

O Lord, begin to clean away from my life all that does not reflect You. Sanctification.

Lord Jesus, nail me to Your cross. Galatians 2:20—crucified with Christ.

I reject every spiritual pollution, in the name of Jesus. 2 Corinthians 7:1—cleanse from all filthiness.

Lord Jesus, break me, shape me, mold me, fill me and use me with the water of Your Spirit. Submission to the Potter.

O Lord, I lose myself in You. Galatians 2:20.

Holy Spirit Fire, ignite me to the glory of God in Jesus' name. Set on fire for God.

Oh Lord, let the anointing of the Holy Spirit break every yoke of backwardness in my life, in the name of Jesus. Isaiah 10:27.

Let my spirit-man become divine fire, in the name of Jesus. Hebrews 12:29.

I frustrate every demonic arrest over my spirit-man, in the name of Jesus. Cancel demonic warrants.

Let the blood of Jesus remove any unprogressive label from every aspect of my life, in the name of Jesus. Labels like "never-do-well," "failure."

Anti-breakthrough decrees, be revoked, in the name of Jesus. Cancel evil pronouncements.

Holy Ghost fire, destroy every satanic garments in my life, in the name of Jesus. Garments of shame, failure, poverty.

Oh Lord, give unto me the key to good success, so that anywhere I go, the doors of good success will be opened unto me. Isaiah 22:22—key of David.

Let every wicked house constructed against me be demolished in the name of Jesus. Demonic structures.

Let the road close against unprofitable visitations in my life, in the name of Jesus. Stop time-wasters, distractions.

Oh Lord, establish me as a holy person unto You, in the name of Jesus. 1 Peter 2:9.

Oh Lord, let the anointing to excel in my spiritual and physical life fall on me, in the name of Jesus. Daniel 6:3—excellent spirit.

I shall not serve my enemies, my enemies shall bow down to me, in the name of Jesus. Isaiah 60:14.

I bind every desert and poverty spirits in my life, in Jesus' name. Spirits of lack and barrenness.

I reject the anointing of non-achievement in my handy work, in the name of Jesus. Deuteronomy 28:12—blessed in all you do.

I pull down all the strongholds erected against my progress, in the name of Jesus. 2 Corinthians 10:4.

I recall all my blessings thrown into water, forest, satanic bank, in the name of Jesus. Reclaim stolen blessings.

Holy Spirit, control my ability to frame my words. Proverbs 15:23—a word in due season.

I cut down all the roots of problems in my life, in Jesus' name. Hosea 14:5—I will be as the dew unto Israel.

Let satanic scorpions be rendered stingless in every area of my life, in the name of Jesus. Luke 10:19.

Let demonic serpents be rendered venom-less in every area of my life, in the name of Jesus. Luke 10:19.

I declare with my mouth that nothing shall be impossible with me, in the name of Jesus. Luke 1:37.

Let the camp of the enemy be put in disarray, in Jesus' name. 2 Chronicles 20:23.

Spiritual parasites in my life, be disgraced, in the name of Jesus. Spirits that feed on your anointing.

Let all my Herod receive spiritual decay, in the name of Jesus. Herod who killed John the Baptist (Matthew 14:10).

Oh Lord, let Your favour and that of man encompasses me this year, in the name of Jesus. Psalm 5:12.

Let evil worms in any area of my life die, in the name of Jesus. Mark 9:48—worm dieth not.

I reject any demonic limitation on my progress, in Jesus' name. Break boundaries set by the enemy.

Let all evil handwriting against me be paralysed, in Jesus' name. Colossians 2:14.

I reject the spirit of the tail, I choose the spirit of the head, in the name of Jesus. Deuteronomy 28:13—the head and not the tail.

Let all those circulating my name for evil, be disgraced, in the name of Jesus. Psalm 35:4.

Lord, put into my hand the gift that will elevate my calling, in the name of Jesus. 1 Corinthians 12:7-11.

Let all evil friends make mistakes that would expose them, in the name of Jesus. Psalm 64:7-8.

I will not lose my calling in the name of Jesus. 2 Timothy 1:12—I know whom I have believed.

Let the strongman from both sides of my family destroy themselves, in the name of Jesus. 2 Chronicles 20:23.

Lord, teach me to be crucified with You. Galatians 2:20.

Let not Your peace depart from me, O Lord. Isaiah 26:3.

I command every blockage in my spiritual pipe to be removed, in the name of Jesus. Unblock the flow.

I refuse to wear the garment of tribulation and sorrow, in the name of Jesus. Isaiah 61:3—garment of praise.

Let every rebellion flee from my heart, in the name of Jesus. 1 Samuel 15:23—rebellion is as witchcraft.

O Lord, let the spirit that flees from sin incubate my life. 2 Timothy 2:22—flee also youthful lusts.

Let the secrets of hidden and open enemies be revealed, in the name of Jesus. Mark 4:22.

I claim all my rights now, in the name of Jesus. Galatians 4:5—redeemed to receive adoption.

I command every satanic net to receive destruction, in the name of Jesus. Psalm 91:3—snare of the fowler.

Holy Ghost, grant me a glimpse of Your glory now, in the name of Jesus. Exodus 33:18.

O Lord, create in me a clean heart by Your power. Psalm 51:10.

O Lord, renew a right spirit within me. Psalm 51:10.

Holy Ghost, pour the Father's jealousy upon me now, in the name of Jesus. Exodus 20:5—jealous God.

I renounce my rights to my anger, in the name of Jesus. Ephesians 4:26—be angry and sin not.

Holy Ghost, quicken me, in the name of Jesus. Psalm 119:25.

O Lord, remove from me the root of irritation that keeps anger alive in me. Ephesians 4:31.

Holy Ghost, breathe on me now, in the name of Jesus. John 20:22.

I reject all thoughts that I will never change, in Jesus' name. 2 Corinthians 5:17—new creature.

Holy Ghost, fill me that I might bring forth healing power, in the name of Jesus. Acts 1:8.

O Lord, produce in me the power of self-control and gentleness. Galatians 5:22-23—fruit of the Spirit.

Beloved, this is your arsenal. This is your prayer field manual. Do not rush through it. Do not treat it lightly. The prayers in this chapter are spiritual explosives—handle them with faith, with fire, with holy aggression.

The battle is not yours; it is the Lord's (2 Chronicles 20:15). But you are the one who must show up on the battlefield, wield the weapons, and enforce the victory Jesus already won.

Pray until something happens. Pray until you feel the shift. Pray until the chains break. Pray until the oil flows. Pray until the fire falls.

Your deliverance is now.

www.ingramcontent.com/pod-product-compliance
Lightning Source LLC
LaVergne TN
LVHW052219200926
848481LV00001B/157